"After the endless, breathless hype about the information superhighway and how it will revolutionize society as we know it come two of America's leading technological thinkers who, in this calm and witty volume, point out that information is inevitably embedded in social relations. If you—like all of us—are living through the Internet revolution, read this book"
—ROBERT D. PUTNAM, Stanfield Professor of International Peace, John F. Kennedy School of Government, Harvard University

"Neither cheerleaders nor debunkers, these knowledgeable and reflective Silicon Valley insiders provide a much-needed critical perspective on the buzzwords, myths, and conventional wisdom of the digital revolution. Brown and Duguid convincingly argue that our future world is evolving from the complex interaction of powerful new technology with resistant existing structures and practices."
—WILLIAM J. MITCHELL, Dean, School of Architecture and Planning, Massachusetts Institute of Technology, and Author of *City of Bits*

"*The Social Life of Information* counters conventional wisdom by reminding us that information technology does not work unless supported by viable communities and institutions. Brown and Duguid argue that communication across distances increases the importance of place, and that the preservation of social knowledge and the art of practice are key to unleashing the economic promise of the new technologies. An artfully crafted and fascinating book that invites the reader to a conversation."
—BRUCE KOGUT, Felix Zandman Professor of International Management, The Wharton School of Business

"This important book provides both the layperson and the technologically adroit with a pragmatic yet visionary perspective on the profound role that information technology will play in reshaping our society and its institutions. By combining their extensive experience in computers and communications technology with an unusually broad understanding of how technology is developed and adopted by contemporary society, the authors provide a realistic yet provocative view of the future."
—JAMES DUDERSTADT, President, Emeritus, and University Professor of Science and Engineering, The University of Michigan

"Fascinating and insightful. Experts Brown and Duguid argue convincingly that the context in which information is embedded is as important as the information itself. If information technology is to realize its promise, technologists must learn to take context into account."
—WILLIAM H. DAVIDOW, General Partner, Mohr, Davidow Ventures

The Social Life of Information

The Social Life of Information

John Seely Brown and Paul Duguid

HARVARD BUSINESS SCHOOL PRESS
BOSTON, MASSACHUSETTS

"Not Waving But Drowning" by Stevie Smith, from *Collected Poems of Stevie Smith*. Reprinted by permission of New Directions Publishing Corp. and James MacGibbon.

Library of Congress Cataloging-in-Publication Data

Brown, John Seely.
The social life of information / John Seely Brown and Paul Duguid.
p. cm.
Includes bibliographical references and index.
ISBN 0-87584-762-5 (alk. paper)
1. Information society. 2. Information technology—Social aspects. I. Duguid, Paul, 1954- II. Title

HM851 .B76 2000
303.48'33--dc21

99-049068

The paper used in this publication meets the requirements of the National Information and Standards Organization as stipulated in *Permanence of Paper for Publications and Documents in Libraries and Archives* Z39.48-1992.

For
Susan and Laura

Contents

Acknowledgments

THE IDEA THAT information and individuals are inevitably and always part of rich social networks is central to this book. Nowhere has the role of such networks been more obvious to us than in the support, help, and contributions—both direct and indirect, explicit and tacit—that we have received from friends, colleagues, and others whose work has inspired us. First and foremost we must acknowledge the contributions, both central and peripheral, of our wives Susan Haviland and Laura Hartman. Both are architects, and in their practice have taught us so much about good design, from a designer's and a user's perspective. We dedicate this book to them, but our gratitude for their support, kindness, and love lies beyond words.

The ideas of Jean Lave and Etienne Wenger, who were colleagues with us at the Institute for Research on Learning, have had an indelible effect on our thinking. Julian Orr and Geoffrey Nunberg from the Xerox Palo Alto Research Center (PARC) have also made particularly important contributions, which will be evident in the essays that follow. We hope in acknowledging them that we do not slight the many other colleagues at PARC who have helped us in a variety of ways. They are so many that we simply could not mention them all. We must, though, mention

Janice Heiler, Mimi Gardner, and Merin Eglington, whose support has been invaluable.

There are many others to whom we are deeply indebted. Among them Paul Adler, Phil Agre and his invaluable RRE Internet Filter <http://www.egroups.com/list/rre>, Bob Anderson, Danny Bobrow, Scott Noam Cook, José Afonso Furtado, Mary Griffin, Bernardo Huberman, Bill Janeway, Martin Kenney, Bruce Kogut, Teresa da Silva Lopes, Peter Lyman, Shawn Parkhurst, Larry Prusak, Dick Rosenbloom, Sim Sitkin, Brian Smith, Frank Squires, Susan Stucky, Roy Tennant and his colleagues at Current Cites <http://sunsite.berkeley.edu/CurrentCites>, Mark Weiser, and Jack Whalen. Ursula Hines provided useful research help, as did Pam Stello with chapter 8 in particular. Softbook Press kindly lent an electronic book. None but ourselves, of course, can be held to account for what we say here.

We are also very grateful for the enthusiastic support of Harvard Business School Press. We thank in particular our energetic editor Hollis Heimbouch, who made us think we could write a book and stuck with us when we thought we couldn't, but also Marjorie Williams who graciously took over the project at a very difficult time and was tactful enough not to sigh aloud with relief when she handed back the reins.

Some of the work in this book develops articles and essays that first appeared elsewhere. In particular, chapter 7 revisits ideas first published as "The social life of the document," and chapter 8 also looks back at an earlier paper, "The university in the digital age."[1]

—JOHN SEELY BROWN AND PAUL DUGUID
SEPTEMBER 1999

The Social Life of Information

Tunneling Ahead

LIVING IN THE INFORMATION AGE can occasionally feel like being driven by someone with tunnel vision. This unfortunate disability cuts off the peripheral visual field, allowing sufferers to see where they want to go, but little besides. For drivers, this full attention to the straight ahead may seem impressively direct. For passengers who can see what the driver does not it makes for a worrisome journey. The car may skirt the mirrors of passing cars, threaten the hands and ankles of nearby cyclists, roll close to the toes of pedestrians, occasionally scrape walls and gateposts, and once in a while take a serious sideswipe that jeopardizes the journey.

Similarly, some of the people driving us all hard into the future on the back of new technologies appear to assume that if we all focus hard enough on information, then we will get where we want to go most directly. This central focus inevitably pushes aside all the fuzzy stuff that lies around the edges—context, background, history, common knowledge, social resources. But this stuff around the edges is not as irrelevant as it may seem. It provides valuable balance and perspective. It holds alternatives, offers breadth of vision, and indicates choices. It helps clarify purpose and support meaning. Indeed, ultimately it is only with the help of what lies beyond it that any sense can be made of the information that absorbs so much attention.

Think of the way people interact. Talk may deliver information—something that can be recorded, transcribed, digitized, and shipped in packets. But as you talk, listeners set what you say in a much larger context. Your appearance, your age, your accent, your background, and the setting all contribute to what they understand. Few people are like Sherlock Holmes, able to spot an ex–Indian Army soldier now working as a billiard marker across a street. But we are all remarkably good at picking up clues and cues that underwrite or undermine what a speaker says. Con artists have to work for their living.

Except, perhaps, in the digital world. It is no surprise, really, that cyberspace has become famous for "identity experiments" and con games.[1] The world of information is often so thin, the cues and clues so few, that in many cases it's easy to pose, even as an ex–Indian Army soldier now working as a billiard marker, and get away with it. In the tight restrictions of the information channel, without the corroboration that broader context offers (or refuses), the powerful detective skills that everyone relies on have little room to work.[2]

TUNNEL DESIGN

Ignoring the clues that lie beyond information doesn't only lead to a narrow world of deception. It leads to a world of what we think of as *tunnel design*—a kind of purblind design of which, in the end, we are all victims. In this world we are often expected to live on a strict information-only diet. Indeed, it's a world that usually addresses worries about information by simply offering more. Yet when only information is on offer, more often means less.

Tunnel design, we suspect, produces technologies that, in Edward Tenner's phrase, "bite back."[3] These are technologies that create as many problems as they solve. Many of the unintended consequences of design that Tenner describes and that make new technologies so frustrating arise from neglecting resources that lie outside the tight focus of information.

If badly designed technologies bite back, the good ones often fight back. Well-designed technologies, that is, refuse to retreat meekly in the face of tunnel design. Futurology is littered with the obituaries of tools that nonetheless continue a robust and healthy life. One of our own favorite examples is the hinge. This seems to be written out of every futuristic movie in favor of the sliding door; yet, it not only hangs on but is vital to many laptops and cell phones.[4] Even the typewriter still finds a place in many "infomated" offices.[5] These are trivial examples. But obituaries are now regularly written not just for tools, but for well-established practices, organizations, and institutions, not all of which seem to be fading away.

The dogged endurance of those that refuse to fade tends to produce opposing responses. Those with tunnel vision condemn the foolishness of humanity for clinging to the past. Those exasperated by tunnel design tend to cheer the downfall of new technology as if it were never likely to come to any good. There is, we believe, a better, more productive approach. It is for the new to learn from the old. Tools fight back when they offer people worthwhile resources that may be lost if they are swept away. So rather than condemning humanity as foolish, primitive, or stubborn for sticking with the old and rejecting the new, it seems better to stop and ask why.

The answer often turns out to be that the new alternatives have underestimated their targets. Paradoxically, tunnel design often takes aim at the surface of life. There it undoubtedly scores lots of worthwhile hits. But such successes can make designers blind to the difficulty of more serious challenges—primarily, to the resourcefulness that helps embed certain ways of doing things deep in our lives. Generations of confident videophones, conferencing tools, and technologies for tele-presence are still far from capturing the essence of a firm handshake or a straight look in the eye.

To say this is not to plead for a return to the buggy cart, the steam engine, or the vinyl record. It is to plead for attention— attention to stubbornness, to what will not budge, to the things that people fight for. So it's to plead for design that takes into account resources that people care about. Such design, we are confident, produces tools that people care about—a kind of tool that seems, despite modern inventiveness, in remarkably short supply. (Take a quick look over the computer applications you have bought, borrowed, or downloaded over the past five years and see how many you would actually fight for.)

Issues about the breadth or narrowness of design are not, we should stress, issues for designers alone. Increasingly, we all live in a heavily designed world and need to understand both the strengths and the limitations of the designs offered to us. In particular, we all need to be able to deal with the hype that accompanies new technological designs. In the digital world, moreover, many of the distinctions between designers and users are becoming blurred. We are all, to some extent, designers now. Many questions about design are thus becoming questions for us all. It is important, then, to understand our own limitations as designers, too, and to know where to look for resources.

FIGHT TO THE FINISH

So where might the resources that we believe are overlooked lie? Despite our metaphor of tunnel vision, our sense of the neglected periphery is not limited to the visual periphery of physical objects.[6] It also embraces what we think of as the *social periphery*, the communities, organizations, and institutions that frame human activities. These, though vital to how we all live and work, are too often missing from the design stylebooks of the information age. Or, if they are included, they come as targets, not resources for design. It is to help draw attention to these hard-to-see (and hard-to-describe) resources that we gave our book the title it has. Attending too closely to information overlooks the social context that helps people understand what that information might mean and why it matters.

Well-honed resources for living tend to fall out of sight, lost to the immediate demands of daily life. New technologies, by contrast, draw and deserve a lot of attention. Consequently, it's easy to overlook the resources that lie beyond the immediacy of the information tunnel, even when they are quite substantial.

For example, a colleague at the University of California, Berkeley, recently sang the praises of the digital world to us. He can now, he told us, through the university's digital library, get direct access to information. He felt, he said, in touch with information as never before.

His enthusiasm was justifiable. New technologies have changed the life of researchers tremendously. Nonetheless, his enthusiasm had screened out an enormous array of people, organizations, and institutions involved in this "direct" touch. The university, the library, publishers, editors, referees, authors, the computer and infrastructure designers, the cataloguers and library collections managers, right down to the students making their way through college by shelving and unshelving books, copying and scanning, and delivering files across the campus had no place in his story. When they do their job well, they do it more or less invisibly. But without them, there would have been no story.

Similarly, those who talk about having direct, unmediated access to the news sometimes sound equally oblivious to how news is made. They sound as if to find the "real" news on Russia, for example, they would expect to pick up the phone and get Boris Yeltsin on the other end of the line. But it requires a profoundly naïve belief in "disintermediation" (see chapter 1) to assume that all the links that fall between Yeltsin and the news are somehow interference in the information channel. Rather, it is in these steps—from sources to reporters to editors and news organizations—that news is made. Without them, again, there would be no story. Nonetheless, when information takes center stage and lights dim on the periphery, it's easy to forget these necessary intermediaries. But while these may be invisible, they are not inconsequential.

Occasionally, the naïve neglect of the world beyond information reminds us of an old Popeye cartoon. In this, if we remember right, Popeye finds Sweet Pea, the baby, crawling along the ledge outside the bedroom, oblivious to the danger below. While Popeye frantically slips, slides, and dangles way above the street trying to reach the baby, Sweet Pea crawls giggling to the end of the ledge and off. But one of those swinging girders that obligingly come by in the cartoon world leads her on undisturbed. Popeye meanwhile, much disturbed, falls down the stairs, trips on the sidewalk, and collides with lamp-posts trying to keep up. From the edge of the swinging girder,

Sweet Pea next crawls onto the roof of a conveniently passing truck. The truck nearly runs Popeye over. And so the chase goes on until Sweet Pea manages to end happily back in the bedroom, all the while oblivious to the extraordinary resources that have provided support and protection. In Sweet Pea's mind, Sweet Pea did it all. Popeye, meanwhile, has met the sharp end of each of these resources.

Some digital champions can appear a little like Sweet Pea, oblivious to the resources of the world that support them. Others, more worryingly, are actively hostile. They see society's resources as constraints on information and yearn to be free of them. Material objects appear as the unwanted antithesis to bits, communities and organizations as enemies to individualism, institutions as "second wave."

It's not hard to understand this antagonism. For the most part people notice these supports primarily when something goes wrong. When everything works well, we are all a little like Sweet Pea, most ignorant of what makes us most secure. When things go wrong, we are more like Popeye, feeling that the stairs betrayed us, the lamppost attacked us, and that the world would be a better place without such things.

We hope that in the course of this book we can steer a path between blindness and bruises. We want to draw attention to the resources people use in the belief that what are resources for people are, by extension, resources for the design of useful tools. Tools that ignore these resources will be, in great part, tools that are at best ignored, at worst a burden on those who have to use them.

To make this case, we look at plans, prognostications, and designs that have been much applauded in theory yet significantly ignored in practice. We include prognostications about, for example, the world of information, digital agents, the home office, the paperless society, the virtual firm, and the digital university. From here we try to explain why so many confident predictions remain just that, predictions. Too often, we conclude, the light at the end of an information tunnel is merely the gleam in a visionary's eye. The way forward is paradoxically to look not ahead, but to look around.

CONVERSATIONS

The essays that follow attempt to address the social context of information from a variety of different perspectives. They have grown out of long-running conversations that the two of us have conducted in public and in private over the last dozen years or so—conversations in which we found that, though the topic shifted, the way in which we addressed it had common threads.

These threads allow us to talk from a single standpoint about the limits of infopunditry (chapter 1), the challenges of software agents (chapter 2), the social character of work and learning—and the limits of management theory (chapters 3–5), resources for innovation (chapter 6), unnoticed aspects of the document and their implications for design more generally (chapter 7), and the future of institutions, in particular the university (chapter 8). Despite what we see as the common threads, each chapter, we hope, can be read on its own.

These essays, like the conversations they reflect, try to avoid the blinkered euphoria of the infoenthusiast. Though we are enthusiasts for technologies, we focus predominantly elsewhere—on society, practice, and institutions. We look this way because we know that while information and its technologies cannot solve all society's problems, society and social resources can solve many of the problems of both information and technology. But it is society and social resources to which many designs are blinkered, if not blind.

Though we point to social resources for solutions, this is, we must admit, more a book of questions than answers. This may not seem a very constructive approach. We are, after all, writing in a genre where people often seem to identify the major problems of the world and then announce that the solution is running on the machine of a colleague in the office next door. We are enormously proud to be associated with our colleagues at the Xerox Palo Alto Research Center (PARC) and of the work they do. And we do point to their work quite often. In general, however, we have tried to avoid short-circuiting the loop between problem and solution. Our aim, though associated as we are with Xerox we are a little hesitant to say it, has been to keep the conversation going and even change its direction a little.

CHAPTER **I**

Limits to Information

On an average weekday the New York Times *contains more information than any contemporary of Shakespeare's would have acquired in a lifetime.*

—ANONYMOUS (and ubiquitous)

Every year, better methods are being devised to quantify information and distill it into quadrillions of atomistic packets of data.

—BILL GATES

By 2047 . . . all information about physical objects, including humans, buildings, processes and organizations, will be online. This is both desirable and inevitable.

—GORDON BELL AND JIM GRAY

This is the datafication of shared knowledge.

—TOM PHILLIPS, Deja News[1]

IT NOW SEEMS a curiously innocent time, though not that long ago, when the lack of information appeared to be one of society's fundamental problems. Theorists talked about humanity's "bounded rationality" and the difficulty of making decisions in conditions of limited or imperfect information. Chronic information shortages threatened work, education, research, innovation, and economic decision making—whether at the level of government policy, business strategy, or household shopping. The one thing we all apparently needed was more information.

So it's not surprising that infoenthusiasts exult in the simple volume of information that technology now makes available. They count the bits, bytes, and packets enthusiastically. They cheer the disaggregation of knowledge into data (and provide a new word—*datafication*—to describe it). As the lumps break down and the bits pile up, words like *quadrillion, terabyte,* and *megaflop* have become the measure of value.

Despite the cheers, however, for many people famine has quickly turned to glut. Concern about access to information has given way to concern about coping with the amounts to which we do have access. The Internet is rightly championed as a major information resource. Yet a little time in the nether regions of the Web can make you feel like the SETI researchers at the University of California, Berkeley, searching through an unstoppable flood of meaningless information from outer space for signs of intelligent life.[2]

With the information spigot barely turned on—the effect has seemed more like breaching a dam than turning a tap—controlling the flow has quickly become the critical issue. Where once there seemed too little to swim in, now it's hard to stay afloat. The "third wave" has rapidly grown into a tsunami.[3]

Faced by cheery enthusiasts, many less optimistic people resemble the poor swimmer in Stevie Smith's poem, lamenting that

> *I was much too far out all my life*
> *And not waving, but drowning.*

Yet still raw information by the quadrillion seems to fascinate.

COULD LESS BE MORE?

Of course, it's easy to get foolishly romantic about the pleasures of the "simpler" times. Few people really want to abandon information technology. Hours spent in a bank line, when the ATM in the supermarket can do the job in seconds, have little charm. Lose your papers in a less-developed country and trudge, as locals must do all the time, from line to line, from form to form, from office to office and you quickly realize that life without information technology, like life without modern sanitation, may seem simpler and even more "authentic," but for those who have to live it, it is not necessarily easier or more pleasant.

Even those people who continue to resist computers, faxes, e-mail, personal digital assistants, let alone the Internet and the World Wide Web, can hardly avoid taking advantage of the embedded microchips and invisible processors that make phones easier to use, cars safer to drive, appliances more reliable, utilities more predictable, toys and games more enjoyable, and the trains run on time. Though any of these technologies can undoubtedly be infuriating, most people who complain want improvements, not to go back to life without them.[4]

Nonetheless, there is little reason for complacency. Information technology has been wonderfully successful in many ways.

But those successes have extended its ambition without necessarily broadening its outlook. Information is still the tool for all tasks. Consequently, living and working in the midst of information resources like the Internet and the World Wide Web can resemble watching a firefighter attempt to extinguish a fire with napalm. If your Web page is hard to understand, link to another. If a "help" system gets overburdened, add a "help on using help." If your answer isn't here, then click on through another 1,000 pages. Problems with information? Add more.

Life at Xerox has made us sensitive to this sort of trap. As the old flip cards that provided instructions on copiers became increasingly difficult to navigate, it was once suggested that a second set be added to explain the first set. No doubt, had this happened, there would have been a third a few years later, then a fourth, and soon a whole laundry line of cards explaining other cards.

The power and speed of information technology can make this trap both hard to see and hard to escape. When information burdens start to loom, many of the standard responses fall into a category we call "Moore's Law" solutions. The law, an important one, is named after Gordon Moore, one of the founders of the chip maker Intel. He predicted that the computer power available on a chip would approximately double every eighteen months. This law has held up for the past decade and looks like it will continue to do so for the next.[5] (It's this law that can make it hard to buy a computer. Whenever you buy, you always know that within eighteen months the same capabilities will be available at half the price.)

But while the law is insightful, Moore's Law solutions are usually less so. They take it on faith that more power will somehow solve the very problems that they have helped to create. Time alone, such solutions seem to say, with the inevitable cycles of the

Law, will solve the problem. More information, better processing, improved data mining, faster connections, wider bandwidth, stronger cryptography—these are the answers. Instead of thinking hard, we are encouraged simply to "embrace dumb power."[6]

More power may be helpful. To the same degree, it is likely to be more problematic, too. So as information technology tunnels deeper and deeper into everyday life, it's time to think not simply in terms of the next quadrillion packets or the next megaflop of processing power, but to look instead to things that lie beyond information.

DROWNING AND DIDN'T KNOW IT

If, as one of our opening quotations suggests, "all information about physical objects, including humans, buildings, processes and organizations, will be online," it's sometimes hard to fathom what there is beyond information to talk about.

Let us begin by taking a cue from MIT's Nicholas Negroponte. His handbook for the information age, *Being Digital,* encouraged everyone to think about the differences between atoms, a fundamental unit of matter, and bits, the fundamental unit of information.[7] Here was a provocative and useful thought experiment in contrasts. Moreover, it can be useful to consider possible similarities between the two as well.

Consider, for example, the industrial revolution, the information revolution's role model. It was a period in which society learned how to process, sort, rearrange, recombine, and transport atoms in unprecedented fashion. Yet people didn't complain that they were drowning in atoms. They didn't worry about "atom overload." Because, of course, while the world may be composed of atoms, people don't perceive it that way. They perceive it as buses and books and tables and chairs, buildings and coffee mugs, laptops and cell phones, and so forth. Similarly, while information may come to us in quadrillions of bits, we don't consider it that way. The information reflected in bits comes to us, for example, as stories, documents, diagrams, pictures, or narratives, as knowledge and meaning, and in communities, organizations, and institutions.[8]

The difficulty of looking to these various forms through which information has conventionally come to us, however, is that infocentric visions tend to dismiss them as irrelevant. Infoenthusiasts insist, for example, not only that information technology will see the end of documents, break narratives into hypertext, and reduce knowledge to data, but that such things as organizations and institutions are little more than relics of a discredited old regime.

Indeed, the rise of the information age has brought about a good deal of "endism." New technology is widely predicted to bring about, among other things,

the end of the press, television, and mass media

the end of brokers and other intermediaries

the end of firms, bureaucracies, and similar organizations

the end of universities

the end of politics

the end of government

the end of cities and regions

the end of the nation–state

There's no doubt that in all these categories particular institutions and particular organizations are under pressure and many will not survive long. There's nothing sacred here. But it's one thing to argue that many "second wave" tools, institutions, and organizations will not survive the onset of the "third wave." It's another to argue that in the "third wave" there is no need for social institutions and organizations at all.

The strong claim seems to be that in the new world individuals can hack it alone with only information by their side. Everyone will return to frontier life, living in the undifferentiated global village.[9] Here such things as organizations and institutions are only in the way. Consequently, where we see solutions to information's burdens, others see only burdens on information.

ORIGIN MYTHS

From all the talk about electronic frontiers, global villages, and such things as electronic cottages, it's clear that the romanticism about the past we talked about earlier is not limited to technophobes.[10] Villages and cottages, after all, are curious survivors from the old world applied to the conditions of the new. They remind us that the information age, highly rationalist though it seems, is easily trapped by its own myths. One of the most interesting may be its origin myth, which is a myth of separation.

Historians frequently trace the beginnings of the information age not to the Internet, the computer, or even the telephone, but to the telegraph. With the telegraph, the speed of information essentially separated itself from the speed of human travel. People traveled at the speed of the train. Information began to travel at the speed of light. In some versions of this origin story (which tends to forget that fire and smoke had long been used to convey messages over a distance at the speed of light), information takes on not only a speed of its own, but a life of its own. (It is even capable, in some formulations, of "wanting" to be free.)[11] And some scholars contend that with the computer, this decisive separation entered a second phase. Information technologies became capable not simply of transmitting and storing information, but of producing information independent of human intervention.[12]

No one doubts the importance of Samuel Morse's invention. But with the all-but-death of the telegraph and the final laying to rest in 1999 of Morse code, it might be time to celebrate less speed and separation and more the ways information and society intertwine. Similarly, it's important not to overlook the significance of information's power to breed upon itself. But it might be time to retreat from exuberance (or depression) at the volume of information and to consider its value more carefully.[13] The ends of information, after all, are human ends. The logic of information must ultimately be the logic of humanity. For all information's independence and extent, it is people, in their communities, organizations, and institutions, who ultimately decide what it all means and why it matters.

Yet it can be easy for a logic of information to push aside the more practical logic of humanity. For example, by focusing on a logic of information, it was easy for *Business Week* in 1975 to predict that the "paperless office" was close. Five years later, one futurist was firmly insisting that "making paper copies of anything" was "primitive."[14] Yet printers and copiers were running faster and faster for longer and longer periods over the following decade. Moreover, in the middle of the decade, the fax rose to become an essential paper-based piece of office equipment. Inevitably, this too was seen as a breach of good taste. Another analyst snorted that the merely useful fax "is a serious blemish on the information landscape, a step backward, whose ramifications will be felt for a long time."[15]

But the fax holds on. Rather like the pencil—whose departure was predicted in 1938 by the *New York Times* in the face of ever more sophisticated typewriters—the fax, the copier, and paper documents refuse to be dismissed.[16] People find them useful. Paper, as we argue in chapter 7, has wonderful properties—properties that lie beyond information, helping people work, communicate, and think together.

If only a logic of information, rather than the logic of humanity, is taken into account, then all these other aspects remain invisible. And futurists, while raging against the illogic of humankind and the primitive preferences that lead it astray, will continue to tell us where we ought to go. By taking more account of people and a little less of information, they might instead tell us where we are going, which would be more difficult but also more helpful.

HAMMERING INFORMATION

Caught in the headlights of infologic, it occasionally feels as though we have met the man with the proverbial hammer to whom everything looks like a nail. If you have a problem, define it in terms of information and you have the answer. This redefining is a critical strategy not only for futurology, but also for design. In particular, it allows people to slip quickly from questions to answers.

If indeed Morse did launch the information age, he at least had the modesty to do it with a famously open-ended question. "What," he piously asked in his first message, "hath God wrought?" Now, "we have answers," or "solutions" or "all the answers you need" (11,000 according to Oracle's Web site). Similarly, IBM claims that a single computer can contain "answers to all the questions you ever had."[17] So if Morse were to ask his question again today, he would no doubt be offered an answer beginning "http://www. . . . ."

True, Microsoft advertises itself with a question: "Where do you want to go today?" But that is itself a revealing question. It suggests that Microsoft has the answers. Further, Microsoft's pictures of people sitting eagerly at computers also suggest that whatever the question, the answer lies in digital, computer-ready information. For though it asks where you want to go, Microsoft isn't offering to take you anywhere. (The question, after all, would be quite different if Microsoft's Washington neighbor Boeing had asked it.) Atoms are not expected to move, only bits. No doubt to the regret of the airlines, the ad curiously redefines "go" as "stay." Stay where you are, it suggests, and technology will bring virtually anything you want to you in the comfort of your own home. (Bill Gates himself intriguingly refers to the computer as a "passport.")[18] Information offers to satisfy your wanderlust without the need to wander from the keyboard.[19]

REFINING, OR MERELY REDEFINING?

In the end, Microsoft's view of your wants is plausible so long as whatever you do and whatever you want translates into information—and whatever gets left behind doesn't matter. From this viewpoint, value lies in information, which technology can refine away from the raw and uninteresting husk of the physical world.

Thus you don't need to look far these days to find much that is familiar in the world redefined as information. Books are portrayed as information containers, libraries as information warehouses, universities as information providers, and learning as information absorption. Organizations are depicted as information coordinators, meetings as information consolidators, talk as information exchange, markets as information-driven stimulus and response.

This desire to see things in information's light no doubt drives what we think of as "infoprefixation." *Info* gives new life to a lot of old words in compounds such as *infotainment, infomatics, infomating,* and *infomediary.* It also gives new promise to a lot of new companies, from InfoAmerica to InfoUSA, hoping to indicate that their business is information. Adding *info* or something similar to your name doesn't simply add to but multiplies your market value.

Undoubtedly, information is critical to every part of life. Nevertheless, some of the attempts to squeeze everything into an information perspective recall the work of the Greek mythological bandit Procrustes. He stretched travelers who were too short and cut off the legs of those who were too long until all fitted his bed. And we suspect that the stretching and cutting done to meet the requirements of the infobed distorts much that is critically human. Can it really be useful, after all, to address people as information processors or to redefine complex human issues such as trust as "simply information?"[20]

6-D VISION

Overreliance on information leads to what we think of as "6-D vision." Unfortunately, this is not necessarily twice as good as the ordinary 3-D kind. Indeed, in many cases it is not as good, relying as it does on a one-dimensional, infocentric view.

The *D* in our 6-D notion stands for the *de-* or *dis-* in such futurist-favored words as

demassification

decentralization

denationalization

despacialization

disintermediation

disaggregation[21]

These are said to represent forces that, unleashed by information technology, will break society down into its fundamental constituents, principally individuals and information. (As we scan the Ds, it sometimes feels as though the only things that will hold up against this irresistible decomposition are the futurists' increasingly long words.)

We should say at once that none of these D-visions is inherently mistaken or uninteresting. Each provides a powerful lens on an increasingly complicated world. They help expose and explain important trends and pressures in society. Nonetheless, the Ds too easily suggest a linear direction to society—parallel movements from complex to simple, from group to individual, from personal knowledge to ubiquitous information, or more generally from composite to unit.

Yet it does not feel that modern life is moving in one direction, particularly in the direction from complex to simple. To most of us, society seems capable of moving in almost any direction, and often in the direction of chaos rather than simplicity. Indeed, many shifts that the 6-Ds reveal are not the first step in an unresisting downward spiral from complex to simple. Rather, they are parts of profound and often dramatic shifts in society's dynamic equilibrium, taking society from one kind of complex arrangement to another, as a quick review of a few Ds will suggest.

Dimensions of the Ds

Much talk about disaggregation and demassification readily assumes that the new economy will be a place of ever-smaller firms, light, agile, and unencumbered. It was once commonplace, for example, to compare the old Goliath, GM, against the new David, Microsoft. As Microsoft's market capitalization passed GM's, the latter had some 600,000 employees and the former barely 25,000. The difference is stark. Not, though, stark enough to step from here to what the business writers Larry Downes and Chunka Mui call the "Law of Diminishing Firms." After all, it's GM that's shrinking. Microsoft continues to grow while other high-tech start-ups compete for the title of "fastest growing ever."[22]

Downes and Mui draw on the theory of the firm proposed by the Nobel Prize–winning economist Ronald Coase. Coase developed the notion of *transaction costs*. These are the costs of using the marketplace, of searching, evaluating, contracting, and enforcing. When it is cheaper to do these as an organization than as an individual, organizations will form. Conversely, as transaction costs fall, this glue dissolves and firms and organizations break apart. Ultimately, the theory suggests, if transaction costs become low enough, there will be no formal organizations, but only individuals in market relations. And, Downes and Mui argue, information technology is relentlessly driving down these costs.

Though he produced elegant economic theory, Coase had strong empirical leanings. He developed his theory of transaction costs in the 1930s to bridge the gap between theoretical accounts of the marketplace and what he saw in the actual marketplace—particularly when he traveled in the United States. There, business was dominated by huge and still-growing firms. These defied the purity and simplicity of the theoretical predictions, which envisaged markets comprising primarily individual entrepreneurs.[23]

In honor of Coase's empiricism, it's important to look around now. When we began work on this book, Justice Department lawyers opened their case against Microsoft, accusing it of monopolistic practices. David now resembles Goliath. At the same time, other Justice Department lawyers were testifying that 1998 would be the first two-trillion-dollar year for mergers. Seven of the ten largest mergers in history had occurred in the first six months alone. We began keeping a list of firms involved. These included Amoco, AT&T, Bankers Trust, BMW, British Petroleum, Chrysler, Citibank, Deutsche Bank, Exxon, Ford, IBM, MCI, Mercedes, Mobil, Travelers, and many more.

Nor were these large firms buying up minnows. They were buying up each other. Ninety years after the era of trust busting, oil, banking, and tobacco, the initial targets, were all consolidating again.[24] As the *Economist* put it, after Exxon's merger with Mobil followed British Petroleum's purchase of Amoco: "Big Oil is Dead. Long Live Enormous Oil."[25]

Whatever else was apparent, we soon realized that whenever the book came out, any list of ours would be profoundly out of date. The only successful strategy in such conditions would be to imitate the great comic novelist of the eighteenth century, Laurence Sterne, who faced with an impossible description inserted a blank page into his manuscript and told the readers to take up their own pen and do it for themselves. As we were revising the manuscript, the two behemoths of the information age, AT&T and Microsoft, began their own extraordinary mating dance. That we found well beyond the reach of our pens.

Undoubtedly, several of the mergers we mentioned may represent the last struggles of dinosaurs to protect their ecological niche before other forces destroy it. Investment and even retail banking, for example, may have particularly precarious futures.

But massification is not occurring in dying "second wave" sectors alone. Many mergers have involved firms based in the "third wave" information sectors. Here mergers often involve not so much dinosaurs as phoenixes rising from the ashes of old business models. These might include AT&T's absorption of TCI and Time-Warner's of Turner Broadcasting. They surely do include Internet-driven combinations such as MCI's merger with WorldCom, IBM's takeover of Lotus, and AT&T's purchase of IBM's Global Network. Meanwhile, firms wholly within the new economy, such as AOL, Microsoft, Amazon, and eBay, go on regular shopping sprees for other companies.

Elsewhere in the information sector, Sir John Daniel, vice-chancellor of Britain's Open University, points to the rise of the "mega-university." Daniel presides over some 160,000 students, but his school hardly qualifies as "mega" in a field in which the largest—China's TV University System—has 580,000 students in degree programs. According to Daniel's figures, two universities break the half-million mark, one exceeds one-third of a million, and three are approaching a quarter million.[26] These are all "distance" universities, using a variety of information technologies to reach their students. So no simple demassification here either. Similarly, the concentration of the media in recent years challenges any simple idea of media demassification.[27]

It doesn't feel then as if firms are shrinking under an iron law. Rather, it feels more as if, as the economist Paul Krugman puts it, "We've gone from an economy where most people worked in manufacturing—in fairly large companies that were producing manufactured goods and engaged in things like transportation—to an economy where most people work for fairly large companies producing services."[28]

The resilience of the large organization is not all that surprising. Given that information technologies are particularly good at taking advantage of large networks, the information economy in certain circumstances actually favors the aggregated, massified firm.[29] These are firms that can or have knit diverse networks together, as AOL hopes to do with its purchase of Netscape or as Microsoft hopes to do with the insertion of Windows into television set-top boxes. Consequently, the small, agile firm with big ideas and little money is less likely to be the viable start-up of legend. (As a recent article in *Red Herring* put it, referring to the famous garage-based start-ups of Silicon Valley, the "garage door slams shut.")[30] And any that do start up in the traditional way are likely to be snatched up by the giants of the industry.

So, while stories abound about the new "niche" markets exploited through the Internet, the examples often come not from niche firms, but from large ones with well-established networks. The paradoxical phrase "mass customizing" suggests that fortune favors the latter. It is possible, for example, to have jeans cut to your personal dimensions. But it is quite probably Levi's that will do it for you. Here the strategy for customized goods relies on a large firm with a large market and a highly standardized product. So the demassification of production relies on the massification of markets and consumption. The Henry Ford of the new economy would tell us that we can all have jeans made to measure, so long as they are Levi's.

Finally, firms are not merely taking power from one another. They are accumulating power that once lay elsewhere. The political scientist Saskia Sassen traces the decline of the nation–state not to the sweeping effects of demassification and disaggregation, but to the rise of powerful, concentrated transnational corporations. The new economic citizen of the world, in her view, is not the individual in the global village but the transnational corporation, often so formidable that it has "power over individual governments."[31] The state and the firm, then, are not falling together along a single trajectory. At least in some areas, one is rising at the other's expense.

In sum, as people try to plot the effects of technology, it's important to understand that information technologies represent powerful forces at work in society. These forces are also remarkably complex. Consequently, while some sectors show disaggregation and demassification, others show the opposite. On the evidence of the 6-Ds, attempts to explain outcomes in terms of information alone miss the way these forces combine and conflict.

So while it might seem reasonable to propose a law of increasing, not diminishing, firms, that too would be a mistake. It would merely replace one linear argument with another. It's not so much the actual direction that worries us about infocentrism and the 6-Ds as the assumption of a single direction. The landscape is more complex. Infocentricity represents it as disarmingly simple. The direction of organizational change is especially hard to discern. The 6-Ds present it as a foregone conclusion.

More Dimensions

Similarly, despite talk of disintermediation and decentralization, the forces involved are less predictable and unidirectional than a quick glance might suggest.[32] First, the evidence for disintermediation is far from clear. Organizations, as we shall see, are not necessarily becoming flatter. And second, where it does occur, disintermediation doesn't necessarily do away with intermediaries. Often it merely puts intermediation into fewer hands with a larger grasp. The struggle to be one of those few explains several of the takeovers that we mentioned above. It also explains the "browser wars" between Netscape and Microsoft, the courtship of AT&T and Microsoft, and the continuing struggle for dominance between Internet Service Providers (ISPs). Each of these examples points not to the dwindling significance but to the continuing importance of mediation on the 'Net (as does the new term *infomediary*, another case of infoprefixation). Moreover this kind of limited disintermediation often leads to a *centralization* of control. These two Ds, then, are often pulling not together, but against one another.

NOT FLATTER. Francis Fukuyama and Abram Shulsky conducted a RAND study in 1997 into the relationship between disintermediation, flat organizations, and centralization on behalf of the army. They began by studying the private sector. Here they give little hope for any direct link between information technology and flatter organizations. Indeed, like us, they believe that the conventional argument that information technology (IT) will lead to flatter organizations is an infocentric one

> *[that] focuses on a single, if very important, function of middle management: the aggregation, filtering, and transmission of information.*

> *It is of course precisely with respect to this function that the advances*
> *in IT suggest that flattening is desirable, since IT facilitates the*
> *automation of much of this work. On the other hand, middle man-*
> *agement serves other functions as well.*[33]

If managers are primarily information processors, then information-processing equipment might replace them, and organizations will be flatter. If, on the other hand, there is more to management than information processing, then linear predictions
about disintermediation within firms are too simple.

Empirical evidence suggests such predictions are indeed over-
simplified. Despite the talk of increasingly flatter and leaner organizations, Paul Attewell, a workplace sociologist, argues that "administrative overhead, far from being curtailed by the introduction of
office automation and subsequent information technologies, has
increased steadily across a broad range of industries."[34] Attewell's
data from the U.S. Bureau of Labor Statistics show that the growth
of nonproduction employees in manufacturing and the growth of
managerial employment as a percentage of the nation's workforce
has risen steadily as the workplace has been infomated.

NOR MORE EGALITARIAN. Fukuyama and Shulsky also argue
that in instances where information technology has led to disintermediation, this has not necessarily produced decentralization. "Despite talk about modern computer technology being
necessarily democratizing," they argue, "a number of important
productivity-enhancing applications of information technology
over the past decade or two have involved highly centralized
data systems that are successful because all their parts conform
to a single architecture dictated from the top."[35] Among the
successful examples they give are Wal-Mart and FedEx, both of
which have famously centralized decision making.

These two are merely recent examples of a clear historical trend whereby information technology centralizes authority. Harold Innis, an early communications theorist, noted how the international telegraph and telephone lines linking European capitals to their overseas colonies radically reduced the independence of overseas administrators. Previously, messages took so long to travel that most decisions had to be made locally. With rapid communication, they could be centralized. Similarly, histories of transnational firms suggest that with the appearance of the telegraph, overseas partners, once both financially and executively autonomous, were quickly absorbed by the "home" office.[36]

Less innocent than infoenthusiasts, commanders in the U.S. Navy understood the potential of information technology to disempower when they resisted the introduction of Marconi's ship-to-shore radio.[37] They realized that, once orders could be sent to them on-board ship, they would lose their independence of action. (Their resistance recalls a story of the famous British admiral Lord Nelson, who "turned a blind eye" to his telescope at the Battle of Copenhagen to avoid seeing his commander's signal to disengage.)[38]

In contemplating assumptions about the decentralizing role of information technology, Shoshona Zuboff, a professor at Harvard Business School, confessed to becoming much more pessimistic in the decade since she wrote her pathbreaking book on the infomated workplace, *In the Age of the Smart Machine*: "The paradise of shared knowledge and a more egalitarian working environment," she notes, "just isn't happening. Knowledge isn't really shared because management doesn't want to share authority and power."[39]

Of course this need not be the outcome. As Zuboff argues,

it's a problem of management, not technology.[40] Smaller organizations, less management, greater individual freedom, less centralization, more autonomy, better organization, and similar desirable goals—these arguments suggest—will not emerge spontaneously from information's abundance and the relentless power of the 6-Ds. Rather, that abundance is presenting us with new and complex problems that another few cycles of Moore's Law or "a few strokes of the keyboard" will not magically overcome.[41] The tight focus on information, with the implicit assumption that if we look after information everything else will fall into place, is ultimately a sort of social and moral blindness.

THE MYTH OF INFORMATION

6-D vision, while giving a clear and compelling view of the influence of the 'Net and its effects on everything from the firm to the nation, achieves its clarity by oversimplifying the forces at work. First, it isolates information and the informational aspects of life and discounts all else. This makes it blind to other forces at work in society. Second, as our colleague Geoffrey Nunberg has argued, such predictions tend to take the most rapid point of change and to extrapolate from there into the future, without noticing other forces that may be regrouping.[42]

This sort of reductive focus is a common feature of futurology. It accounts, for example, for all those confident predictions of the 1950s that by the turn of the century local and even domestic nuclear power stations would provide all the electricity needed at no cost. Not only did such predictions overlook some of the technological problems ahead, they also overlooked the social forces that confronted nuclear power with the rise of environmentalism. (Fifties futurism also managed to miss the significance of feminism, civil rights, and student protest while continually pointing to the imminence of the videophone and the jet pack.)

We began this chapter with a brief look back to the industrial revolution. In many ways the train epitomized that earlier revolution. Its development was an extraordinary phenomenon, spreading from a 12-mile line in the 1830s to a network of nearly 25,000 miles in little more than a decade.[43] The railway captured the imagination not only of Britain, where it began, but of the world. Every society that could afford a railway, and some that couldn't, quickly built one. Standards were developed to allow for interconnections. Information brokers emerged to deal with the multiple systems involved.[44] The train also sparked an extraordinarily speculative bubble, with experienced and first-time investors putting millions of pounds and dollars into companies with literally no track record, no income, and little sign of profitability. Unsurprisingly, in popular imagination, both at the time and since, the train has presented itself as a driving force of social and economic revolution.

Economic and social historians have long argued, however, that the story of the industrial revolution cannot be told by looking at the train alone. Historians might as well whistle for all the effect they have had. The myth of the train is far more powerful.

Today, it's the myth of information that is overpowering richer explanations. To say this is not to belittle information and its technologies. These are making critical and unprecedented contributions to the changes society is experiencing. But it is clear that the causes of those changes include much more than information itself. So the myth significantly blinds society to the character of and forces behind those changes.

In particular, the myth tends to wage a continual war against aspects of society that play a critical role in shaping not only society, but information itself, making information useful and giving it value and meaning. It's hard to see what there is other than information when identity is reduced to "life on the screen," community thought of as the users of eBay.com, organization envisaged only as self-organization, and institutions merely demonized as "second wave."

We do not believe that society is relentlessly demassifying and disaggregating. Though we admit it would be much easier to understand if it were. The social forces that resist these decompositions, like them or not, are both robust and resourceful. They shaped the development of the railroad, determining where it ran, how it ran, and who ran it. And they will continue to shape the development of information networks. As we hope to show in the course of this book, to participate in that shaping and not merely to be shaped requires understanding such social organization, not just counting on (or counting up) information.[45]

CHAPTER 2

Agents and Angels

I'm sorry to hear that you are depressed.
> It's true, I am unhappy.

Do you think coming here will help you not to be unhappy?
> I need some help, that much seems certain.

What would it mean to you if you got some help?
> Perhaps I could learn to get along with my mother.

Tell me more about your family.

IN THIS EXCHANGE, the therapist was Eliza, a legendary computer program written in 1966 by Joseph Weizenbaum of MIT. The identity of the patient is fortunately unknown. According to folklore, Eliza software persuaded many people to pour out their souls in the belief that a person, not a software program, was responding.

The software behind Eliza has since developed in many directions, including, for example, customer service. (This is not all that surprising. Irate customers often resemble the deranged and customer service agents, automatons.) On the Web site of Neuromedia, for example, you can meet the prototype, Shallow Red, who will greet you as follows:

> *Hello. I'm Shallow Red. I'm a Virtual Representative made with NeuroStudio™. What is your name?*
> John
>
> *Are you ready to ask some questions, John?*
> Yes
>
> *What would you like to know about Neuromedia?*
> What does Neuromedia do?
>
> *Neuromedia makes authoring and serving tools to assist people in the development and deployment of VSRs.*

Eliza and Shallow Red are both examples of "chatterbots." These are software programs that will simulate a human response to typed questions. There's an old joke (old, that is, by Internet standards) with the tag line "on the Internet, nobody knows you're a dog." And sometimes it can be quite hard to tell if what you are dealing with is a chatterbot. There's one, apparently, that plays Jeopardy with great skill.[1]

Chatterbots, in their turn, are instances of "autonomous agents" (familiarly known as "bots"). These agents, it seems likely, will play an increasingly critical role in the organization, in particular the self-organization, of social life. First, they help deal with the cascades of information that many people find so threatening. Second, they promise to handle many intricate human tasks. If they can, they promise to sweep away many conventional organizations and institutions previously involved in those tasks. So bots offer an interesting way to evaluate some of the endisms threatened by information technology.

These agents are not just the dream of eager futurists. Many are already hard at work. Without them the Internet, which has grown so dramatically in the past few years, would by now be unmanageable. Diligent agents that endlessly catalogue the World Wide Web for such familiar services as Yahoo!, Lycos, Excite, and Alta Vista have helped to manage it. As a result, you can find needles of information in the Web's vast haystack and order in the midst of its apparent chaos. Indeed, it was the search-and-catalogue capability of their agents that principally transformed these sites from mere search engines into lucrative *portals*—points where people plan and begin their voyages on the 'Net (and so points of great interest to advertisers).

Agent software also runs on the sites of major Internet retailers. When a regular shopper arrives, for example, at the sites of the bookseller Amazon.com or the CD seller CDNow, a personalized list of suggestions greets him or her. Agents track the customer's preferences and purchases and, by "collaborative filtering," compile these lists dynamically. The suggestions reflect purchases made by others with apparently similar tracks (and so, presumably, tastes).[2] Agents will trim the virtual "shop window" that a customer sees on arriving at the retailer's site to reflect his or her interest. In some cases they may also offer personalized discounts tailored to particular buying patterns and not available to other shoppers.

Agents don't only work for portals, retailers, and similar organizations. Increasingly people have agents at their personal disposal, even on their desktop. Macintosh computers, for example, come with "Sherlock," a customizable agent that will orchestrate many of the Web's different search engines into a collective search on a user's behalf. (Search engines don't catalogue the Web in the same way, and none catalogues more than a fraction, so orchestration is more powerful than solo performance.) Web users also have access to shopping agents or "shopbots" that on request will roam the Web sites of different vendors, comparing prices.

There are many plans for agents to perform other tasks and responsibilities on behalf of individuals. Already they undertake highly complex institutional financial trading, so it isn't surprising that developers envisage them trading for individuals. Already, too, NASA's infomatics division has a "smart T-shirt," remotely connecting its wearer's body to large central computers that can track vital signs and provide medical advice or summon assistance as necessary. This work, done for the military, is expected to migrate to civilian use.[3]

These examples seem part of a general trend leading from institutional agents to individual, personalized ones. As one book puts it, over the next few years, bots will be ever "more tightly woven into the fabric of our daily lives."[4] By 2005, a study offering more precision predicts, "at least 25 percent of the then-current PC/workstation user base will allow their personal agents to anticipate their needs."[5]

THE ROAD AHEAD

There's undoubtedly a great deal of reasonable forecasting in such predictions. There's a good deal of technological evangelism, too.[6] Indeed, in the hands of some futurists, agents appear more as angels offering salvation for encumbered humanity than as software programs. They will hover over our virtual shoulders, monitoring our good deeds and correcting our failings.

They will have all the advantages of their ethereal, wholly rational character to see past our earthly foibles and overcome our bounded rationality. But they will also be capable of entering into the material side of life, mowing lawns, stocking the refrigerator, and driving the car.

The evangelistic view, however, may overlook some significant problems on the road ahead. And in overlooking those problems, it may actually miss ways in which agents can and will be practically useful, preferring instead to trumpet ideal but ultimately impractical uses. In considering agents in this chapter, then, our aim is not to dismiss them. We are great admirers. But we seek to ground them in social life rather than "information space."

The problems bots face, however, may be hard to see. Agents are victims of the sort of procrustean redefinition we mentioned in chapter 1. The personal names—Sherlock, Jeeves, Bob, or Red—though they are surely harmless enough on their own, hint that the gap between digital and human is narrow and narrowing. Using human job titles such as "personal assistant" or "agent" for digital technologies closes this gap a little further, suggesting that these jobs might soon be open to real or virtual applicants alike. Other terms, "digital broker" or "electronic surrogate," also elide the world of software and the world of humans, suggesting the possibility of having the best of both worlds. And many accounts simply endow digital agents with human capacities. They talk of bots' "decision-making powers," "social abilities," "learning capacities," and "autonomy."[7] Bill Gates confidently predicts that bots will soon develop personality.[8]

Redefinition comes from the other direction, too. That is, some accounts don't so much make bots sound like humans as make humans sound like bots. One definition puts both in a broad class of "goal pursuing agents, examples [of which] are to be found among humans (you and I), other animals, autonomous mobile robots, artificial life creatures, and software agents."[9] This kind of redefinition not only makes humans seem like bots, but makes human activity—learning, developing taste, wanting, choosing, pursuing, brokering, negotiating—appear principally as different kinds of individual information processing done equally by software goal-pursuing agents or by "wetware."[10]

Faced with such redefinitions, it becomes important to pay attention to ways that human learning, developing taste, wanting, choosing, pursuing, brokering, and negotiating are distinct. In particular, these human practices reflect social and not simply individual activities. Redefinition, however, makes it easy to overlook the significant challenges that this social character presents. As the history of artificial intelligence shows, computer science has long found social issues particularly hard to deal with (as, indeed, have social scientists). Social issues are remarkably hard. "It isn't that these issues aren't interesting," Robert Wilensky, a professor of computer science of the University of California, Berkeley, put it succinctly, "it's just that these problems, like so many social/psychological issues, are *so* hard that one had to hope that they weren't on the critical path."[11]

But with the sort of agenda for agents that we have summarized above, technologists and designers have now put these issues directly on the critical path. So whether as designers, producers, or users, we will all have to confront them, asking to what extent agents should or can be woven into the fabric of human life in all its complexities. These are issues that everyone must face.

Furthermore, they are issues that, from a technological point of view, cannot simply be read off from past successes with agents, admirable though these successes are. If social and psychological issues lie ahead (and they surely do when dealing with taste, style, and judgment), and if Wilensky's insight that such matters have been avoided in the past is right, then the road ahead is not likely to continue directly from the one behind. We cannot cry "full speed ahead" and trust that the outcome will be desirable. A tight focus on information and behaviorist aspects of individuals has propelled development successfully to its current position. But it will probably not suffice to take us to the less restricted future laid out for bots. To understand where to go next, it's time to open the aperture and look around. In what follows, we try to raise some of the social and psychological issues that, for good reasons, have usually been left out of discussions, both of the past and of the future.

RANKS OF AGENTS

To understand the strengths and limits of agents, let us look primarily at personal assistants and some of the tasks planned for them. First, we look at the sort of information brokering done by the Macintosh's Sherlock. We then consider three categories of what might be thought of as market brokering. Here Pattie Maes (a professor at MIT's Media Lab and one of the most insightful designers of collaborative filters) and two colleagues distinguish three stages in the overall "buying process" that bots can handle. They are "product brokering," "merchant brokering," and "negotiation."[12]

Information Brokering

Information brokering puts agents in their own backyard, weeding and selecting from among the very stuff that is central to their existence—information. As we said, there are many successful information brokers currently in use, not only combing the World Wide Web as a whole but also, for example, gathering market information from the major exchanges, collecting weather information from diverse sources, indexing online newspapers, updating citation links between on-line journals, and gathering, "mining," and processing information from multiple databases. From here, it's easy to assume that these sorts of agents might make those classical providers and selectors of information—newspapers, publishers, libraries, and universities—redundant. Another handful of institutions appears set to disappear.[13]

To explore the strengths of information-brokering bots, however, it's important also to recognize their limitations. We sent Sherlock out on a relatively simple search, and to keep it well within its own interests, we asked it to search for *knobot*. Orchestrating half-a-dozen major search engines, Sherlock very quickly returned 51 "hits." That is, it pointed to 51 documents in the vast cornucopia of the Web containing the word *knobot*—an apparently rich return in such a short time. But an hour or so of follow up exposed some limitations.

7 were simple repeats (different search engines turned up the same site and Sherlock failed to filter them out).

3 more were simple mirrors. Here, a site on one server carries the direct image of a site on another, so although the addresses were different, the document containing *knobot* was exactly the same.

11 pointed directly or indirectly to a single document apparently held at an "ftp" site of the Corporation for National Research Initiatives (NRI), a high-powered research center

in Reston, Virginia. NRI computers, however, refused to acknowledge the existence of this document.

2 pointed indirectly to a document at the Johnson Space Center (JSC) via the word Knobot (TM). *TM* (trademark) suggested that the JSC has some proprietary interest in the term and so its site might be particularly rewarding. Alas, the link to the JSC was dead, and a search using the JSC's own knobot returned the answer "Your search for knobot matched 0 of 418337 documents."

2 others led to documents that did not contain the word *knobot*. Here the document itself had probably changed, but not the index.

14 led to a single document maintained by the World Wide Web consortium. Unfortunately, the word *knobot* seemed more or less irrelevant to the document.

2 led us to the Music Library at Indiana University, which curiously was peripherally involved in some rather overblown claims about the digital library and the Internet.[14] The documents there, alas, only pointed us on to the World Wide Web consortium again, but this time to a document apparently removed.

2 pointed to papers using the word *knobot* in passing.

4 led to glossaries defining the word *knobot* to help people read documents using the word *knobot*.

4 led to two documents at Stanford University, two chapters in a report outlining how agents could make searches of the Web and digital libraries more usable.[15]

We cannot read too much significance into this outcome of a single search. Sherlock is a relatively crude engine and our single-word search, with no refinements, was itself yet more crude. Our results primarily serve to remind us that the Web is a vast, disorderly, and very fast-changing information repository with enormous quantities of overlapping and duplicate information and that all its catalogues are incomplete and out of date. That in itself, however, is a useful lesson when we consider whether the Web, self-organized but patrolled by bots, might be an alternative to libraries. Automatic organization, like automatic search, has its perils.

More significantly, perhaps, Sherlock's objective search, conducted on relatively friendly territory, hints at difficulties that might lie ahead in sending out a Sherlock-like surrogate with requests to "get me a knobot," let alone to get the "best," the "most interesting," the "most useful," or the "most reliable" knobot. This brings us to the marketplace kinds of brokering discussed by Maes and her colleagues.

Product Brokering

Product brokering, the first in their basket of shopping agents, involves agents that alert people to the availability of particular items that, given a person's previous track record, might be of interest. It's the sort of brokering done by the bots at Amazon and CDNow. Like Ian Banks? Well, there's a new William Gibson book available. Listen to the MJQ? Well, there's a new issue of John Lewis. eBay, the on-line auction offers agents to alert users when a particular type of item comes up for sale. This kind of brokering is enormously useful. But because it is so useful, all sorts of people are interested in it, both as producers and consumers.

When interests conflict, they can lead to major problems for brokers and their users.[16]

The flap over Amazon's endorsements indicated the potential for difficulties. The Amazon site offers, among other things, recommendations and endorsements for books it stocks. In this it recalls conventional book (or wine) stores, where staff often provide personal recommendations, and customers come to rely on them. Such recommendations thus have something of a "mom and pop" or corner-store charm to them and can draw people who might otherwise resist the impersonal character of the on-line retailer. But when it was revealed that publishers paid Amazon for some endorsements, that charm dissipated. Amazon was quick to insist that it would always indicate which endorsements were paid, but the fall was irreversible. Innocence was lost, and faith in good agents on "our" side had to face the specter of bad agents purporting to represent "our" interests but in fact secretly representing someone else's.

The Amazon problem recalls the famous case against American Airlines' SAABRE system. Ostensibly this system would find all available flights from a computer database. In fact, it was subtly weighted to favor American's flights. Both examples raise questions of technological transparency. We might all be able to use agents, but how many are able to understand their biases among the complex mathematics of dynamic preference matching? Is your agent, you must ask, neutral, biased, or merely weighted? And can you tell the difference? Who really controls your agent, you, the designer, or the person feeding it information? How can you be sure that your agent has not been "turned," being now a double agent? As with the SAABRE case, will we all need to rely on some supervening agencies, rather than agents, to ensure fair play? An infocentric approach does not resolve these questions.

Merchant Brokering

Maes and her colleagues' second category, merchant brokering, includes agents that can roam the 'Net comparing prices and so report back on "best buy" options. Again, these sorts of bots are already in use and are helpful resources, providing the sort of information that makes markets more efficient, removing layers of intermediation in the process.

But again, too, they present some problems for the idea of the Web that they are assumed to promote. The buzz is all about personalization, product diversity, the demassification of production and consumption, and niche markets. Merchant brokering, however, heavily favors standardization.

Consider, for example, that despite all the rhetoric about the Internet "killing" the book and tailoring information, the first great flagship of Internet enterprise was a book retailer. There is no real surprise here. Books are the oldest mass-produced commodity. They are wonderfully standardized, with each copy of a particular edition being almost identical to its fellows. And markets, particularly long-distance markets, work best with standardized measures and standardized products.[17] The integration of the European market, for example, has driven nonstandard varieties of fruit and vegetables out of the market altogether, while wine regions that once blended seventy varietals now find themselves with five. So the first concern about merchant brokering is whether it may lead to less choice, not more as is often promised.

A second problem is that, as part of the process of price competition and standardization, subjective issues such as quality and service disappear. Both service and quality, the economists Brad de Long and Michael Froomkin have argued, tend to get squeezed out of markets when low price becomes the decisive factor.[18] From the decisive factor, low price soon becomes the only factor. Network effects will tend to marginalize merchants who try to resist. With bots, which are not well suited to weigh subjective issues such as quality and service, these will probably disappear much more quickly.

In fact, though, quality and service don't simply disappear in these conditions. They can become highly problematic "externalities," not subject to the sales and purchase contract, but imposing heavy burdens after the fact. Low-bid environments have frequently shown this. Many government agencies award contracts to the lowest bidder to eliminate costly corruption. Instead they get costly headaches from inept or deceptive bidding, poor service, cost overruns, supplemental negotiations, "change orders," out-of-their-depth firms going bankrupt, and complicated litigation—all of which must ultimately be paid for. Led by Rhode Island and Washington, several states are now exploring alternative, more reliable indicators than the lowest price to choose suppliers.[19]

And as with product brokering, the question of good and bad agents also haunts merchant brokering. This time the user must ask not "Is this recommendation really what I wanted?" but "Is the price quoted in fact the lowest price available?" Amazon again became involved in such a question when it stepped from the market of highly standardized commodities, new books, to the far less standardized one of out-of-print books. These are priced from the subjective influence of such things as provenance (who owned the book before), author signatures, wear and tear, scarcity, and the like, so prices can vary significantly. Amazon offers a bot to search for out-of-print books for customers with the promise that this would recommend the lowest-priced book. But people who used the service have claimed that it would often recommend a copy that was not the lowest priced available.

Again the questions arise, "Is this an inept or a corrupt agent?" and perhaps more important "Can you tell the difference?" The 'Net, some economists believe, will become home to perfect information. It will be harder to make it a place of perfect (and trustworthy) informers.

Negotiating

These problems suggest that agent brokering is more problematic than it may first appear. The difficulty of agent negotiating is already well known. Despite the way many pundits talk of their presence just over the horizon, true negotiating bots do not yet exist. Maes and her colleagues are more circumspect about their development. And experimental results show serious problems. Nonetheless, it's easy to find confident talk about the speedy appearance of "Situations where your software agent meets my agent and they negotiate for prices and conditions."[20]

Difficulties with bots arise because human negotiating is an intricate process that tends to keep an eye on externalities such as the social fabric as well as on the immediate goal. This social fabric embraces such things as social capital and trustworthiness, things that make social relations, including market relations, possible. The confident predictions about markets of negotiating bots, however, tend to assume that negotiating is little more than a matter of matching supply and demand.

The first thing to notice is that people negotiate all the time. These negotiations, however, are only occasionally over price. Usually, humans negotiate behavior. They continually accommodate themselves to one another, and in the process construct and adjust the social fabric. In negotiating this way, people are barely conscious that they are negotiating at all. Indeed, when negotiations surface and people do become aware of them, it is usually a sign that implicit negotiation has broken down or that there is a tear in the social fabric.

Consider, for example, the way people negotiate with one another in the flow of collective conversation. Conversations demand individual and collective decisions over who will speak, when, and for how long. But in informal conversation the negotiations involved in such turn taking, though rapid and efficient, are all but invisible. To claim a turn, people will merely shift their gaze, subtly alter body position, or wait for a break to interject. Others will turn from or toward them, inviting them in or leaving them out. Speakers will hand off the conversation with a look, rising intonation, or a direct question to another person. Or they may attempt to keep hands on by avoiding eye contact, speaking rapidly, rejecting counteroffers, or pausing only at words like *and* or *so*. (One of the reasons that conference calls can be so awkward is that they remove many of these cues used for effective negotiation.)

Or consider a speechless negotiating practice: the way people on a crowded street negotiate a passage, pulling to one side or another, standing back, hurrying forward, dropping into single file then falling back to two abreast, and so forth. All of this is done with rarely a word among people who have never seen each other before and will never see each other again. Such negotiation does not rely on simple rules like "keep left" or "keep right." Rather it is a dynamic process. It too only becomes noticeable when it fails, when, for example, both pull in the same direction, stepping toward the street, then toward the wall, then back again, each time finding the same person in their way. (Such accidental deadlocks have been nicely called *faux pas de deux*.)[21]

In conversation, such impasses might be called a committee. In committees, particularly acrimonious ones, such implicit negotiations often don't work. Then participants have to invoke formal rules: the right to speak, the right to resist interruption, the order of speakers, the topics permitted, the length of time allotted, points of order, and so forth. This sort of explicit, rule-governed negotiation is clumsy, but necessary when the social fabric will not bear implicit negotiation. It looks more like the sort of thing developers have in mind when they talks of bots negotiating, but it is only a small portion of what human negotiation involves.[22]

HUMAN FOIBLES. To understand human negotiation and imitate it, then, requires understanding humans as more than simple "goal pursuing agents." For humans, rules and goals bear a complicated relationship to the social fabric. Both may shift dynamically in practice depending on the social conditions that prevail.

This human shiftiness is present even when people shop, let alone when they talk. In shopping, as elsewhere, humans have the awkward habit of changing rules and shifting goals in mid-negotiation. The Berkeley anthropologist Jean Lave discovered this in her studies of people shopping in the supermarket.[23] The people that she and her colleagues studied set out with a list that looks like a bot's instructions. When they returned, they accounted for their behavior in bot-like terms, talking about "best buys," "lowest prices," and so on. But studying their actual shopping behavior revealed something quite different. In between setting out and coming back, they continually shifted their goals, their preferences, and even their rules without hesitation. Shopping was in many ways a process of discovering or creating underlying preferences rather than acting in accordance with them.

This sort of goal shifting is even more evident when people negotiate directly with one another. (In a supermarket, we are often more in negotiation with ourselves than with anyone else. "Do I really want this?" "Is this worth it?" "Will the family eat it?" are questions we try out on ourselves, not on other people.) In interpersonal negotiation, people change their immediate goal for the sake of the higher goal of preserving the social conditions that make negotiation possible. For example, people will back off demands, even if they are in the right, because asserting rights may damage the social fabric.

People don't only abandon goals. They abandon rules, too. Authorities, for example, turn a blind eye if they sense that enforcing the law could be more damaging.[24] Stock exchanges not only suspend trading (particularly electronic trading), they may even suspend the rules when to do otherwise would damage the exchange or the market. In such circumstances, people implicitly invoke the axiom that if following the rules causes damage, then abandon the rules—an axiom it's hard for bots to follow. Immediate goals, longer-term relationships, and creation and preservation of the social fabric are always in balance in this way. Indeed, this interdependence paradoxically affects even those who deliberately break the rules. Liars have a heavy investment in truth telling, opportunists in dependability, speculators in stability.

BOT FOIBLELESSNESS. Negotiating bots favor the direct and explicit side of human negotiation. They are the economist's idealized "homo economicus," anonymous traders working in a spot market. They are blind to the complex social trade-offs between goals, rules, and the social fabric. So it's no surprise to find that they are capable of tearing rents in that fabric.

Experiments at both IBM and MIT with bots in apparently frictionless markets indicate potential for destructive behavior. Not "subject to constraints that normally moderate human behavior in economic activity," as one researcher puts it, the bots will happily destabilize a market in pursuit of their immediate goals. In the experiments, bots engaged in savage price wars, drove human suppliers out of the market, and produced unmanageable swings in profitability. "There's potential for a lot of mayhem once bots are introduced on a wide scale," another researcher concluded.[25] The research suggests that frictionless markets, run by rationally calculating bots, may not be the efficient economic panacea some have hoped for. Social friction and "inertia" may usefully dampen volatility and increase stability.

De Long and Froomkin even suggest that such frictionlessness might disable the "Invisible Hand." The great classical economist Adam Smith used the image of the invisible hand to describe forces that reconcile the pursuit of private interests through markets with the public good and with what we have called the social fabric. If not actually producing good, at least the invisible hand prevents the pursuit of private interests from doing harm. "Assumptions which underlie the microeconomics of the Invisible Hand," de Long and Froomkin conclude, "fray badly when transported to the information economy."[26]

Better bots, then, will require a better understanding of human negotiation, the contribution of the social fabric, and the role of human restraint in the functioning of the invisible hand. Development will be ill served by people who merely redefine elaborate social processes in terms of the things that bots do well.

HOW AUTONOMOUS?

If human negotiation is a delicate and complex art, it is inevitably more delicate and more complicated when conducted by proxies. And bots are proxies. They act not on their own behalf, but on behalf of others. As such, they also lead us to questions about delegation and representation, which will take us once more to the issue of transparency.

Delegates

One account of bot delegation, defining it in human terms, explains it as follows: "Just as you tell your assistant, 'When x happens, do y' an agent is always waiting for x to happen!"[27] The first and most obvious question to confront is: Is that really how human assistants work?

If humans are not, as we suggested, strict in following rules, they are far worse at laying them out. Human delegation relies as much on sympathetic disobedience when circumstances change as it does on strict obedience. As people working with computers have long known, strict obedience leads to disaster. Internet stock traders are becoming increasingly aware of this problem as on-line trades are executed as ordered in conditions of insufficient liquidity—conditions in which a broker would wisely have disobeyed the order. Labor organizations have long known that by "working to rule," following only the letter but not the spirit of a work contract, work becomes impossible.

Behind the stock traders' difficulties and labor tactics lies the simple truth that giving orders that have to take account of all possibilities is impossible in all but the simplest tasks. Consequently, rules, contracts, delegation, and the like rely on unspecifiable discretion and judgment on the part of the person following those orders. These return us once again to the differences between bots and people. Judgment and discretion are not features of software. They are products of human socialization and experience. As the political philosopher Michael Oakeshott has argued, they are learned not by the acquisition of facts and rules, but through social relations and participation in human activities.[28] As Mark Humphrys of the School of Computer Applications, Dublin University, points out, even if bots could learn like humans, they lack the rich stimuli that humans depend on to develop such things as judgment. Bots, in contrast to humans, live a wretchedly impoverished social existence.[29]

Representatives

Of course, the view of bots as blindly obedient, "doing x when y happens," denies them much of the autonomy that is central to their identity as autonomous agents. Consequently, it is more usual to think of bots as having "control over their own actions and their own internal state," as one account puts it.[30] While it might solve the problem of blind obedience, this autonomy raises problems of its own. If bots make decisions and give advice autonomously, who takes responsibility for those decisions? Can Eliza be sued for medical malpractice? And if not, should the programmer be sued instead? Can Shallow Red be sued for business malpractice? And if not, who should be sued, the programmer or the company that the chatterbot represents?

If the owner of a bot should take responsibility for those actions, then that owner must have some control over and insight into them. Yet for most bot users, the digital technology around which bots are built is opaque. Because bots are autonomous, it can be difficult to know what decisions a bot has taken, let alone why.

Once, as promised, bots start interacting with one another, understanding bot behavior may become impossible. Anyone who has had to call a help line with a problem about the way an operating system from one vendor and a program from another are working together—or failing to work—knows how hard it is to get anyone to take responsibility for software interactions.[31] Support staff rapidly renounce all knowledge of (and usually interest in) problems that arise from interactions because there are just too many possibilities. So it's easy to imagine sophisticated programmers, let alone ordinary users, being unable to unravel how even a small group of bots reached a particular state autonomously. The challenge will be unfathomable if, as one research group has it, we can "anticipate a scenario in which billions of intelligent agents will roam the virtual world, handling all levels of simple to complex negotiations and transactions."[32]

If human agents are confused with digital ones, if human action is taken as mere information processing, and if the social complexities of negotiation, delegation, and representation are reduced to "when x, do y," bots will end up with autonomy without accountability. Their owners, by contrast, may have accountability without control.

These are not trivial matters. As we have seen, people are being asked to put everything from the food in their refrigerator to their cars, houses, assets, reputation, and health in the hands of these agents despite the difficulty of understanding what these agents actually do or why.

One of the remarkable features of the recent failures of derivative traders (such as Barings Bank, Long-Term Capital, and Orange County) has been how little investors, even major financial institutions, have understood about the ventures to which traders armed with highly complex mathematical calculations and software programs were committing them. They took it all on trust, had insufficient safeguards (though somewhat paradoxically they called themselves "hedge" funds), and lost disastrously. The question "Do you know what your agent is doing tonight and with whom?" and the worry that their agent is no angel may loom increasingly large in the already overburdened late-night worries of executives.

"THE BRIGHTEST FELL"

Once you worry about bots that represent, you also have to worry about bots that misrepresent. Bots may not be like people in every way, but they can give a good imitation of human deceit and in so doing be quite disruptive. And as with humans, it can be difficult to distinguish good from bad. "There's no way," one system administrator insists, "to tell the difference between malicious bots and benign bots."[33] The similarity is already significantly changing the way the 'Net is viewed.

Since its early days, the 'Net has been an extraordinary source of free help and information. Some have suggested that it is an example of a "gift economy." One of the most useful areas of this economy has been the newsgroups. Though these are probably more famous for their pornographic content, newsgroups provide a great deal of esoteric and not just erotic information. Divided into groups by subject, they allow people interested in a particular topic to pose questions and receive advice and suggestions from people with similar interests. There are, for example, multiple Microsoft Windows discussion groups where people having difficulty with everything from basic use to Visual Basic programming can get help.[34]

Given this aspect of the 'Net, it wasn't too surprising to get some helpful advice when Paul put an advertisement to sell a car in Yahoo!'s classifieds. This is a free service that allows you to describe the car in your own words and provide details of how you can be reached. Within twenty-four hours a friendly message came back:

From: shelby@dallas.quick.com

Subject: FYI ON AUTO SALES

Date: Tue, 21 Jul 1998 17:33:22 -0600

X-Mailer: Allaire Cold Fusion 3.0

X-UIDL: 8e772fe616fe165b05ca43f75d8ea500

i saw your vehicle ad on the internet. i just wanted to let you know about the realy neat system i found where mine sold after many inquiries shortly after listing it. you can get to that system by clicking on the following link:
http://www.aaaaclassifieds.com

just thought you might be interested.

dan

Thanking Dan for his kind recommendation, however, was more difficult than it first appeared. "shelby@dallas.quick.com" turned out to be a bogus address. The message, ingenuous misspelling and all, had come from an anonymous remailer in the

Czech Republic designed to conceal the identity of the actual sender. "Dan" was no doubt little more than a software program, combing the 'Net for postings on car lists and sending out this advertisement disguised as a personal recommendation from a "user like you."[35] As the political scientist Peter Lyman points out, strange things happen when a gift economy and a market economy collide.[36]

WAR IN HEAVEN

Dan is only a minor case of what has become close to bot warfare on the 'Net. While bots have yet to develop personality, they have already been involved in "personality theft," sending out messages in the names not only of people who do not exist but also of people who do exist but did not send the message. One journalist found he had been widely impersonated by a bot that sent e-mail and joined chat rooms using his name.[37]

Besides creating messages in others' names, bots can also erase them, wiping out messages that people have sent. *Cancelbots*, as these are sometimes called (perhaps they could more simply be called *Nots*), are an unfortunate case of good intentions gone awry. They developed in response to a notorious newsgroup incident. Two lawyers used a bot to post a message offering immigration assistance on 6,000 newsgroups. Angry newsgroup users took corrective action, developing cancelbots, which could patrol newsgroups and remove messages that were posted indifferently to multiple groups. Such a design, however, was too tempting to remain only a force for good. One night in September 1996, a rogue cancelbot wiped out 30,000 bona fide newsgroup messages.[38]

The 'Net now has a robust army of antisocial bots. These

attack the innocent and the guilty alike. They make misleading recommendations and erase useful ones. They throw dust in the eyes of the collaborative filters and others tracking patterns of use.[39] And they overload mailboxes and attack Web sites until they crash. As rapidly as the diligent bots find ways to see through their ruses and overcome these tactics, others find new ways to produce mayhem.

Meanwhile, the line between good and bad becomes increasingly hard to draw. Intel, for example, recently persuaded Symantec, maker of antivirus software to take action against what was deemed by Intel "hostile" code written by a company called Zero-Knowledge Systems. People who rely on Symantec's software now get a warning when they visit Zero-Knowledge's site that they may be at risk from viruses. Zero-Knowledge, however, insists that its software is not a virus, but a program designed to reveal a flaw in Intel's chips. Intel's categorization, Zero-Knowledge maintains, was deliberately self-serving.[40]

MOORE SOLUTIONS

Faced with the rebellions of these fallen agents, people often suggest that another cycle of Moore's Law will produce suitably powerful encryption to resist them.[41] Better encryption (and fewer government restrictions) will almost undoubtedly be advantageous. But it is important to realize that it alone cannot solve the problems at issue. Why not? First, the same power that is used for defense can be used for attack. As a (perhaps apocryphal) detective from London's Scotland Yard is said to have put it fatalistically, in fifteen years computers will be involved in the solution of most crimes, but they will also be involved in the perpetration of most crimes.

Second, solutions that rely on encryption already focus too tightly on information systems, ignoring the fact that these are always and inevitably part of a larger social system. Just as bots only deal with one aspect of negotiation, the information-exchange part, so cryptography deals only with one part of technological systems, the classical information channel. The human activity that encryption is designed to protect, however, usually involves much more.

For example, in the 1990s a number of companies have produced strategies for secure and private digital cash transactions over the Internet. Some of these—in particular David Chaum's company DigiCash, founded in 1994—matched powerful technologies and admirable social goals. Futurists have greeted each such company and its encryption tools with confident claims that here was the "killer application" of the era. It would allow secure microtransactions (cash exchanges worth pennies), provide suitable anonymity and thereby unleash net commerce, dismantle the current financial system, and undermine the power and authority of major banks. It all sounded plausible, with more institutions satisfyingly looking to fall.

Unfortunately, DigiCash itself, like other similar efforts before it, fell, filing for bankruptcy in November 1998. It failed not because encryption isn't important, nor because DigiCash's encryption wasn't good (it was very good), but because encryption isn't enough. A viable system must embrace not just the technological system, but the social system—the people, organizations, and institutions involved. It must be able to verify not just the encryption, but a user's right to use the encryption, that this right has not been revoked, and that it is being used correctly. "A digital signature," says Dan Geer, an encryption specialist and chief strategist for CertCo, "is only as valid as the key (in which it was signed) was at the moment it was signed, it is only as good as the procedural perfection of the certificate issuer and the timely transmission of subsequent revocation."[42] In short, encryption is a strong link in a long chain whose very strength points up the weakness of other links, which cannot be made so secure. Overall, such systems, Geer argues, are only as secure as the financial and institutional investment committed. Consequently, interactions over the 'Net, financial or social, will be as secure not as its digital encryption, which is a relatively cheap fix, but as the infrastructure—social as well as technological—encompassing that interaction.[43]

SEPARATE SPHERES

The human and the digital are significantly, and usefully, distinct. Human planning, coordinating, decision making, and negotiating seem quite different from automated information searches or following digital footsteps. So for all their progress, and it is extraordinary, the current infobots, knobots, shopbots, and chatterbots are still a long way from the predicted insertion into the woof and warp of ordinary life. Current successes may not, as some hope, point directly to the grander visions laid out for agents. Optimists may be underestimating the difficulties of "scaling up" from successful but narrow experiments to broader use. (It's been said that computer scientists have a tendency to count "1, 2, 3, one million, . . . ," as if scale were insignificant once the first steps were taken.)

Digital agents will undoubtedly play a central part in future developments of the 'Net. They are powerful resources for all sorts of human interactions. But to pursue their development needs more cold appraisal and less redefinition or evangelism.

First, developers and futurists must recognize that their goals address fields of human activity that lie well beyond the simple realm of information. "The humanizing of technology," the sociologist Anthony Giddens argues, "is likely to involve the increasing introduction of moral issues into the now largely 'instrumental.'"[44] Designing bots to imitate or replicate human actions introduces both moral and social-institutional questions. Your willingness to put your paycheck into a slot in the wall is, in many ways, remarkable. But it relies on much more than the instrumental reliability of the ATM. Indeed, for most people a particular ATM isn't transparent enough for us to judge whether it is instrumentally reliable or not. Instead, we look for reliability, both instrumental and moral, in the organizations represented by the ATM and by the institutions regulating those organizations.[45]

But, as Robert Wilensky rightly points out, such issues have not been on the critical path of much computer science. They are now on the road that lies all before us. They are not insurmountable roadblocks. But if people do not open their eyes a little wider, they will act as potholes into which much research may unprofitably stumble.

Second, and most important, bots and humans operate in different, if overlapping, spheres. By redefining one as the other, or reducing both to information-processing or goal-pursuing agents, these differences are submerged or confused. Some futurists seem continuously anxious to replace humans with bots in certain tasks without quite appreciating how *people* accomplish those tasks. In general, it will be better to pursue not substitution but complementarity. (We want ATMs that will supply us with money, not ones that will spend it for us.) But complementarity requires seeing the differences between information-processing agents and human agency.

CHAPTER 3

Home Alone

MONDAY: *Cannot access personal e-mail box from home using company's Internet access. Call company. Unbeknown to me or support services, I have been accessing my personal e-mail for four years through a leak in the company's firewall. Will no longer be able to access this e-mail account, where most of my mail accumulates, an e-mail message tells me, adding a smiley face for consolation. Suggests opening a third ISP [Internet Service Provider] in addition to company and remote site in order to dial locally and use remote mail address. (The alternative is to close the remote account and lose mail from people who still have that 10-year-old address or who continue to get it from records remaining on the Web, over which I have no control.)*

TUESDAY: *After a little research, choose local Baby Bell as a cheap, reputable ISP from a large enough company with a large enough interest to do it well. Go to their Web site to download Internet access software. Download crashes my machine. Try again. Successful after two more crashes and an hour. Next, install software. Crash. Try again. Success. Reboot. New software starts automated registration process. Crashes. Reboot. Recrash. Have to*

63

remove ISP sign-up software to start machine successfully. Try to install once again. Same problems. Same crashes. Same process to remove. Call service center. Polite confession, download is "a little buggy." Recommended the more reliable CD kit. Will send. In all about 5 hours lost. CD takes 5 days to arrive. The provider's compelling slogan "How will you use it?" remains moot.

MONDAY (following week): *Try to install Internet kit using CD-ROM. Invokes Crashguard (designed to prevent crashes) and brings everything to a halt. Remove Crashguard. Load Provider kit successfully. Start installation again. Crashes. Repeat. Repeats. Use a second computer to reach ISP's "Help me find a solution" Web site. Apparently if the version of Netscape already on your machine is newer than the one in Provider's kit, a Java bug may cause installation to fail. Discard my better version of Netscape. Run registration kit. Refuses to recognize modem. Contact provider. Apparently, if the modem is very new, the installation kit doesn't contain initialization information. My modem is two years old; the company that made it has long been taken over. About 4 hours lost.*

TUESDAY: *Call ISP. Tell them I would prefer to do my own manual installation if they would let me have the necessary details. Service center discourages this, politely but firmly. I tell them the troubles I have had with their automation, tell them I believe I am competent to do a manual installation but cannot find details (phone numbers, TCP/IP numbers) on their Web site. The details are not there. They exist on an automated fax system. Obligingly, provider representative agrees to fax them. Sit, wait. Nothing happens. Call provider. Tell details to a new (equally polite) provider representative, who again tries to discourage me from going it alone, who again agrees to fax, but who acknowledges automated fax system can sometimes take a long time—even days, apparently. Kindly agrees (probably against rules) to copy the details into an e-mail message and send it to the one account I still have easy access to. Sends it. Insert details. Log on successfully. Open an account successfully. Try to log onto 'Net. Fails. All settings work for registration only. Must remove all settings, reinsert a new list to use for all other purposes. Finally, 9 days later, with the help of two computers, three e-mail accounts, phone, fax, and the best part of four days lost, I'm on the 'Net. It's just a click away.*

THURSDAY: *Automated fax with details for manual installation chugs slowly through my fax.*

—Home Office Diary

INFORMATION, AS THE PHRASE HAS IT, "wants to be free," and that freedom, it is widely hoped, will in turn make people free. In particular, many people hope that it will free them from the ties of the office and the firm. The era of "organization man" may be coming to an end, and a society of entrepreneurs emerging. There are certainly many reasons to hope for this and some to believe it might be possible.

The idea that the individualized technology of the information revolution will undo the massification produced by the technology of the industrial revolution underlies most such scenarios of disaggregation. Steam mills brought people together to work at single sites. They thus helped to drain the countryside of its inhabitants and concentrate the population in factory towns. Information technologies, many hope, might at least halt this two-century-long process. Supported by the 'Net, people can drift apart to hot desks, home offices, and telecenters. The drain from the countryside appears pluggable with technology.

YEARNING TO BREATHE FREE

Thus Microsoft, for example, emphasizes the value of its technologies to the survival of the small town (pop. 1,500) of Lusk, Wyoming. "The people of Lusk," Microsoft's Web site proclaims, "are using Microsoft software and technology as a means to preserve their way of life."[1] Others hope that this trek from country to city may not just stop, but reverse. In the view of some futurists, information technology will help rediscover *gemeinschaft*, the sort of small, local, community-based way of life broken down, according to some sociologists, by industrialization. Hence the quasi-rural talk of "televillages" and "electronic cottages."[2] Somewhere in here, then, is that familiar hope that the road to the future will somehow take us back to the simplicities of the past.

Yet other enthusiasts see no reason to stop at the village. The cyberguru and writer John Perry Barlow extols the nomadic life. He was a rancher in Wyoming, but now believes his laptop and cell phone, allowing him to work anywhere, free him from ties to place or community, making him an itinerant citizen of the global village of cyberspace (for which he issued a declaration of independence).[3]

In all of this, there is a mixture of hype and hope with some quite reasonable forecasting. The idea that technology can untie the unwanted ties that bind people together seems to have been around since those ties started to bind. The canal, the railway, the telephone, and rural electrification were all taken as signs of hope. With the Internet, that hope seems more reasonable. Now, people truly can reach colleagues, correspondence, conferences, customers, and so forth instantly and remotely.

Yet the slow pace of transformation to, for example, the home office suggests that some critical challenges are being glossed over and some important questions left unasked. Is it, for example, only "path dependency" (the legacy of history) and inertia that keep people together in conventional offices? Can innovation pick apart the uncomfortable social ties that bind, but leave the wanted ones intact? Can it undo the unprofitable ties, but leave the profitable ones? Are these two goals the same? And, to return to the question we raised in the last chapter, is the current approach to technology design leading in the right direction, or may it again be focusing too tightly on an idealized view of information and how it—and individuals—work?

JUST A CLICK AWAY?

The home office may seem little more than a click away, but predictions have put it just over the horizon for some time now. In 1980, Alvin Toffler predicted that within our lifetime urban downtowns would "stand empty, reduced to use as ghostly warehouses or converted into living space." Yet a 1998 survey shows that the office vacancy rate dropped to single digits for the first time since 1981, despite office completions doubling in 1997.[4]

Another prediction claimed 66 percent of workers would work from home by the millennium.[5] Though reliable figures are hard to find, it would take a startling burst between now and 2000 to reach even 6 percent. And the greater part of the jobs would probably still be in farm work or child care. In the late 1980s, the pace was so timid that one disgruntled researcher (who had tried a home office and found how difficult it was) claimed, "if things go well for high-tech homeworking, we may get back to 1950s levels of self-employment some time in the 21st or 22d century."[6] Going forward to the past can be slow work.

The data on which such assessments are made, we need to stress, are highly ambiguous, and it is easy to make the proportions look much more favorable. Figures for home workers in the United States swing wildly from one million to 41 million, depending on how the category is defined. The low-end figure comes from government data (and includes 300,000 self-employed, the balance working at home but for someone else).[7] Higher figures (which usually come from people with something to sell) tend to bundle in anyone who takes any work (except their own housework) home, including, for example, teachers who take home papers to grade.[8]

Even the direction of trends can be hard to read. Some people trace a rise in home working in the early 1990s to the explosion of the Internet and related technologies. Others attribute it to the last major round of corporate downsizing. If the latter explanation is right, this trend may have gone into reverse with the "upsizing" of the late 1990s. What little valuable research there is shows that even for those who triumphantly set themselves free from the prison of the office, recidivism is quite high. One study of a telecenter found that 25 percent of the participants gave up within the first five months, and 50 percent within a year.[9]

LEAVING HOME

A couple of articles in *Wired*, emblematically in issues 2.07 and 7.02, illustrate such reverses. The first profiled a company restructuring its offices to accommodate the new wired future in 1994.[10] Five years later, in 1999, *Wired* reported on the same company's retreat to conventional offices.[11] The two stories both looked at "hot desking," the strategy of abandoning fixed desks and providing laptops, cell phones, and Internet connections so employees can work where they choose. Though some may have chosen to take their hot desk home, hot desking is clearly different from the canonical home office. But it provides some insight into the difficulties of getting out of the conventional office and offers some explanations of why some who return home to work leave home again before too long. [12]

First, many of the difficulties reflect a misunderstanding of office work, which is too easily painted as information handling.[13] This sort of redefinition drives Toffler's analysis. He built his argument for the "electronic cottage" on firms that had seen significant shifts from manual to managerial work. At one such firm, Toffler was told that "fully half of the 2,000 workers now handle information instead of things, and much of their work can be done at home." Others firms concluded, "fully 75 percent could work at home if we provided the necessary communications technology."[14] The idea of managers working remotely with information inevitably ignores the much more difficult, intangible, but inevitably face-to-face side of management, the management not of things or of information, but of people.[15]

Second, bold predictions about the spread of hot desking and electronic cottages may also ignore the frailty of technological systems.[16] The more cavalier futurists sometimes appear to work with a magical brand of computer not available to the rest of us. It's hard to believe that if they had to deal with the inexplicable crashes, data corruption, incompatibilities, buggy downloads, terrifying error messages, and power outages that are standard fare for most, they could remain quite so confident about the ease of hot desking and home working. As the home office diary we began this chapter with shows, simply downloading Internet software can lose many billable hours and cause nightmares. [17]

And third, by overlooking both the social aspects of work and the frailty of technology, design that attempts to replace conventional work systems may often merely displace the burdens of work. In the transition to home offices, these burdens pass from the social system, where tasks are shared, onto the lap of individuals. The desire to show that with a computer one person can do everything may look not forward, but back to the stage in social evolution before anyone noticed the advantages of the division of labor.

In all, to achieve the goals that technologists themselves set out, it will become increasingly important both to reconceive work and to retool design. In particular, design needs to attend not simply to the frailty of technological systems and the robustness of social systems, but to the ways in which social systems often play a key part in making even frail technology robust.

NO ROOM OF ONE'S OWN

The *Wired* hot desking stories that we mentioned earlier covered the famous attempt by the advertising company Chiat/Day to reconceive work in a new way and a new building. The first story followed the firm into its new offices.[18] The second, five years later, watched its retreat to a more conventional way of working.[19] The agency is well known for producing Apple advertisements, including the famous 1984 Superbowl ad, which portrayed Apple as champions of individualism, and the later "Think Different" campaign. The new offices of the early nineties (in Los Angeles and New York) suggested that Chiat/Day, too, could both champion individualism and think differently.

The exterior design of the Los Angeles building (by the architect Frank Gehry) expressed the forward-looking approach directly—it resembled a pair of binoculars. But inside, it was even more unconventional. Arrangements were based on the simple principle that no one should have a room of his or her own. Instead, if they came to the office, employees could check out a laptop and a cellular phone and then look for somewhere to sit. At the end of each day, they had to check these back in again—so there were no tools of one's own, either. In a curious way, then, Chiat/Day managed to be individualistic and collectivist at the same time.

Not only did people not have offices, they also were not supposed to sit in the same place on consecutive days. Jay Chiat, the CEO, occasionally walked the floors asking people if they had been where they were sitting on the day before and, if they had, would move them on. Anything not stored in digital form on the company's servers via the laptops—retrograde stuff like books, papers, and files—had to be put away in hall lockers at the end of each day and taken out again in the morning. There were meeting rooms for formal meetings, but all other deskwork and communication was to be done digitally.

COOLING OFF

With hot desking, Chiat/Day sought to keep people on the creative edge of the business. All reports suggest that it primarily just kept them on edge. Chaos rather than dynamism was the most noted result. But for observers, the Chiat/Day experiment (which the company's new owners abandoned) exposes to view some of the underlying needs of people working together that the infocentric view too easily overlooks.[20]

First, it made some simple material needs clear. Desks are useful things and provide more than a surface to balance a laptop on. Moreover files, documents, and even those wobbly stacks people build on their desks often have a useful sequential order in their disorder (which is why tidying can be so disruptive). Similarly, people customize phones and laptops to fit personal ways of working. Having to rebuild your conventional or your digital desktop every morning is a highly disruptive chore that ignores the needs of work and the nature of technology.

Second, the experiment also showed that, constraining though they sometimes are, offices keep people together for good reasons as well as bad. Good office design can produce powerful learning environments. But much of that power comes from incidental learning. For example, people often find what they need to know by virtue of where they sit and who they see rather than by direct communication. At Chiat/Day people were spread around roughly in the order in which they arrived. People who worked together didn't necessarily sit together or see each other. (Chiat/Day account managers reported coming back from client meetings and being unable to find their department.) With such lottery seating, incidental learning is much harder to come by. As a result, the need for more cumbersome formal learning and informing processes increases.

Third, the Chiat/Day experiment also showed that, despite the power of technologies, robust work patterns are hard to disrupt. To get things done, people rebelled. They filled their lockers and the trunks of their cars with the files they needed. They refused to turn in their laptops and telephones. And they used various strategies to build "virtual" departments. Here, being virtual was not an aspect of the digital realm. These were physical areas of the office that people tried to occupy collectively so that they could re-create the useful connections of conventional departments.

Finally, accounts of this office-based civil disobedience throw an interesting light on other social implications of office design. One metaphor for the Chiat/Day office was the campus. Students on a college campus don't have offices, the masterplan argued. They move from classrooms, to libraries, to lounges. The same model was expected to work for the office. As some employees pointed out, however, at Chiat/Day the result was more like high school. In particular, the redesign appears to have unleashed the office equivalent of high school bullying. The daily unsettled space created daily turf wars. Departments tried to pull rank on each other, each claiming favored areas because it was "more important." Account executives and creative departments went to battle over pecking order. People with sufficient authority and power pulled rank on those without, seniors shooing juniors away from comfortable spots. Executives with assistants would order the latter in early to hold a place for their boss. And so on.

Petty though this might seem, the turf wars remind us that offices involve much more than the simple flow of information. Office space is not neutral ground. Everyone who works in one knows that, for better and for worse, offices are dense with highly charged social relations. Power, tension, authority, and insecurity are all closely interwoven. They can help get work done, and they can hinder it. The troubles at Chiat/Day indicate how the structure of the conventional office, while it may pander to petty fiefdoms and yearnings for a window or a corner office, helps keep social tensions and turf war in check. Any one settlement may appear less than optimal, but it may nonetheless be better than no settlement at all.

Breaking up such a settlement has different consequences, depending on where you stand (or sit) in an organization. The urge for radical reorganization, such as tearing the walls down and throwing away all badges of rank, generally comes from the top. But it is usually those in less secure positions who bear the adverse consequences. Bosses lose little else when they lose their space. Their status is usually still quite evident. Others lower in the pecking order, where authority and control are far more tenuous, may find they lose a good deal more. Middle management, one of the most insecure points in any organization, may find managing increasingly difficult.

Undoubtedly, making people justify their position and authority, challenging old alliances and divisions, and generally trying to transform office culture by transforming its infrastructure can be a good way to destroy inertia and drive new thinking. Breaking from a structured office to hot desking, however, suggests that the only two alternatives are closed stables or a stampede. Between these two lie more subtle uses of office space that can enhance working conditions, build channels of coordination and communication, and improve the quality of work done.

Indeed, while Chiat/Day has taken many of the headlines, both euphoric and damning, elsewhere modern office design has proceeded along much more interesting lines. Plans more closely relate physical structure and social structure, revealing the pecking order without either reinforcing it or concealing it behind a faux egalitarianism. External models have been internalized, so that the floor plans of some offices now resemble town plans with streets, squares, parks, and locales. While the accolade "community" is often used to make the most tawdry design seem respectable, this "community-based planning" at its best can both reflect and magnify the social resources for getting work done.[21] Forward-looking companies are finding that designing a new company and designing its offices are intricately related processes, with each feeding off and into the other. Such designs are expected to be dynamic as well, with businesses looking for designs that do not lock the company into a single model of work but can grow with the company.[22]

At their best, such design reflects the social character of work—the way in which people act as resources for one another, rather than just as one another's information provider. Given the nature of this resourcefulness, severing the ties that bind people together in work may be as damaging as binding them together more tightly. Finding the balancing point between the mix of centrifugal and centripetal forces needs to be the goal. It is admittedly a challenging one, which may involve alternative or even shifting points of equilibrium.

MAINTAINING BALANCE

Information technology undoubtedly must play an increasingly important part in this balancing act. Yet none but an evangelist could claim that technology will find the balance point automatically. Introducing new technologies and overestimating what they could do played a role in the imbalance felt at Chiat/Day, as it has elsewhere.

More generally, new technology often threatens not to help find a new equilibrium but rather to unsettle equilibria whenever they are found. The rapid innovation endemic to the technology can be destabilizing, even for large organizations with copious resources. In well-supported offices, users often look to the next upgrade with much the same relish with which they greet the annual visit of the winter flu. They know it will precipitate crises and shortages, increase the burdens of those still up and running, and take weeks for the headaches to pass. They also know that just about the time that things return to balance, another disruptive strain will come through. Where there aren't technicians to manage the transformation or peers to share the burdens with, the weight of continuous product innovation can be unsupportable.[23]

The instability that rapidly changing technology brings, however, often lies less in the technology itself than in enthusiastic expectations that everything being "just a click away" or "at your fingertips" will make life easy. Battered by such hype, it's easy to believe that everyone except *you* knows how to use this stuff without a problem.

We saw this pressure at work on a new employee at Xerox PARC. She was intelligent and hard working, but got mired in difficulties with the office computer system. That system came with the usual promises of "usability" and self-explanatoriness, but she found it impossible to use or understand. Being a newcomer, she was reluctant to keep asking for help. Suffering in silence, it seemed daily more likely that she would have a breakdown if she didn't quit.

Then chance moved her desk from an isolated office into the center of a group of offices. There she immediately benefited from the incidental learning that we mentioned earlier. She saw that these "stable" machines crashed for everyone. She saw that there was no more "ease" for experienced assistants, longtime employees, or PARC's hallowed computer scientists than for her. And she also saw that when a machine did crash, its user would without shame look around for help from someone else who, whatever their status, had successfully steered around that particular problem. No one person knew how to handle these temperamental machines. But spread around the office was enough collective knowledge to keep them up and running.

Office help systems, this story indicates, are not limited to manuals, vendor Web sites, IT departments, or on-line files. The office social system plays a major part in keeping tools (and people) up and running. The "geek" who understands the network, the secretary who knows the secrets of Word, the one colleague proficient with databases, the other who has learned Java in her spare time, and the one who knows how to nurse the server all contribute.

Most systems, amalgams of software and hardware from different vendors, rely on social amalgams of this sort to keep everything running. (One of the first people mentioned on the Microsoft Web page about Lusk, the Wyoming town, is a teenager who "doesn't mind sharing his expertise.") In this way, the facts of office life reveal a combination of technological frailty and social resourcefulness. Infoenthusiasts, however, tend to think of these the other way around, missing the role of the social fabric and assuming that individuals in isolation can do it all.

Paul Strassmann, former vice president of Xerox's Information Products Group and onetime chief information technologist for the Department of Defense, argues that most businesses that are well endowed with computer technology lose about $5,000 a year per workstation on "stealth spending." Of this, he argues, "22% [is] for peer support and 30% for the 'futz factor.'" The second includes "time users spend in a befuddled state while clearing up unexplained happenings [and] overcoming the confusion and panic when computers produce enigmatic messages that stop work."[24]

Home office workers usually lack this sort of cash. More significantly, they lack necessary peer support. Consequently, with current technology, money-losing futzing, late at night and early in the morning, is endemic to the home office. Lacking the boundaries and structures provided by office life, work spills relentlessly over into private and family life.

INVISIBLE HANDS

Within organizations, this stealth spending is readily hidden from those at the top. Unfortunately, so is the need for such spending. Life at Xerox brought us face to face with this issue, too, this time over the matter of copier design. Xerox has long made usability a critical issue for the design and marketing of its photocopiers. With one series of copiers, however, reports came back from the field saying that machines were proving unmanageable for most people. Management disregarded these reports, however, because when they used the copiers, they found them thoroughly usable.

Only in time did it become clear why. The most common encounters between senior management and copiers came when new machines were presented for their inspection. Inevitably, in such encounters, the managers were surrounded by people whose jobs depended on all going well. Consequently, as managers experimented, the right finger was edged toward the right button at the right time, in a thousand barely perceptible ways. What everyone took to be a successful encounter between an individual, instructions, and the copier was actually an encounter made successful by an informal and almost invisible social network working hard to prevent the embarrassment of failure for all.

Like the story of the Xerox assistant, once again we see that the office help system is significantly a social system. It is also something that home office workers don't have. But instead of trying to overcome this deficit, futurists and technologists instead lead people to believe that they don't need to rely on social systems and would be better without them. "Put a computer in people's homes," Toffler insists, "and they no longer need to huddle,"[25] as if huddling were always a waste. But it isn't. It's often a way of getting things done through collaboration. At home with frail and fickle technologies and unlimited configurations, people paradoxically may need to huddle even more, but can't. After all, as Craig Mundie, a senior vice president at Microsoft acknowledges "there's no IT manager in the home"—though much of the technology seems to require one.[26] These cumulative problems may lead to the curious paradox that information technology, by ignoring the role played invisibly by the social system, is keeping people out of the home and in the conventional office, and not the other way around.

CONCENTRATED EFFORT

In a home office the only IT manager is the person who wants to spend time working with the tools, not on them. When tools fail, home workers have to provide their own variety of the peer support Strassmann mentions. All problems and all futzing, shared elsewhere, fall into the lap of the idealized, individualized entrepreneur. Nor is this concentration limited to malfunctions. In attempting to replace outmoded ways of doing things, new technologies also displace work tasks that were once successfully shared across a group. These are now concentrated on an individual.

Desktop publishing, for example, tries to put in a box on the desktop all the tools that previously were distributed among authors, editors, copy editors, proofreaders, designers, typesetters, and printers, each with their own embodied, inarticulate skill and judgment built out of experience. On the one hand, concentrating tools like this produces enormous benefits. An individual gains, at least potentially, tremendous freedom and control. On the other, that individual now lacks the experience and support that was distributed among those different roles. Inevitably, much of this sort of concentration takes place on the assumption that the task involved, typesetting for example, is purely "mechanical" so the experience is of no interest once the mechanisms change.

The purely mechanical is rarely so pure. There's a story told of a typesetter working on a Greek text at the Oxford University Press who announced he'd found a mistake in the text. As the typesetter couldn't read Greek, his colleagues and then his superiors dismissed his claim. But the man insisted. So finally an editor came down to the compositing room. At first, she, too, dismissed the idea, but checking more closely, she found there was an error. Asked how he knew, the typesetter said he had been hand picking letters for Greek texts for most of his professional life and was sure that he'd never made the physical move to pick the two letters in that order before.

The story may well be apocryphal, but it does illustrate the diverse sorts of knowledge, including the "embodied" knowledge, which people in different roles possess. (And may account for the absence of cogent editing or design in many modern books.) Putting this all on the desktop, while supporting the individual in some ways, ignores the support and knowledge latent in systems that distribute work. The apparent "ease" offered by these technologies hides much of the extra work they involve. So teachers are encouraged to "put their materials up on the Web," as if that task too were merely a click away. Anyone who tries will quickly find how demanding making and maintaining a worthwhile Web page can be.

The displacement and concentration provided by digital technology may be a legacy of its design. The legend of the 'Net, after all, is littered with stories of people "hacking" around the clock, oblivious to time or sleep. It's still a young person's medium, calling for intense concentration and few distractions.[27] Andrew Odlyzko, a mathematician at Bellcore who has pioneered studies of Internet design and behavior, argues that most systems development serves the interests of such dedicated users. In so doing, it ignores the demands such development places on ordinary users. In consequence, there has been, he argues, a "migration of administrative and maintenance duties" toward the edges of the system—to the individual user, who is the person least equipped to deal with these problems. When that person is isolated in the home office, the migrants all beat a path to a single door.[28]

SOMETHING FOR NEXT TO NOTHING?

For the home office, one of the most significant things displaced to the margin is cost. We all know that the cost of hardware is dropping precipitously. The $500 computer with Internet access already looks expensive. It's easy, then, to imagine setting up a home office for a few thousand dollars. But infoenthusiasts, who tend to underestimate many challenges, often underestimate costs, too. Odlyzko estimates that capital costs are only about 20 percent of total costs for a networked environment; as Strassmann argues, many of the true costs are often hidden "stealth" fashion, in budgets.

Even without the stealth portion, costs are high for both conventional and unconventional offices. Figures for the 1990s show Microsoft spending $16,000 per annum for each of its workstations on maintenance and upgrading.[29] (Given these expenses and the difficulties, it's not surprising to read that some companies are "downgrading and 'de-automating'; Chrysler Financial Corp. and Pacific Gas & Electric, among others, search for perfect blend of manpower and technology.")[30] These figures are not that different from those provided by the California advertising agency CKS (now USWeb/CKS). It had about one quarter of its employees working at home, but estimateed that new technologies there cost the firm between $10,000 and $15,000 per employee per year—though employees were still paying half the costs of the hardware.[31]

Not only are these costs hard for a small office to bear. It's hard, too, to bear the hype which claims that a principal advantage of the home office is that it's cheaper. "The reason why companies are going towards telecommunications is simple," one advertisement argues: "They save millions." They usually do not. Indeed, some people have claimed that many of Chiat/Day's problems followed from its unwillingness (or inability) to meet the true costs, visible and invisible, of hot desking.

Trying to transform the way work is done and simultaneously save money is usually a mistake, even when moving from cost-laden atoms to near-free bits. The demands of turning work that has been well supported by the local social system into work produced without most or any of that system requires a commitment to transformation, not a commitment to cost cutting. For when costs are not met up front in the home office, they are deducted, stealth fashion, from the unbudgeted and unbillable time of the home worker.

PARADOX LOST

Frailty, displacement, and cost, then, are significant and continuously underestimated factors in the evolution of work. Consequently it's no surprise that the introduction of computers has caused widespread economic disruption not only locally, but nationally, limiting growth in productivity. While multifactor productivity (which takes labor and capital into account) produced a growth rate of 2.5 percent from 1948 to 1973, it produced a rate of growth of 0.7 percent from 1973 to 1990. The numbers may seem abstract, but their significance can be directly grasped from average earnings. Had growth continued at the 1948 to 1973 rate, U.S. average income in 1994 would have been $47,600. It was, in fact, $35,300.[32] Economists refer to this surprising decline in productivity growth despite massive investment in computers as the "productivity paradox."

Paul David, an economist at Stanford University, has argued, however, that the paradoxical slowdown was not such a paradox at all. Looking to the past, he points out that a slump in productivity followed the appearance of industrial-strength dynamos in the 1880s. Economically beneficial effects of the dynamo, David shows, did not appear in productivity data for another three decades. Over those decades, industry underwent a major retooling as the old, heavily centralized, steam-driven processes gave way to methods that took advantage of dispersed, localized electrical power. A similar process has been underway with the computer, David suggests. It has taken time for society to transform the "mature, ossified, Fordist regime of mass production" to the new regime of digital tools and demassification.[33]

Productivity remained stagnant for almost a decade after

David first made this argument. But recent productivity figures lend support to his case. Manufacturing productivity has been especially high, and for the economy as a whole, the figures for 1995 to 1998 show a return to about 2 percent growth. Those for 1999 may approach 4 percent, a much more impressive rate, though still some distance from the sustained boom of the 1950s.[34]

In less careful hands, however, the thesis about a lag can be quite misleading. It's easy to find people claiming that society falls behind while technology streaks ahead. Writing during the period that David studied, the early technological futurist H. G. Wells (who admired the dynamos at Niagara Falls more than the falls themselves), for example, already claimed to see society falling behind electrical technology.[35] It's harder, by comparison, to find explanations for how society catches up. Yet catch up it must, if only to be in a position to lag again in subsequent technological waves, as, for example, the computer scientist Douglas Englebart, the inventor of the mouse, argues it is in danger of doing today:

> *Real social danger today is that the technology is erupting and moving so much faster than it ever ever ever has in all of our historical experience. . . . [It's] time to start adapting society to this revolution in the technology. There's a lot of potential dangers ahead if we don't adapt it successfully.*[36]

The business writers Downes and Mui turn this sort of argument into their "Law of Disruption," which holds that "[s]ocial, political, and economic systems change incrementally, but technology changes exponentially."[37]

The implications of this formulation depend heavily on what sort of increments and adaptation society is capable of. If society cannot make occasional, huge leaps and transformations, it will forever lag technology. On the other hand, David's argument would suggest that society did adjust. If so, we would expect to see signs of major social transformation and disruption in periods of catch-up. Yet, if we set aside the appearance of the Soviet Union and the defeat of the Axis powers as not germane, it is hard to see a major social transformation in the industrial countries between 1890 and 1920 or (setting aside the collapse of the Soviet Union, this time) in the 1980s. Change, yes; progress, yes; but not the sort of leap that would be necessary to keep pace with "exponential" growth.[38]

It may be, instead, that thinking this way about technology and society is backward. It's a wrong way, moreover, that can have serious consequences. To accuse society of lagging lets technology and design off the hook too easily. It implies, in the end, that you can tear down walls, issue laptops and cell phones, or send people home with industrial-strength technology and then blame them if they don't adjust.

Our argument, in the course of this chapter, by contrast, is that technology design has not taken adequate account of work and its demands but instead has aimed at an idealized image of individuals and information. We would argue, then, that the predictions about demassification and the home office inherent in this idealized view cannot come about until not society, but design adjusts. (At which point, the idealized view will have to adjust a little, too.)

Again, parallels with the development of electricity are worth noting. For example, the 1920s and 1930s, particularly with the development of rural electrification, also produced familiar-sounding claims that, with this new technology, work and workers would move from the cities to the countryside

once they adjusted.[39] Seventy years later, cities are still growing
and rural communities still shrinking.

Furthermore, a long view of the dynamo would start not
with the first generating plants, as David does, but with the first
dynamo. Michael Faraday invented this in 1831. Initially, it was
too frail and too expensive for much practical use. For some
forty years, its principal use was to drive the telegraph. Only by
1890 was it "tamed," in the words of the economic historian Joel
Mokyr. Then electric motors and dynamos had become robust
enough to make adjusting to factories and cities worthwhile.[40]
(This is roughly the point at which David takes up his story.)
Inevitably, that adjustment took time and proceeded in a series
of feedback loops along with developments in the technology.
But this was a matter not of society "catching up" with technology, but of society adjusting technology to its needs.

The computer would seem to follow a similar trajectory.
Whenever we start its process of development (some would go
back to Charles Babbage, a contemporary of Faraday's; others to
the adding and calculating machines of the turn of the century),
there follows a long period in which it also is both too expensive and too frail for widespread social adoption. Gradually, it has
become more robust, cheaper, and more useful. Only in the past
few years has it begun to be "tamed" for general use. For the
home office, there is still some house training to do.[41]

SOCIALIZING TECHNOLOGY

While we don't want to let design off the hook, we must also
say as forcefully as possible that good design is very hard to do.
It is easy and understandable to make fun of bad technologies.
It is not easy to make good ones. Given the difficulties of design,

however, it is important not to misrepresent the task it faces. Too often, information technology design is poor because problems have been redefined in ways that ignore the social resources that are an integral part of this socialization process. By contrast, successful design usually draws on these social resources, even while helping them change.[42]

One way to engage such resources is to help build them, engendering a sufficient number of competent users that they can start to help each other. Apple, for example, liberally provided computers for schools. This built a loyal user base and positioned the computer in a social system that provided both formal and informal help for struggling users. IBM and Microsoft, by contrast, benefited from the corporate preference for IBM's machines. The necessary informal resources then developed within the formal workplace.

It's much harder to go into the home, a more isolated social setting. So it's also hard to be as confident as Sun Microsystems in its prediction that using Java to connect household appliances will make them easier to use. People still have difficulties with much simpler appliances like the VCR. They continue to confess (or maybe boast) that they cannot record or set the clock. Were there a social context for VCR recording (as there is for watching), the problem would probably disappear (see chapter 5).

Yet it is possible to socialize domestic appliances. Consider Alexander Graham Bell's strategy for introducing the telephone, which drew both on the office and on other situations for social resources. By 1878, Bell's English shareholders were becoming impatient with the slow development of this new technology that no one could really understand. The well-entrenched telegraph with its reach and increasingly sophisticated switching seemed far ahead of what appeared to be an interesting but limited point-to-point gadget.[43] Both Western Union in the States and the post office in Britain had refused the offer to buy the patents, though Bell's partners had been willing to all but give these away.

To a great extent, the experts put their faith in the telegraph because the telegraph was in the hands of the experts. It needed operators to encode messages at one end and to decode messages at the other end. And it worked through august organizations—Western Union and the General Post Office—that lent significant weight to the system. It was generally felt that only organizations like these could introduce the telephone to society. When they proved unwilling, the venture looked increasingly unlikely.

Bell, however, invited the shareholders to put their faith not in sophistication and organizational expertise, but in popular use. The company needed, Bell argued, to abandon specialists and specialist training and put phones in people's hands. In the right circumstances, the practicality of the device would do the rest. So he crafted the circumstances. Early on, he put telephones in hotel rooms and encouraged guests to use them in the familiar task of talking to the front desk. In engaging a regular practice, he subtly taught people the use and the ease of use of his new device. He also promoted their use for office intercoms, drawing in the resources of the office while nonetheless helping it to change. Later, to pursue new users unlikely to stay in hotels or use office intercoms, the company developed a new strategy. It put phones near lunch counters. That way, it reasoned, people who didn't know how to use them would be likely to see people who did know how and in this way learn about the phone system.[44]

As new technologies cascade into society, Bell's approach strikes us as illuminating. Though the telephone was a transforming technology, Bell nonetheless worked with the social context of his day, not against it or in isolation from it. In the collective understanding of groups, Bell found the resources for individuals. Similarly, e-mail and collaborative games have had profound socializing effects on some fairly antisocial technologies.

Paradoxically perhaps, such social resources are nowhere more important than in the home, because there they are fewest. In such isolation, the limitations of usability, self-explanatoriness, and ease and the gap between promise and performance are most cruelly exposed. People need to reach out from the home to find social resources.

Already, it has become law that the way to learn to use a home computer is to get a kid. Senior citizens are also proving adept at learning to use computers and are currently the second-fastest-growing group of customers (after kids) for computer manufacturers. Both, we should note, tend to have available the time that such learning can call for (showing that the technology is not yet quite ready for "plug and play" and that users still cut producers more slack than the latter deserve). And both tend to be fairly well tied into peer groups, who provide support. Each of these groups, young and old, is well positioned to help those in between.

These examples continue to suggest that, in order for people to be able to work alone, technology may have to reinforce their access to social networks. The home worker, from this perspective, resembles not the frontier pioneer, striking out alone and renouncing society, but more a deep-sea diver. The deeper a diver works alone beneath the ocean, the more sturdy the connections to the surface have to be.

CHAPTER 4

Practice Makes Process

A company must continue to focus on its processes so that they stay attuned to the needs of the changing business environment. . . . A process-centered organization must strive for ongoing process improvement. To accomplish this, the company must actively manage its processes. Indeed, we can now see that the heart of managing a business is managing its processes: assuring that they are performing up to their potential, looking for opportunities to make them better, and translating these opportunities into realities.

—MICHAEL HAMMER, Beyond Reengineering[1]

BY THE LATE 1980S the cumulative effects of the productivity paradox, the dramatic changes fostered by information technology, the general slowdown in the economy, and the rise in global competition were making business life hell.[2] It was clear that current organization structures were not producing a "virtuous circle" between investment and production. But few could imagine what the right organization structure might be.[3]

The pressure to do something, anything, gave birth to innumerable fashions and fads in management. Consultants firmly told managers how to run their businesses. Many of their imperatives, however, had people running in circles or opposing directions. Focus only on quality, on customer satisfaction, or on shareholder value, some said. Pursue core competency or diversification. Internalize, internationalize, divest, or merge. Integrate backward, forward, or outsource. Go hollow, flat, or virtual.

One of the many virtues of "business process reengineering," by contrast, was that it was clear, direct, and consistent. Michael Hammer and James Champy developed reengineering in response to "the crisis that will not go away."[4] It presented a clear antidote to organizational inconsistency, inertia, and gradualism. Reengineering manifestos assumed that business organizations were similar to other bureaucracies. Over time, they come to serve themselves first, customers and investors next. As a consequence, established businesses are rife with divisions and diversions that drain resources but, from the customer's point of view, add no value. Taking "a clean sheet of paper," reengineering teams were told to reorganize their organizations around the processes that did add value, making these the center of the new organization.

With this sharp distinction between value-adding and non–value-adding processes, reengineering insisted on sweeping away old practices. "Forget all you know," managers were told. "Don't automate, obliterate." Like all organizational fads, it also puffed itself up with some grandiose claims. Hammer and Champy, for instance, insisted they were transcending Adam Smith, one of the most enlightened thinkers of the eighteenth century and a pervasive influence on modern economics.

Slogans aside, there was enough substance for reengineering to acquire an impressive following. Hewlett-Packard, AT&T, IBM, Xerox, Ford, NYNEX, Seagram, and a host of other corporations great and small reengineered. Soon, 50 percent of Fortune 500 companies had vice presidents of reengineering.[5] Results, too, were impressive. Reengineering seems to have been behind the transformation of several dinosaurs of the industrial age into phoenixes for the digital age (see chapter 1).

Nonetheless, by the mid-1990s, reengineering's stock was plummeting. Some critics claimed that this "pernicious panacea" never came close to the results promised (such as a 75 percent drop in overheads).[6] Moreover, while the changes in output were often trumpeted, they were not always set against the costs of input.[7] Other critics claimed that reengineering was obsessed with technology, to which reengineered firms became subservient. And for many people, *reengineering* was little more than a euphemism for downsizing.[8]

As reengineering stumbled, reengineering consultants themselves began to be downsized. They received little sympathy from those who had seen reengineering as a consultant's mint. (A senior partner in Andersen consulting apparently intoned, "God Bless Mike Hammer," as company revenues reached $700 million.)[9] They probably needed little sympathy, for many moved swiftly across the hall to the suites reserved for the next fashion, "knowledge management."

This succession strikes us as particularly interesting. Was it merely a case of a new fad fortuitously and fortunately succeeding an exhausted old one? Or was there, perhaps, more than chance to the sequence? Did the focus on process, perhaps, overlook the increasing demand for knowledge in modern organizations? We suspect it did. Consequently, looking at reengineering in the light of knowledge, as we do here, may help reveal both the strengths (often hidden behind catcalls) and the weaknesses (equally hidden behind cheerleading) of reengineering.

PERFECTING PROCESS

It is perhaps significant that many of the celebrated cases of business process reengineering come from a fairly narrow band of operations. Procurement, shipping and receiving, warehousing, fulfillment, and billing are favorites. These generally account for the most impressive results, with inventories transformed into just-in-time delivery, fulfillment and billing accomplished in days rather than weeks.

In these areas of work, processes are relatively well defined. They usually have clearly measurable inputs and outputs. And, as we might expect from a process-oriented view, they emphasize a linear view of how organizations work. To complete a process, something passes from *A* on to *B* ending with *C*—from, for example, receiving to manufacturing to shipping. In such well-defined processes, it is the "longitudinal" links between each stage that appear to matter. Lateral ties among people doing similar tasks—among, for example, the people in shipping—appear at a heavy discount from a process-based perspective. They are generally regarded as non–value-adding.

Consequently, with regard to information, reengineering directs attention to the information that flows across longitudinal links. This information helps to coordinate the complementary activities that make up a firm's critical process. So, for example, the sociologist Charles Sabel stresses how just-in-time processes both require and generate "a rich flow of precise and targeted information about what was happening throughout the production process."[10]

Such a focus is undoubtedly invaluable for organizations. Nonetheless, focusing on longitudinal process and the information that goes with it may lead to tunnel vision. Although reengineered organizational charts may happily represent organizations in terms of these types of process, neither linear processes nor charts encompass all that goes on in organizations.

It is not surprising, then, that business process reengineering has had less success in the parts of organizations that are less linear and less clearly defined by process and information. Management, for example, has proved notoriously hard to reengineer. So has R&D. In such areas, life is less linear; inputs and outputs are less well defined; and information is less "targeted." These are, rather, areas where making sense, interpreting, and understanding are both problematic and highly valued—areas where, above all, meaning and knowledge are at a premium.

MEANING AND ENDS

Process perspectives are not necessarily indifferent to meaning. James March, one of the preeminent figures in organization studies, sees a close link between the two. "It is," he argues, "process that gives meaning to life, and meaning is the core of life." For March, however, "Outcomes are generally less significant . . . than process."[11] Curiously, reengineering tends to see things the other way around. It focuses most heavily on the input and output of the stages in a process. It is relatively indifferent to the internal workings of these stages—to the particular practices that make up a process and the meaning they have for those involved.

Given this indifference, it was perhaps inevitable that studies of workplace practice, of the internal life of process, would reveal tensions between the demands of process and the needs of practice. Nor is it surprising that these tensions are often the result of struggles over meaning. These struggles, furthermore, are not confined to the "thinking" parts of organizations. They occur throughout, pitting the process-focused need for uniform organizational information against the practice-based struggle for locally coherent meaning.

Etienne Wenger, formerly of the Institute for Research on Learning, revealed this tension, for example, in his study of the comparatively "lowly" and well-defined process of claims processing.[12] He found that many of the problems faced by the health-insurance claims processors he studied could be traced to clashes over meaning and sense making—over such things as what a form signifies, why similar claims elicit different reimbursements, and who does or does not qualify for reimbursement. In the end, these problems for the claims processors create problems for the company.

To do their job, processors need to be able to make sense of what they do. The company offers explanations. But, from the processors' point of view, the organization's information and explanations are difficult to use. They explain things in terms of the company's overall goals and processes, but they take little account of the immediate practicalities of the claims processors' work. Indeed, many of the company's explanations have the ring of those parental imperatives that skip explanation and simply say "Do it this way because I say so."[13] Such imperatives make life easier for the company, but difficult for the processors, who need to understand what they do to do it well and also must justify their actions to customers.

Wenger's work reminds us that, while process is clearly important to the overall coherence of an organization, in the end it is the practice of the people who work in the organization that brings process to life, and, indeed, life to process. Organizations, then, should not attend to the process and process-related explanations only. They must also attend to practice. By practice, of course, we do not mean the sort of rote exercises people associate with phrases like *piano practice*. Rather we mean the activity involved in getting work done—the sort of activity that lies at the heart of medical practice or legal practice, for claims processors are practitioners of their own craft just as doctors and lawyers are practitioners of theirs.

LOOKING THE OTHER WAY

These two aspects of organizations, one process based and the other practice based, not only look from different directions—from outside a process and from within—they also look in different directions for the resources for understanding. From outside, people find meaning in functional explanations. They rely on process-based, cross-functional, longitudinal accounts of why things are done. From inside, people take a lateral view. The claims processors, for example, look less to their superiors or to the people to whom their work goes next than to their peer group for explanations of what they do and why. For them, knowledge comes more from fellow practitioners than from cross-functional connections.

These contrasting sources of meaning and understanding present business process reengineering and process views of organization with difficulties for several reasons. First, business process reengineering tends to be somewhat monotheistic. There is not much room for variation in meaning in its camp. The process view is expected to explain all.

Second, despite talk of rebuilding from the bottom up and empowerment, business process reengineering tends to be relentlessly top down. Indeed, some suggest that it is of necessity a top-down, command-and-control procedure.[14] (It is not surprising that one of the most enthusiastic and successful reengineers has been the army.) Together, these two biases of business process reengineering make it hard to see and harder to understand the needs of people whose practices make up processes.

Third, the top-down view tends to give a bloodless account of businesses, as the quotation with which we opened this chapter suggests. Reengineering begins with processes into which people are then inserted as needed. "Process owners," as Hammer puts it, "are focused on process, not on personnel."[15] Personnel, for their part, seem to face the option of getting on board or getting out. Opportunities for them to craft, change, own, or take charge of process in any meaningful way are limited.[16] While lip service is paid to them, improvisation and "local" knowledge have little place in these schema, particularly if they challenge the coordination of process.

And fourth, business process reengineers tend to discourage exactly the sort of lateral links that people pursue to help make meaning. Focused on longitudinal cross-functionality, they dislike, and often try to discourage or even disempower, occupational groups, job categories, and local workplace cultures. Encouraging cross-functional links between occupations, business process reengineering tends to see the contrasting links within occupational groups as non–value adding. Here, then, we see in another form the problems that beset the worker at home alone, which we discussed in chapter 3. Focusing on individuals, process accounts overlook social resources that people in similar occupations provide one another. Tunnel-visioned process accounts rarely understand the importance of these resources. (In an exemplary piece of partial blindness, for example, British Telecom did notice the damaging isolation of its home workers. As a remedy, however, it decided to pipe the sound of canned background chatter into their home offices.)[17]

These four biases, as we said, make it difficult for business process reengineering to deal with practice. Yet the tensions between process and practice, between the structure provided by one and the spontaneity provided by the other, are key structuring forces in an organization. Consequently, you can't redesign process effectively if you don't understand practice.

REPRESENTING PROCESS

Let us take an example of the contrasting perspectives of process and practice at work. Results from a study by Julian Orr, an organizational consultant and former colleague at Xerox PARC, help clarify what is missing from the process-centered perspective.[18] An anthropologist, Orr studied the Xerox technical representatives (reps) who service and repair the company's copiers at customers' sites.[19] The reps' work is critical to the company's overall purpose and so falls well within the class of value-adding processes. Nonetheless, as Orr found out, the reps might almost be said to succeed despite the company's best intentions. Their success is in good part a triumph of practice over the limits of process.[20]

As a process with clear input and output, the repair work Orr studied could be described easily. Customers having difficulty called the Customer Service Center. This in turn notified the reps. A rep would then go to the customer's site, identify the problem with the help of the machine's error codes, find the right response from the machine's documentation, and, having fixed the problem, "clear" the call with the service center.[21]

The company tried to provide the reps with the targeted

information they would need. First, it provided training courses to familiarize new technicians with the company's machines and to familiarize established technicians with new machines. Second, it provided them with documentation to do the job. This "directive" documentation provides a map to repair work, with directions guiding the rep from problems (which appear as error codes in the machine) to repair solutions. Through these courses and documents, the reps gathered the information that, from the company's perspective, is needed to see the process from beginning to end.

UNDERSTANDING PRACTICE

Given this clear view of the process, Orr's voyage into the reps' world seemed superfluous to some colleagues when he embarked on it. Everyone knew what reps did. But Orr argues forcefully that work is rarely well understood. Neither management nor management theorists, he points out, are adequately "concerned with work practice," by which he means they "do not focus on what is done in accomplishing a given job."[22] He was not surprised, then, to find that what looked quite clear and simple from above was much more opaque and confusing on the ground. Tasks were no longer so straightforward, and machines, despite their elegant circuit diagrams and diagnostic procedures, exhibited quite incoherent behaviors. Consequently, the information and training provided to the reps was inadequate for all but the most routine of the tasks they faced. Although the documentation claimed to provide a map, the reps continually confronted the question of how to travel when the marked trails disappeared and they found themselves surrounded by unmarked poison oak.

For example, in the process view, machines work quite predictably.[23] A part malfunctions. The malfunction produces an error code. And the error code leads, by way of the map, to a solution. Yet large machines, comprising multiple subsystems, are not so predictable. Any one machine may have profound idiosyncrasies, for each inevitably reflects the age and condition of its parts, the particulars and patterns of use, as well as the distinctive influences of the environment in which it sits—hot, cold, damp, dry, clean, dusty, secluded, in traffic, and so forth. (Reps know the machines they work with, Orr suggests, as shepherds know sheep. So, while everyone else assumes each machine is like the next, a rep knows each by its peculiarities and has to sort out general failings from particular ones.) All this undirected machine behavior inevitably undermines the very premise of directive documentation.

Anyone who has had trouble with a piece of information technology (surely that is everyone who has a piece of information technology) has trawled through manuals and indexes and help systems and never found the problem in front of him or her described. All, too, probably know the frustration of "!FATAL ERROR!" messages that no one, not even the people in customer service and tech support, can explain.[24]

The reps' real difficulties arose, however, not simply because the documentation had lapses. They arose more problematically because it told them what to do, but not why. It gave instructions, but it didn't explain. So when machines did something unpredicted, reps found themselves not just off the map, but there without a compass or tools for bushwhacking. At this point, reps needed to bridge the gap between the limits of prediction and reality. In short, they needed to make some sense of the machine in order to fix it. Directive documentation, however, wasn't designed for sense making. It was designed for rule fol-lowing.[25] So, Orr found, when the reps fell off the map of process, they went to breakfast.

WHEN THE GOING GETS TOUGH

Orr begins his account of the reps' day not where the company process begins—9 o'clock at the first call—but at breakfast beforehand. From a conventional perspective, the reps' job was highly individual. There was a "team" that covered the same geographical area (though individual reps carry the responsibil-ity for specific accounts), and there were specialists whom a rep could call on if he or she got into difficulties. Routine work was carried out alone, however, at the customer's site. Yet Orr found that the reps were remarkably social, getting together on their own time for breakfast, lunch, coffee, or at the end of the day—and sometimes for all of the above.

This sociability wasn't simply a retreat from the loneliness of an isolating job. At these meetings, while eating, playing crib-bage, and engaging in what might seem like idle gossip, the reps talked work, and talked it continuously. They posed questions, raised problems, offered solutions, constructed answers, and dis-cussed changes in their work, the machines, or customer rela-tions. In this way, both directly and indirectly, they kept one another up to date with what they knew, what they learned, and what they did.

The constant exchanges the reps engaged in are similar to the useful background updating that goes on constantly in any ordinary work site where people simply become aware of what others are up to because it's evident. There, too, this sort of chat usually passes unnoticed unless someone objects to it as "time wasting." Yet, though only a fraction may involve directly informing others about explicit business matters, this talk is valuable. Chat continuously but almost imperceptibly adjusts a group's collective knowledge and individual members' awareness of each other. Providing information directly is a little like the chiming of an alarm clock. This constant chatter is more like the passage of the sun across the sky, a change hard to see directly yet one that continuously reorients people to the progress of the day.

The reps' chatter stood out, however, because the process view assumed that they worked alone and had adequate resources in their training, tools, and documentation. Time spent together would, from the process perspective, be non–value adding. It might at best be the sort of problem someone might try to remedy with British Telecom's canned chatter. But, as Orr showed, the reps provided much more than comforting noises. They were critical resources for each other. The informal and extracurricular group helped each member to reach beyond the limits of an individual's knowledge and of the process documentation.

THE PRACTICE IN THE PROCESS

Not all problems, however, can be solved over breakfast. One day, Orr studied a rep at work with a finicky machine. It had been recently installed, yet never worked satisfactorily. Each time it failed, it produced a different error message. But following the prescription for each report—replacing or adjusting parts—didn't fix the overall problem. And collectively, the messages made no sense. The rep's path to a solution, then, shows how people do explore territory when they fall off the maps that process provides.

Having reached his limits, the rep summoned a specialist. But the specialist could not understand what was going on either. So the two spent the afternoon cycling the machine again and again, waiting for its intermittent crashes and recording its state at the time. Simultaneously, they cycled stories about similar-looking problems round and round until these stories, too, crashed up against the peculiarities of this machine. In Orr's account, the afternoon resembles a series of alternating, improvisational jazz solos, as each took over the lead, ran with it for a little while, then handed it off to his partner, all against the bassline continuo of the rumbling machine until finally all came together.

For in the course of the afternoon, the two gradually brought their separate understandings closer together and simultaneously came closer to a collective understanding of the machine. Eventually, late in the day, the different cycles achieved collective understanding. The machine's previously erratic behavior, the experience of the two technicians, and the stories they told finally formed a single, coherent account. They made sense of the machine and as a result could fix it and satisfy the customer.

In approaching the machine this way, these two reps were traveling off road and without maps, but they got to where they needed to go, nonetheless. We can understand this journey better by approaching it in terms of collaboration, narration, and improvisation.

Collaboration

The reps' practice involved both collaborative problem solving and collective sharing in the solution. The end result, the final insight of the particular problem-solving episode we described, became available for all the area's reps to draw on. Orr later heard a group discussing the story in the course of a long cribbage game.

In chapter 3, we discussed individualized work in terms of "displacement." There we argued that tasks better shared are often pushed into the lap of individuals, in the name of "empowerment." Orr's study suggests that a process view of work can result in similar displacement, cutting off lateral ties in the name of cross-functional efficiency. The result is quite disempowering and inefficient, burdening people with individual responsibility that is better shared by the group. The reps responded by developing their own lateral ties, drawing on their peers in their occupational community.

Some of these ties are company sanctioned. The reps, for example, filled in for one another as they were needed. But their collaboration was evident in other, less clearly approved ways. For instance, the reward structure made it difficult for each rep to hold expensive parts critical for certain types of infrequent failure. Reps (and the company's) relations with customers, however, suffer if too long a delay occurs between identifying the problem and providing the part to fix it. To get around this problem, the reps implicitly formed a collective pool of parts, so that each could draw readily on the other in times of need, and the necessary parts were always available.

More important, the reps also developed a collective pool of knowledge and insight on which they drew. Where, then, the reps may have had similar cases of tools, their knowledge in some way resembled the pool of parts they held collectively. All contributed from personal stock, and there was a great deal of overlap, but each had his or her strengths, which the others recognized and relied on.

We advance this analogy with some hesitation. Shared knowledge differs significantly from a collective pool of discrete parts.[26] In this pool of knowledge, where one person's knowledge ends and another's begins is not always clear. In the example we gave above, it took the collaboration of the two technicians working together to come to a coherent conclusion. But neither had a decisive "piece" of knowledge. Nor was the final solution the property of either one. It was a collective process that created an indivisible product. Thus we tend to think of knowledge less like an assembly of discrete parts and more like a watercolor painting. As each new color is added, it blends with the others to produce the final effect, in which the contributing parts become indivisible.

Narration

Narration is another key, if unexpected, aspect of the reps' approach. The constant storytelling—about problems and solutions, about disasters and triumphs, over breakfast, lunch, and coffee—serves a number of overlapping purposes.

Reps tell stories about unsolved problems in an attempt to generate a coherent account of what the problem is and how to solve it. They may do this individually, putting their own story together. Or they can do it collectively, as they draw on the collective wisdom and experience of the group.

Stories are good at presenting things sequentially (this happened, then that). They are also good for presenting them causally (this happened because of that). Thus stories are a powerful means to understand what happened (the sequence of events) and why (the causes and effects of those events). And so storytelling is indispensable for the reps for whom what and why are critical matters yet often hard to discern.[27]

More generally, people tell stories to try to make diverse information cohere. Economists tell stories in their models, scientists tell stories in their experiments, executives tell stories in their business plans, lawyers tell stories in their briefs, and so on. Indeed, the business processes written down on Hammer and Champy's blank piece of paper are another example of storytelling.

Stories, then, can be a means to discover something completely new about the world. The value of stories, however, lies not just in their telling, but in their retelling. Stories pass on to newcomers what old-timers already know. Stories are thus central to learning and education, and they allowed the reps to learn from one another.[28]

Stories, moreover, convey not only specific information but also general principles. These principles can then be applied to particular situations, in different times and places. So the reps find that they carry back what they have learned from their colleagues in the coffee shop to a different site and a different problem.

While it may appear at first that the reps used stories to circulate information, they were actually doing much more. For it is not shared stories or shared information so much as shared interpretation that binds people together.[29] In their storytelling, the reps developed a common framework that allowed them to interpret the information that they received in a common light. To collaborate around shared information you first have to develop a shared framework for interpretation. "Each of us thinks his own thoughts," the philosopher Stephen Toulmin argues. "Our concepts we share."[30]

Learning to tell their war stories, then, was a critical part of becoming a rep. It allowed newcomers to see the world with a rep's eyes. And it allowed all to share in their major resource— their collective, collaborative wisdom. "When technicians gather, their conversation is full of talk about machines," Orr concludes,

> *This talk shows their understanding of the world of service; in another sense, the talk creates that world and even creates the identity of the technicians themselves. But neither talk nor identity is the goal of the technicians' practice. The goal is getting the job done.*[31]

Improvisation

As we hoped to indicate with our jazz metaphor earlier in this chapter, the reps' work has a clear improvisational component. Though they are supplied with routines and information, they have to rely heavily on improvisation to close the gap between the world as they find it and the inevitably limited model of that world embedded in routines and processes.

People in organizations continuously wrestle with the problem that, while their organization may be a haven of routine, the rest of the world is not. Part of the skill of work, all work, then is *routinization,* adapting the particulars of the world so that they fit within the general schemas of the organization. The gap to be bridged lies between reality and process, and it is bridged by the improvisation inherent in practice—so deeply inherent that the practitioners themselves are barely aware of it.

This adaptation is aptly reflected in the wonder (and the problems) of forms.[32] Forms are the crucial means by which an organization brings the heterogeneous world into line with its processes. Consequently, you don't get very far into an organization until you fill out the forms or answer the questions—in short, till you make yourself formulaic. Everyone knows what it is like not to fit within the standard form that gets things going.[33] And everyone knows, too, the value of the skilled representative who understands how to fit you into the form and the firm without causing problems for either. ("We'll just leave that box blank, but we'll put a check down here, even though it doesn't apply, because that will ring a bell in accounting, and then they will know what to do.") Such gap-closing improvisation is one example of what another former colleague and organizational ethnographer, Lucy Suchman, describes as "endless small forms of practical 'subversion' taken up in the name of getting work done."[34]

PROCESSING

In providing standard output, routines permit the ready coordination of business processes. Consequently, organizations have a heavy investment in routine behavior—it is the key to orderly process, to process improvement, and to process coordination.[35]

On the other hand, to survive in a changing world, organizations also need to improvise, to break routine by trying new things, exploring new regions, finding new markets, developing new models. Improvisation, however, inevitably disrupts routine. Consequently, all organizations have to balance routine and improvisation.[36]

Some people—those in R&D or in business planning, for example—are expected to improvise. Others, like the reps, are not. In general they are expected to do things the organization's way. There are penalties—formal and informal, explicit and implicit—for those who don't follow routines, don't carry out processes as defined. Such pressures produce what we think of as *processing*. These are attempts to disguise unauthorized behavior so that it looks authorized, to justify improvisation in terms of routine. Employees negotiate the gap between their actual practice and recognized routines and process by making the former appear to be the latter.

In all walks of life, processing provides a screen between what people do and what people say they do. It helps turn unauthorized practice, however effective, into authorized routine, however inept. It makes us all appear "rational" and rule governed to the world, even though a great deal of what everyone does is, of necessity, guesswork and intuition.[37] Most people, indeed, are not even aware of the implicit improvisation they engage in to bridge the gap between these two. They simply assume that what they do and what their job description says are one and the same. People thus keep their own skills hidden even from themselves. (Even braggarts usually brag about the wrong things.)

Back to our example, the reps actually improvised at a couple of distinct points in their work. First, they improvised to close the often-wide gap between machine behaviors and their own understanding. This required skill and collaboration, but these generally passed unnoticed and unappreciated in good part because, second, the reps disguised this improvisation through a little improvisational processing. They made it look as though they performed according to plan.

Directly or implicitly, organizational routines and processes encourage this sort of processing. In doing so, organizations make themselves blind to what lies outside the narrow tunnel of process. Improvisation, for example, can be a useful indicator of problems or change in the environment. The greater the improvisation, the less adequate the routine. But routines and processes encourage employees to hide their insights and improvisations. So, by subordinating practice to process, an organization paradoxically encourages its employees to mislead it. Valuing and analyzing their improvisations, by contrast, can be highly informative. Indeed, it's been suggested that Xerox stumbled so badly in the 1970s in part because it failed to gather evidence of poor quality from its field representatives. This sort of self-deception is, we suspect, especially acute in organizations who focus on process, unreconstructed or reengineered, and the information it provides to the exclusion of all else.

LATERAL THRUST

We have described the process view as a "longitudinal" view. It seeks to overcome divisions of labor and establish cross-functional links. As such, its goals are admirable. Business processes provide the backbone of organization, structure amid the spontaneity of practice. But in pursuit of this backbone, business process reengineering has generally been indifferent to practice and even hostile to the solidarity of occupational groups and occupational cultures. *Specialist* in Hammer and Champy's work is almost a term of abuse.[38] Lateral ties, ties that do not follow the lines of process, are readily dismissed as "non–value adding."

Yet research into work groups, like research into the difficulties of home working (see chapter 3), suggests that people rely heavily on lateral, occupational ties to overcome the limits of process-based information. Peers, engaged in parallel not sequential practices, provide valuable resources for each other.

As a result of Orr's work, rather than trying to support the reps with yet more information from outside the reps' community, Xerox turned instead to reinforcing internal ties. The first step was simple. Reps were given two-way radios, which allowed them to continue to talk to one another even when working apart. This intervention both supported and acknowledged the reps' ways of collaboration, narration, and improvisation.

The second step was more ambitious, but it too reflected the resources the reps provided for themselves and tried to amplify this resourcefulness. Though passed on in war stories, the insight reps developed in the course of their work tended to have a short reach, traveling primarily in local groups, and a short life, fading from memory even locally. Consequently, reps near and far ended up reinventing fixes that might have been known elsewhere. The Eureka project set out to create a database of this useful knowledge, preserving over time and delivering over space resourceful ideas.

Of course, a database for technical information is not in itself original. But most such databases are, like the reps' documentation, top-down creations. People who are not themselves reps usually fill these databases with what they think reps ought to know. (In this way, databases resemble those "FAQ" sheets found on the Web, which the designers fill with their ideas of what their public should know.)[39] Eureka was designed differently, however. It drew directly on the reps own insights and their own sense of what they needed.

Of course, such a database would be no use to anyone if it filled up with everybody's favorite idea (which is exactly why the Web can be so hard to use). Such a database must be selective. But again it would be a mistake to filter these from a top-down, process perspective. Instead, as with scientific articles, the reps' tips are subject to peer review, drawing on those same lateral ties that make the reps resources for one another. A rep submits a tip, peers review it, and if it stands up to scrutiny—is original, is useful—then it is added to the database. There, other reps can find it over Web-based links.

For the reps, this database has become more than an indispensable tool (reckoned to save the company up to $100 million per year in service costs). It is also a recognition of the value of their own knowledge and knowledge creation, which was previously disregarded by most of the corporation. And it is a means by which individual reps build social capital and recognition among their peers. At a recent meeting of reps in Canada, a rep who provided highly useful tips was given a standing ovation by his peers.

Identity, as we argue in chapter 5, provides a key aspect of work, learning, and understanding. Orr's work and the reps' response to Eureka emphasize the way in which the reps (like many similar occupational groups) find their identity: not only through longitudinal process, through identity with the corporation but to a significant degree through peer recognition.

The virtual connections among reps provided by the database suggest that virtual groups—the fabled virtual teams of the cyberworkplace—tend to mirror conventional groups, not transcend them. A study of such teams, conducted by Andrea Hornett, indicates that going virtual does not thereby allow you to go vertical. Lateral ties are as significant in cyberspace as in the old world. Cross-functionality is no easier.[40]

BEYOND EITHER/OR

The view we have offered in this chapter implicitly contrasts the formal view of structured organization—the process view—with the informal, improvisational practices that actually keep the organization going. This distinction between formal and informal is, the Stanford sociologist Mark Granovetter notes, "one of the oldest in the literature."[41] Its age is testament not only to our lack of originality but also to the distinction's robustness. For attempts have repeatedly been made to iron out the improvisational and informal—or perhaps to iron them *in* to routines. Frederick Taylor's "scientific management" sought to program every move of workers into a tightly choreographed and coordinated routine. And Chester Barnard, the grandfather of organizational studies at Harvard Business School, portrayed the informal as deviant behavior, something to be stamped out.[42]

Standard notions of process, too, give primacy to the formal—the account that can be written on that blank sheet of paper. People are to forget all that they know, including all their hard-won, practice-based knowledge, business process reengineering implies, and learn again in accordance with organizationally ordained process. What isn't ordained from above as part of process risks being labeled "non–value adding" and therefore suspect.

Given the radical reorganization demanded by the conditions that we outlined at the beginning of this chapter, this tilt toward a top-down view is not surprising. Businesses had to kick themselves through discontinuous change under enormous pressure. Practice-driven change, by contrast, tends to be more continuous and continual. For that very reason, overlooking practice risks cutting organizations off from such continuous change. And if they are cut off like this, organizations can only expect to lurch from one top-down "palace revolution" to another.

Of course, practice-based views have their own blind spots. The current interest in virtual organizations, for example, downplays the uses of formal organization and structure, while self-organization abandons it almost entirely.

In this chapter we have weighed in favor of practice over process. As should become clear in later chapters, however, our view attempts to see the strengths that come from balancing the two, favoring neither but balancing both formal and informal, structure and spontaneity. The process view is important, giving shape and direction to an organization. It always risks, however, binding people too tightly to process, cutting them off from their "lateral" resources, blinding the organization to improvisation and new ideas, which may enter organizations along the lines of these peer groups.

Practice suffers from the opposing danger—of allowing itself to evolve too independently and so become too loosely "coupled" to the organization. The balancing act, as we shall see, requires developing coupling loose enough to allow groups to develop their own new knowledge, but tight enough to be able to push that knowledge along the lines of process. The idea that all that matters here is information woefully underestimates the challenges involved, which are ultimately, as we shall see, challenges of organization, knowledge, and innovation.

CHAPTER 5

Learning — in Theory
and in Practice

*Knowledge management is the use of technology to make informa-
tion relevant and accessible wherever that information may reside.
To do this effectively requires the appropriate application of the
appropriate technology for the appropriate situation.*

*Knowledge management incorporates systematic processes of find-
ing, selecting, organizing, and presenting information in a way that
improves an employee's comprehension and use of business assets.*[1]

WE BEGAN THE LAST CHAPTER contemplating the trend from
business process reengineering to knowledge management.
There, we focused primarily on the limits of process, which we
suggested was an infofriendly concept, but one that might be
blind to other issues.

In this chapter, we take up the other half of the matter and
consider knowledge and learning, again in relation to practice

and again as distinct from information. We do this with some trepidation. On the one hand, epistemology, the theory of knowledge, has formed the centerpiece of heavyweight philosophical arguments for millennia. On the other, knowledge management has many aspects of another lightweight fad. That enemy of lightweights, *The Economist,* has pronounced it no more than a buzzword. We may then, be trying to lift a gun too heavy to handle to aim at a target too insubstantial to matter.

Certainly much about knowledge's recent rise to prominence has the appearance of faddishness and evangelism. Look in much of the management literature of the late 1990s and you could easily believe that faltering business plans need only embrace knowledge to be saved. While it's often hard to tell what this embracing involves, buying more information technology seems a key indulgence.

Nonetheless, people are clearly taking up the idea of knowledge in one way or other. From within organizations come sounds of fighting between the IT (information technology) and HR (human resources) factions over who "owns" knowledge management.[2] Similarly, technology giants have entered a propaganda war over who best understands knowledge.[3] Elsewhere, the management consultants are maneuvering for high ground in the knowledge stakes.

In the process, *knowledge* has gained sufficient momentum to push aside not only concepts like reengineering but also *information*, whose rule had previously looked so secure. To be, in Peter Drucker's term, a "knowledge worker" now seems much more respectable than being a mere "information worker," though for a while the latter seemed very much the thing to be. Similarly, pundits are pushing "information economy" and the venerable "information age" aside in the name of the more voguish "knowledge economy" and "knowledge age." There's even a bit of alternative prefixation in such terms as *knobot*, which we talked about in chapter 2, where the buzz of bots and the buzz of knowledge meet.

Beyond its buzz, however, is there any bite to these uses of *knowledge*? When people talk about *knowledge*, are they just clinging to fashion (as many no doubt are), or might some be feeling their way, however intuitively, toward something that all the talk of information or of process lacks? Is there, we begin by asking, something that *knowledge* catches, but that *information* does not?

PERSONAL DISTINCTION

Twenty-five hundred years of unresolved epistemological debate from the Sophists to the present argue that we would be unwise to seek the difference by pouring over rigorous definitions. Moreover, whatever differences abstract definitions might clarify, persuasive redefinition now obscures. People are increasingly eager that their perfectly respectable cache of information be given the cachet of knowledge. Such redefinitions surreptitiously extend the overlapping area where *knowledge* and *information* appear as interchangeable terms.

Nevertheless, if we check the language of knowledge management at the door, there do appear to be some generally accepted distinctions between knowledge and information. Three strike us as particularly interesting.

First, knowledge usually entails a knower. That is, where people treat information as independent and more-or-less self-sufficient, they seem more inclined to associate knowledge with someone. In general, it sounds right to ask, "Where is that information?" but odd to ask, "Where's that knowledge?" as if knowledge normally lay around waiting to be picked up. It seems more reasonable to ask, "Who knows that?"

Second, given this personal attachment, knowledge appears harder to detach than information. People treat information as a self-contained substance. It is something that people pick up, possess, pass around, put in a database, lose, find, write down, accumulate, count, compare, and so forth.[4] Knowledge, by contrast, doesn't take as kindly to ideas of shipping, receiving, and quantification. It is hard to pick up and hard to transfer. You might expect, for example, someone to send you or point you to the information they have, but not to the knowledge they have.

Third, one reason knowledge may be so hard to give and receive is that knowledge seems to require more by way of assimilation. Knowledge is something we digest rather than merely hold. It entails the knower's understanding and some degree of commitment. Thus while one person often has conflicting information, he or she will not usually have conflicting knowledge. And while it seems quite reasonable to say, "I've got the information, but I don't understand it," it seems less reasonable to say, "I know, but I don't understand," or "I have the knowledge, but I can't see what it means." (Indeed, while conventional uses of *information* don't necessarily coincide with the specialist uses, as we noted earlier, "information theory" holds information to be independent of meaning.)[5]

WHERE IS THE KNOWER LOST IN THE INFORMATION?

Knowledge's personal attributes suggest that the shift toward knowledge may (or should) represent a shift toward people. Focusing on process, as we argued, draws attention away from people, concentrating instead on disembodied processes and the information that drives them. Focusing on knowledge, by contrast, turns attention toward knowers. Increasingly, as the abundance of information overwhelms us all, we need not simply more information, but people to assimilate, understand, and make sense of it.

The markets of the knowledge economy suggest that this shift is already underway. Investment is no longer drawn, as postindustrial champions like to point out, to bricks and mortar and other forms of fixed capital. Nor does it pursue income streams. (In some of the newest knowledge organizations there is as yet barely enough income to puddle, let alone stream.) Instead, investors see value in people and their know-how—people with the ability to envisage and execute adventurous new business plans and to keep reenvisaging these to stay ahead of the competition.

So, while the modern world often appears increasingly impersonal, in those areas where knowledge really counts, people count more than ever. In this way, a true knowledge economy should distinguish itself not only from the industrial economy but also from an information economy. For though its champions like to present these two as distinct, the information economy, like the industrial economy, shows a marked indifference to people. The industrial economy, for example, treated them en masse as interchangeable parts—the factory "hands" of the nineteenth century. The information economy threatens to treat them as more or less interchangeable consumers and processors of information. Attending to knowledge, by contrast, returns attention to people, what they know, how they come to know it, and how they differ.

The importance of people as creators and carriers of knowledge is forcing organizations to realize that knowledge lies less in its databases than in its people. It's been said, for example, that if

NASA wanted to go to the moon again, it would have to start from scratch, having lost not the data, but the human expertise that took it there last time. Similarly, Tom Davenport and Larry Prusak argue that when Ford wanted to build on the success of the Taurus, the company found that the essence of that success had been lost with the loss of the people that created it. Their knowledge was not stored in information technologies. It left when they left.[6]

Mistaking knowledge and its sources for information and its sources can, then, be costly. In her book *Wellsprings of Knowledge*, Dorothy Leonard-Barton of Harvard Business School tells the story of one firm, ELP, taking over a rival, Grimes, primarily to capture Grimes's impressive intellectual capital. Only after it had paid generously for the business, machine tools, and research did ELP find that Grimes's real competitive advantage had lain in the operating knowledge of its line employees, all of whom had been let go.

Similarly, the sort of blind downsizing produced by business process reengineering has caused organizations to lose "collective memory."[7] It's impossible to assess the value of such layoffs. But the business journalist Thomas Stewart estimated the cost of AT&T's last round as equivalent to an $8 billion capital write-off.[8] In all, the job of knowledge management cannot involve just the protection and exploitation of patents. It must include the cultivation of knowledgeable workers. Focusing on information, however, makes this kind of cultivation difficult.

KNOWN PROBLEMS

Curiously, if knowledge will go out of the door in the heads of people who have developed and worked with that knowledge, it seems reluctant to go out (or stay behind) in the heads of people who have not been so involved. The CEO of the innovative steel manufacturer Chaparral Steel told Leonard-Barton that for this reason the firm has no problem with competitors touring their plant. Chaparral, he said, is willing to show just about everything "and we will be giving away nothing because they can't take it home with them."[9] Unlike information, knowledge, as we said, is hard to detach.

While the challenge of detaching knowledge from some people and attaching it to others may protect some knowledge assets, it makes management of the knowledge much more difficult. The difficulty has revealed itself in, for example the struggle over "best practices." To maintain competitive edge, firms first search for the best practices either within their own or in their competitors' units. Once identified, they then transfer these to areas where practices are less good. The search part has led to a great deal of useful benchmarking. The transfer part, however, has proved much more awkward.

Robert Cole of the University of California at Berkeley's Haas Business School has investigated this difficulty in a recent study of best practice strategy. He looked at, among others, Hewlett-Packard's attempts to raise quality levels in its plants around the globe by identifying and circulating the best practices within the firm. Even internally, Cole showed, transfer was uncertain.[10] Cole's findings seem to justify the now-famous lament of HP's chairman, Lew Platt, as he considered how much better the firm would be "if only we knew what we know at HP."[11]

Although, as Cole emphasizes, HP works across continents and countries, failure to transfer practice is not simply a matter of national or linguistic boundaries. Best practices can have as much trouble traveling across town as they do across continents. As one winner of the prestigious Baldridge prize who grappled with this problem told researchers in frustration, "We can have two plants right across the street from one another, and it's the damndest thing to get them to transfer best practices." Similarly, Jeff Papows, president of Lotus, whose Notes is a widely used tool for knowledge management, acknowledges that for all the power to communicate that Notes and similar groupware provide, "spreading the practice has not been easy."[12]

IN DEFENSE OF LEARNING

Circulating human knowledge, these experiences suggest, is not simply a matter of search and retrieval, as some views of knowledge management might have us believe. While knowledge is often not all that hard to search, it can be difficult to retrieve, if by *retrieve* people mean detach from one knower and attach to another.

So learning, the acquisition of knowledge, presents knowledge management with its central challenge. The defense of intellectual property, the sowing and harvesting of information, the exploitation of intellectual capital, and the benchmarking of competitors' intellectual assets are all important parts of the knowledge management game. But all of these are subordinate to the matter of learning. For it is learning that makes intellectual property, capital, and assets usable.

The difficulty of this central challenge, however, has been obscured by the redefinition that, as we noted earlier, infoenthusiasts tend to indulge. The definitions of knowledge management that began this chapter perform a familiar two-step. First, they define the core problem in terms of information, so that, second, they can put solutions in the province of information technology.[13] Here, retrieval looks as easy as search.

If information retrieval were all that is required for such things as knowledge management or best practice, HP would have nothing to worry about. It has an abundance of very good information technology. The persistence of HP's problem, then, argues that knowledge management, knowledge, and learning involve more than information. In the rest of this chapter we try to understand what else is involved, looking primarily at knowledge and learning on the assumption that these need to be understood before knowledge management can be considered.

COMMUNITY SUPPORT

To understand learning in the context of knowledge management, let's begin by asking in what conditions do knowledge and best practice move. In chapter 4, we saw the reps sharing their knowledge, insights, and best practices quite effectively. These traveled first among the small group of coworkers and then, with the help of the Eureka database, across larger groups of company reps. To understand how these best practices travel, this example suggests, requires looking not simply from knowledge to information, but (as the idea of best practice might suggest) from knowledge to practice and groups of practitioners. For it is the reps' practice shared in collaborative communities that allowed them to share their knowledge.

As we saw, the reps formed themselves into a small community, united by their common practice, servicing machines. The members of this community spent a lot of time both working and talking over work together. In Orr's account, the talk and the work, the communication and the practice are inseparable. The talk made the work intelligible, and the work made the talk intelligible. As part of this common work-and-talk, creating, learning, sharing, and using knowledge appear almost indivisible. Conversely, talk without the work, communication without practice is if not unintelligible, at least unusable. Become a member of a community, engage in its practices, and you can acquire and make use of its knowledge and information. Remain an outsider, and these will remain indigestible.

Two learning researchers, whose individual work we mentioned earlier, Jean Lave of the University of California, Berkeley, and Etienne Wenger, a consultant formerly of the Institute for Research on Learning, explain this sort of simultaneous working, learning, and communication in terms of both the practice and the community. Learning a practice, they argue, involves becoming a member of a "community of practice" and thereby understanding its work and its talk from the inside.[14] Learning, from this point of view, is not simply a matter of acquiring information; it requires developing the disposition, demeanor, and outlook of the practitioners.

Like Orr's study of reps, Wenger's study of claims processing (see chapter 4) showed the importance of the group to both what people learn and how. Within the group, Wenger's study reveals, knowledge, traveling on the back of practice, was readily shared.

It may at first seem that group practice and community support are only appropriate for the tedium of "lowly" claims processing. They might seem to have little do with the "higher" altitudes of knowledge work, where the image of the lone, Rodinesque "thinker" is more common. Yet the value of communities of practice to creating and sharing knowledge is as evident in the labs of particle physicists and biotechnologists as in the claims processing unit.[15] The apprenticeship-like activity that Lave and Wenger describe is found not only on the shop floor, but throughout the highest reaches of education and beyond. In the last years of graduate school or in internships, scientists, humanists, doctors, architects, or lawyers, after years of schoolroom training, learn their craft in the company of professional mentors. Here, they form learning communities capable of generating, sharing, and deploying highly esoteric knowledge.

Recently a computer engineer described a group that he led on a difficult project that, despite the difference in subject matter, resembles the groups of interdependent technicians and claims processors:

> *[It] was less than half a dozen people; and the group that did the software and hardware never did get to be more than about a dozen people. It was a tiny enough group that everyone knew everything that was going on, and there was very little structure . . . there were people who specifically saw their role as software, and they knew a lot about hardware anyway; and the hardware people all could program. There wasn't a great deal of internal difficulty. There's always a little, I don't think you can get even six people together without having some kind of a problem. . . . There was amazingly little argument or fighting.*[16]

This description catches central properties of the community of practice. In particular, it notes how, in getting the job done, the people involved ignored divisions of rank and role to forge a single group around their shared task, with overlapping knowledge, relatively blurred boundaries, and a common working identity. The speaker in this case is Frank Heart of Bolt Beranek and Newman; the group's task, designing the core computers for what came to be the Internet.

In all, whether the task is deemed high or low, practice is an effective teacher and the community of practice an ideal learning environment.

TO BE OR NOT TO BE

Of course, whatever the strengths of communities of practice, people learn on their own, picking up information from numerous sources about numerous topics without ever becoming a "member." We can learn something about Tibetan medicine or racing without needing to work with Tibetan doctors or become a Formula 1 driver. The critical words here, however, are *about* and *become*. They point to a distinction made by Jerome Bruner, a professor of psychology at New York University, between *learning about* and *learning to be*. Certainly, most of anyone's knowledge might best be described as knowledge "about." Many people learn *about* a lot of things—astrophysics, Australian Rules football, Madagascan lemurs, or baseball statistics. In the age of the Web, this learning about is easier than ever before.

But, picking up information about Madagascan lemurs in the comfort of our home doesn't close the gap between us and Madagascan field zoologists. Learning to be requires more than just information. It requires the ability to engage in the practice in question.

Indeed, Bruner's distinction highlights another, made by the philosopher Gilbert Ryle. He distinguishes "know that" from "know how." Learning about involves the accumulation of "know that": principally data, facts, or information. Learning about does not, however, produce the ability to put "know that" into use. This, Ryle argues, calls for "know how." And "know how" does not come through accumulating information. (If it did, "know that" and "know how" would, in the end, be indistinguishable—build up enough "know that" and you would become a practitioner.) "We learn *how*," Ryle argues, "by practice." And, similarly, through practice, we learn to be.[17]

Ryle's philosophical argument may have brought us danger-
ously near the realm of abstruse epistemology that we promised
to avoid. But it helps explain why the same stream of information directed at different people doesn't produce the same
knowledge in each. If the people are engaged in different practices, if they are learning to be different kinds of people, then
they will respond to the information in different ways. Practice
shapes assimilation.

The practice of managing a baseball team, for example, is not
the same as the practice of playing on a baseball team. The
"know that" for each job may be fairly similar. Managers and
players gather a lot of the same information. But the "know
how" for the two (thus the way each makes use of their "know
that") is quite different. One's practice is to manage; the other's
is to play. Similarly, while management theorists and managers
may posses similar "know that," their different practices keep
them apart. The two can read the same books, magazines, and
journals, but these don't allow either to do the other's job. A
good management theorist may explain the practice of management well, but never make a good hands-on manager. Similarly, an excellent manager may prove an inept theoretician.[18]

LEARNING IN PRACTICE

Practice, then, both shapes and supports learning. We wouldn't
need to labor this point so heavily were it not that unenlightened
teaching and training often pulls in the opposite direction. First,
they tend to isolate people from the sorts of ongoing practice of
work itself. And second, they focus heavily on information.

Nowhere is this isolation more true than in the workplace.
Or perhaps we should say than *not* in the workplace. For while

many of the resources for learning to work lie in the workplace, training regularly takes people away from there, to learn the job in classrooms. The ideal of learning isolated from the "distractions" of work practice still influences many training regimens. So let us look briefly at a couple of examples that suggest some of the limits of the classroom and the resources of practice.

Limits to Going by the Book

The first example draws on research by two educational psychologists, George Miller and Patricia Gildea, into how children learn vocabulary. Miller and Gildea compared learning words in the everyday practice of conversation with trying to learn vocabulary from dictionaries.[19]

In the everyday case, they found that learning is startlingly fast and successful. By listening, talking, and reading, the average 17-year-old has learned vocabulary at a rate of 5,000 words per year (13 per day) for over 16 years. The children know both what these words mean and how to use them.

By contrast, learning words from abstract definitions and sentences from dictionaries is far slower and far less successful. Working this way, the children in the study acquired between 100 and 200 words per year. Moreover, much of what they learned turned out to be almost useless in practice. Despite their best efforts, looking up *relate, careful, remedy* and *stir up* in a dictionary led to sentences such as, "Me and my parents correlate, because without them I wouldn't be here"; "I was meticulous about falling off the cliff"; "The redress for getting sick is staying in bed"; and "Mrs. Morrow stimulated the soup."

Most of us have seen the workplace equivalent of this—the eager young intern with all the right information but none of the practical knowledge that makes the job doable. Similarly, a lawyer friend of ours recalled how the first days at work were a nightmare because, despite all her excellent results in law school and on the law board exams, nothing in the classroom had prepared her for the realities of having a client on the other end of the telephone.

The Practical Value of Phone Cords

Another colleague, Jack Whalen, showed the power of practice in his study of learning in a service center taking the calls from customers and scheduling technicians.[20] Sending technicians to fix broken machines is an expensive undertaking. It is a waste if the problem does not really require a technician. So the people who take the calls can save the company money by diagnosing simple problems and telling the customer how to fix these for themselves. It makes customers happy, too. They don't have to sit with a dead machine, waiting for a technician to bring it back to life.

The phone operators are not, of course, trained as technicians. In the past, however, they learned from the reps when the latter called in to pick up their next job. The reps would then explain how trivial the last one had been, and in the process the phone operators could learn a lot from these mentors. When they next took such a call, they could offer a solution. As a result of a change in communications technology, however, technicians no longer pick up their calls this way. Consequently, operators no longer pick up insights. Their opportunity for inherent learning has been lost.

The company has tried to replace this kind of learning with the more explicit support of a "case-based expert system." This is an information-based system that prompts operators to ask the customer a series of questions. The operator types the responses into the system, which then searches for a ready solution. This alternative has not worked well. As the reps found with "directive documentation," it can be surprisingly difficult to get a clear diagnosis and solution this way. Moreover, such a system doesn't help the operators understand what they are doing. And that lack of understanding undermines the customer's confidence. It's hard to put faith in people who are obviously reading instructions off a screen. As a result, customers will ask for a technician anyway, and so defeat the whole expert-system strategy.

To overcome these problems, the company contemplated new training courses with several weeks off site to better prepare new operators. Whalen and his fellow researchers took a slightly different route, however. They studied one service center and the quality of diagnosis its staff provided. There they found two operators who gave especially reliable answers. One, unsurprisingly, was an eight-year veteran of the service center with some college experience and a survivor from the days when reps served as mentors. The other, however, was someone with only a high-school diploma. She had been on the job barely four months.

The researchers noticed, however, that the newcomer had a desk opposite the veteran. There she could hear the veteran taking calls, asking questions, and giving advice. And she began to do the same. She had also noticed that he had acquired a variety of pamphlets and manuals, so she began to build up her own stock. Moreover, when she didn't understand the answers the veteran gave, she asked him to show her what he meant, using the service center's own copier.

So instead of training courses, the sociologists suggested restructuring the phone center. They sought to draw on its reservoir of knowledge by putting all its operators in positions to learn from each other. By opening the place up to this collective knowledge, the redesign effectively created a small laboratory of what Whalen calls "indigenous sharing and collaborative learning." The new plan also asked technicians to come in and take calls intermittently. As a result, operators could learn from them once again.

From these changes, the operators were up to speed in about the time it took to plan a training course for them and in far less time than was set aside for actual training. Ultimately, Whalen concluded, given the amount and level of knowledge already available in the room, what the operators needed were not so much expert systems or new training courses, but "longer phone cords."[21] (These allow an operator taking a call to slide over to the desk and the screen of a resourceful colleague who could provide the necessary help.) Both examples, the classroom and the workplace, indicate how the resources for learning lie not simply in information, but in the practice that allows people to make sense of and use that information and the practitioners who know how to use that information. Where in other circumstances knowledge is hard to move, in these circumstances it travels with remarkable ease.

PHILOSOPHICAL EXPLANATIONS

To venture cautiously again onto philosophical grounds, the distinction between explicit and implicit dimensions of knowledge can help illuminate why practice is so effective. It's possible, for example, to learn about negotiation strategies by reading books about negotiation. But strategy books don't make you into a good negotiator, any more than dictionaries make you into a speaker

or expert systems make you into an expert. To become a negotiator requires not only knowledge of strategy, but skill, experience, judgment, and discretion. These allow you to understand
not just how a particular strategy is executed, but when to execute it. The two together make a negotiator, but the second
comes only with practice.

The chemist and philosopher Michael Polanyi distinguished
these two by talking about the explicit and the tacit dimensions
of knowledge. The explicit dimension is like the strategy book.
But it is relatively useless without the tacit dimension. This,
Polanyi argues, allows people to see when to apply the explicit
part.[22]

To take another simple example of this sort of tacit "seeing,"
consider dictionaries again. These are the guidebooks of language and particularly for spelling. But if you lack the tacit
dimension required for spelling, shelves of dictionaries do you
no good. For being able to use a dictionary (the explicit part) is
not enough. You have to know when to use a dictionary. A good
speller will say, "I just know that doesn't look right." This is the
tacit part. Once it has done its work, you can turn to the explicit
information in the dictionary. The problem for a bad speller, of
course, is that if he or she lacks the tacit knowing that makes
words look wrong, then a dictionary's use is limited. In the end,
paradoxically, you only learn to use a dictionary by learning to
spell.

In making his distinction between explicit and tacit, Polanyi
argues that no amount of explicit knowledge provides you with
the implicit. They are two different dimensions of knowledge,
and trying to reduce one to the other is a little like trying to
reduce a two-dimensional drawing to one dimension. This
claim of Polanyi's resembles Ryle's argument that "know that"

doesn't produce "know how," and Bruner's that *learning about* doesn't, on its own, allow you to *learn to be*. Information, all these arguments suggest, is on its own not enough to produce actionable knowledge. Practice too is required. And for practice, it's best to look to a community of practitioners.

PRACTICAL IMPLICATIONS

Teach these boys nothing but Facts. Facts alone are wanted in life.
Plant nothing less and root out everything else. You can only form
the minds of reasoning animals upon Facts. . . . Stick to Facts, Sir.
—CHARLES DICKENS, Hard Times[23]

The view of knowledge and practice we have put forward here has several implications for how to think about learning—and related issues such as spreading best practice, improving performance, or innovating—as well as training and teaching.

In the first place, it takes us beyond information. The idea of learning as the steady supply of facts or information, though parodied by Dickens 150 years ago, still prevails today. Each generation has its own fight against images of learners as wax to be molded, pitchers to be filled, and slates to be written on.

Literature about workplace learning is still laced with ideas of "absorptive capacity," as if humans were information sponges. Indeed, the idea that learning is mere information absorption may be on the rise today because it allows for more redefinition. If we accept this view of learning, then it's a short step to talking about such things as computers or bots learning, as if what they do is just what people do. Looking beyond information, as we have tried to do, provides a richer picture of learning. From this picture, the following features stand out for us.

Learning on Demand

Learning is usually treated as a supply-side matter, thought to follow teaching, training, or information delivery. But learning is much more demand driven. People learn in response to need. When people cannot see the need for what's being taught, they ignore it, reject it, or fail to assimilate it in any meaningful way. Conversely, when they have a need, then, if the resources for learning are available, people learn effectively and quickly.

In an essay we wrote about learning some years ago, we referred to this aspect of learning as "stolen knowledge." We based this idea on a short passage in the biography of the great Indian poet and Nobel Prize winner Rabindrath Tagore.[24] Talking of an instructor hired to teach him music, Tagore writes, "He determined to teach me music, and consequently no learning took place." Tagore found little to interest him in the tedious tasks he was given as practice for these involved not the authentic activity itself, but only a pale imitation. "Nevertheless," he continues, "I did pick up from him a certain amount of stolen knowledge."[25] This knowledge, Tagore reveals, he picked up by watching and listening to the musician when the latter played for his own and others' entertainment. Only then, when what was evident was the practice of musicianship and not dismembered teaching exercises, was Tagore able to see and appreciate the real practice at issue.

A demand-side view of this sort of knowledge theft suggests how important it is not to force-feed learning, but to encourage it, both provoking the need and making the resources available for people to "steal." We regard this as the paradoxical challenges of encouraging and legitimating theft. Organizations have become increasingly adept both at provoking and at responding to changes in their clients' needs. They need to consider how to do this for their employees as well.

Social Learning

Despite the tendency to shut ourselves away and sit in Rodinesque isolation when we have to learn, learning is a remarkably social process. Social groups provide the resources for their members to learn. Other socially based resources are also quite effective.

For example, people who are judged unfit to learn to operate simple tools or who fail to master domestic appliances nevertheless learn to operate complex machines that present users with hazardous, changing environments and sophisticated technologies. We refer, of course, to the car. Technologically, cars are extremely sophisticated. But they are also extremely well integrated socially. As a result, learning becomes almost invisible. Consider, by contrast, the triumphal despair with which people frustratedly boast that they still can't program their VCR. The success of learner drivers—with or without instruction—should undoubtedly be the envy of many who design far less difficult consumer or workplace appliances.

The car and the VCR make an interesting contrast. Almost everyone in our society who learns to drive has already spent a great deal of time traveling in cars or buses, along roads and highways. New drivers begin formal instruction with an implicitly structured, social understanding of the task. Now consider the VCR. Most people can use their machine to play tapes. What they find difficult is recording, though that's not a much more complex task. The central distinction between these two functions is that one is often a social act, the other highly individual. You might invite a group over to watch a movie. You are unlikely to invite one over to watch you record.[26]

Learning and Identity Shape One Another

Bruner, with his idea of learning to be, and Lave and Wenger, in
their discussion of communities of practice, both stress how
learning needs to be understood in relation to the development
of human identity. In learning to be, in becoming a member of
a community of practice, an individual is developing a social
identity. In turn, the identity under development shapes what
that person comes to know, how he or she assimilates knowledge and information. So, even when people are *learning about*,
in Bruner's terms, the identity they are developing determines
what they pay attention to and what they learn. What people
learn about, then, is always refracted through who they are and
what they are learning to be.[27]

So information, while a critical part of learning, is only one
among many forces at work. Information theory portrays information as a change registered in an otherwise steady state. It's a
light flashing out on a dark hillside (to borrow an example from
the philosopher Fred Dretske[28]) or the splash of a pebble breaking the calm of a still lake. In either case, the result, as the
anthropologist Gregory Bateson puts it neatly, is "a difference
that makes a difference."[29]

The importance of disturbance or change makes it almost
inevitable that we focus on these. We notice the ripple and take
the lake for granted. Yet clearly the lake shapes the ripple more
than the ripple shapes the lake. Against a different background,
the pebble would register a different change or perhaps, in Bateson's terms, make no difference at all. So to understand the
whole interaction, it is as important to ask how the lake is
formed as to ask how the pebble got there. It's this formation
rather than information that we want to draw attention to,

though the development is almost imperceptible and the forces invisible in comparison to the drama and immediacy of the pebble. It's not, to repeat once more, the information that creates that background. The background has to be in place for the information to register. The forces that shape the background are, rather, the tectonic social forces, always at work, within which and against which individuals configure their identity. These create not only grounds for reception, but grounds for interpretation, judgment, and understanding.

A Brief Note on the "Social"

We emphasize the social side of learning and identity with some caution. The economist Friedrich Hayek claims that *social* is a weasel word.[30] Moreover, people readily point out that they can learn a great deal sitting alone in an office or a library. And you don't have to go very far with the thesis that learning is significantly social to encounter the question "What about Robinson Crusoe?"[31]

Early economists liked to present Crusoe as an example of the *homo economicus*, the universal economic man, learning and working in splendid individual independence. And that's the idea behind this question. It took Karl Marx to point out, however, that Crusoe is not a universal. On his island (and in Defoe's mind), he is deeply rooted in the society from which he came:

> *Our friend Robinson . . . having rescued a watch, ledger, and pen and ink from the wreck, commences, like a true-born Briton, to keep a set of books. His stock book contains a list of the objects of utility that belong to him, of the operations necessary for their production; and lastly, of the labour time that definite quantities of those objects have, on average, cost him.*[32]

Robinson is not just a man in isolation, but a highly representative member of what Napoleon was to call a "nation of shopkeepers." It is, of course, not only the British who play to type, even when alone. The French philosopher Jean-Paul Sartre, in a famous passage, illustrates how that true-born Frenchman, the café waiter, though working alone, conforms his actions to society's idea of what a waiter does:

> *He returns, trying to imitate in his walk the inflexible stiffness of some kind of automaton while carrying his tray with the recklessness of a tight rope walker by putting it in a perpetually unstable, perpetually broken equilibrium which he perpetually re-establishes by a light movement of the arm and hand. . . . We need not watch long before we can explain it: he is playing at being a waiter in a café . . . . [T]he waiter plays with his condition in order to realize it.*[33]

So while people do indeed learn alone, even when they are not stranded on desert islands or in small cafés, they are nonetheless always enmeshed in society, which saturates our environment, however much we might wish to escape it at times. Language, for example, is a social artifact, and as people learn their way into it, they are simultaneously inserting themselves into a variety of complex, interwoven social systems.

LEARNING DIVISIONS

Looking at learning as a demand-driven, identity forming, social act, it's possible to see how learning binds people together. People with similar practices and similar resources develop similar identities—the identity of a technician, a chemist, a lepidopterist, a train spotter, an enologist, an archivist, a parking-lot attendant, a business historian, a model bus enthusiast, a real estate developer, or a cancer sufferer. These practices in common (for hobbies and illnesses are practices too) allow people to form social networks along which knowledge about that practice can both travel rapidly and be assimilated readily.[34]

For the same reason, however, members of these networks are to some degree divided or separated from people with different practices. It is not the different information they have that divides them. Indeed, they might have a lot of information in common. Rather, it is their different attitudes or dispositions toward that information—attitudes and dispositions shaped by practice and identity—that divide. Consequently, despite much in common, physicians are different from nurses, accountants from financial planners.[35]

We see two types of work-related networks that, with the boundaries they inevitably create, are critical for understanding learning, work, and the movement of knowledge. First, there are the networks that link people to others whom they may never get to know but who work on similar practices. We call these "networks of practice." Second, there are the more tight-knit groups formed, again through practice, by people working together on the same or similar tasks. These are what, following Lave and Wenger, we call "communities of practice." Here we sketch the two briefly before elaborating their role in later chapters.

Networks of Practice

While the name "networks of practice" helps us to emphasize what we see as the common denominator of these groups—practice—elsewhere they go by the name of "occupational groups" or "social worlds."[36] People in such networks have practice and knowledge in common. Nevertheless, most of the members are unknown to one other. Indeed, the links between the members of such networks are usually more indirect than direct—newsletters, Web sites, Bulletin boards, listservs, and so forth keep them in touch and aware of one another.[37] Members coordinate and communicate through third parties or indirectly. Coordination and communication are, as a result, quite explicit.[38]

The 25,000 reps working for Xerox make up, in theory, such a network. They could in principle be linked through such things as the Eureka database (though it is in fact not worldwide) or corporate newsletters aimed at reps. Their common practice makes these links viable, allowing them to assimilate these communications in more-or-less similar ways. By extension, the network could also include technicians in other companies doing the same sort of work, though here the connections would be weaker, grounds for common understanding more sparse.

Networks of this sort are notable for their reach—a reach now extended and fortified by information technology. Information can travel across vast networks with great speed and to large numbers but nonetheless be assimilated in much the same way by whomever receives it. By contrast, there is relatively little reciprocity across such network; that is, network members don't interact with one another directly to any significant degree. When reach dominates reciprocity like this, it produces very loosely coupled systems.[39] Collectively, such social systems don't take action and produce little knowledge. They can, though, share information relating to the members' common practices quite efficiently.

Communities of Practice

Lave and Wenger's notion of communities of practice, which we mentioned earlier, focuses on subsections of these larger networks of practice. These subsections stand in contrast to the network as a whole in several ways. They are relatively tight-knit groups of people who know each other and work together directly. They are usually face-to-face communities that continually negotiate with, communicate with, and coordinate with each other directly in the course of work. And this negotiation, communication, and coordination is highly implicit, part of work practice, and, in the case of the reps, work chat.[40]

While part of the network, groups like this cultivate their own style, their own sense of taste, judgment, and appropriateness, their own slang and in-terms. These things can distinguish members of one community within a network from others. In networks of scholars, for example, while all may be from one field, it's often easy to guess who trained together in a particular lab or school by their style and approach.

In these groups, the demands of direct coordination inevitably limit reach. You can only work closely with so many people. On the other hand, reciprocity is strong. People are able to affect one another and the group as a whole directly. Changes can propagate easily. Coordination is tight. Ideas and knowledge may be distributed across the group, not held individually. These groups allow for highly productive and creative work to develop collaboratively.

UNDERSTANDING DIVISION

The divisions marked by the external boundaries of these groups have significant implications for the development of organizations, technologies, and indeed of societies as a whole. Yet they are divisions that discussions of such developments easily overlook.

For example, discussions of the emerging "network society" suggest that society is becoming a single, uniform entity. The network stretches indefinitely, linking the individuals that stand at each node to one another and providing them with common information. Communities, organizations, nations, and the like disappear (victims of the 6-Ds discussed in chapter 1). The network is all, configuring itself more or less as the vaunted global village.

From the perspective of practice, rather than of process or information, a rather different picture emerges. From this viewpoint, any global network has a highly varied topography. While the whole may ultimately be global, within it there are networks of practice with lines of reach that are extensive but nonetheless bounded by practice. And there are communities of practice, with dense connections of both reach and reciprocity, which again put limits on extent. These two, networks and communities, produce areas marked by common identity and coordinated practice within any larger network. And as a consequence of these areas, information does not travel uniformly throughout the network. It travels according to the local topography.

Curiously, organization theory suffers from similarly homogenizing vision. It has been fashionable of late to talk of workplace culture or organizational culture as if these made organizations internally uniform. But divisions created by practice produce significant variation here as well. Within organizations as without, connections are dense in some places and thin in others. Sometimes these networks extend across the boundaries of the organization. Elsewhere, they may confront discontinuities within, where meaningful communication breaks down.

Business process reengineering, in particular, ignores divisions created by different practices. Indeed, Hammer and Champy's *Reengineering the Corporation* seeks to supersede the division of labor that the economist Adam Smith saw as central to capitalist production.[41] Consequently, business process reengineering fails to understand the internally varied terrain of organizations and its fractures and divisions.

Sim Sitkin of the Fuqua School of Business at Duke University and a colleague revealed similar blindness in "Total Quality Management." Managers of one large organization, Sitkin and his colleague found, attempted to implement a single scheme uniformly across a company. The approach overlooked the different ideas of quality that different practices develop. Pursuing a common goal in the face of these divisions made the different groups feel that they were being judged by the standards of others, and in consequence, fear their work would either be undervalued or unrecognized. Rather than spreading quality, the researchers concluded, the scheme only spread dissent and distrust.[42]

Failure to read the topography may be at its most damaging as people try to predict the effects of new information technologies on organization. One of the remarkable things about these technologies is their reach. Consequently, they are well suited to support, develop, and even strengthen the networks of practice we have described. As these networks readily span the borders of organizations, their increasing strength will affect those organizations. Whether networks will grow at the expense of organizations is a question needing further research, not the linear assumptions of infoenthusiasts. It seems improbable that they will simply dissolve organization any more than, as we claimed in chapter 1, they will necessarily damage local communities, which remain robust.

New technologies may, though, spread these communities out more than before. The growing reciprocity available on the

'Net, while probably underused at the moment, is helping people separated by space maintain their dense interrelations. Yet for the sort of implicit communication, negotiation, and collective improvisation that we have described as part of practice, learning, and knowledge sharing, it's clear that there are advantages to working together, however well people may be connected by technology. Indeed, one of the most powerful uses of information technology seems to be to support people who do work together directly and to allow them to schedule efficient face-to-face encounters. Looking too closely at the progression from atoms to bits may miss the role the bits play in allowing us to reinforce the valuable aspects of the world of atoms. Critical movements in the knowledge economy may go not just from atoms to bits, but from atoms to bits and back again.

CHAPTER 6

Innovating Organization, Husbanding Knowledge

Electronic commerce is the single greatest change in business since the invention of money. . . . On the Internet there's perfect information. . . . Location doesn't protect you any more. It's a truly global economy.

—National Public Radio Business News[1]

IF THE RECESSION OF the early 1990s disrupted U.S. business, as we noted in chapter 4, the long expansion that has followed has not, as might have been expected, brought calm. Far from it. As the recovery got under way, the World Wide Web arose out of nowhere, popularizing the Internet, populating cyberspace, and bringing on its back the turmoil of "e-commerce" and the challenges of "globalization."

At first e-commerce was seen as a matter for hobbyists only. (The personal computer was greeted in much the same way.) Economic reality soon changed that opinion. In 1995, Web sales accounted for some $436 million. By 2000, the Department of Commerce estimates, it will be $30 billion.[2] The landed gentry of the business world, who once looked aloof from their upholstered carriages at e-commerce, suddenly found themselves scrambling to get on the bus. The aristocratic brokerage house Merrill Lynch, for example, treated on-line traders as if they were dumpster scavengers. In 1999, it finally realized that it had to scavenge too. One of every seven trades was being made online. And the portion would only grow.

As they move onto the 'Net, firms find themselves competing in a strange world where apparently insignificant competitors transform themselves into market leaders almost overnight. In 1995, Barnes & Noble felt secure in its successful chain of bookstores. By 1997, the upstart Amazon.com presented it with the stark choice of going on-line quickly or out of business slowly. It's a world where an absence of fixed assets, profits, and even income can be an advantage. A world where firms appear to thrive, as one commentator put it, by selling a dollar for 85 cents.[3] A world, too, where distance appears to be dead and the economy global—though at the same time, local "clusters" like Silicon Valley seem ever more important. Indeed, the person interviewed on the death of location at the head of this chapter was, paradoxically, chosen because he comes, as NPR put it, from the "technology stronghold" of the San Francisco Bay Area.

In such strange conditions, no one feels secure. Those so far unaffected see tornadoes touch down in a new sector every day. Those already hit, meanwhile, find that these tornadoes don't touch down and move on. They come to stay. The painfully steep part of the curve keeps getting steeper. E-commerce plans, perfected one day, have to be torn up the next. Income streams get quickly diverted. Long-term investments evaporate. Once bankable customer loyalty suddenly disappears. Within this storm, it remains very difficult to say what is simply churning and what is a trend.

Faced with constantly changing conditions, the pressure for firms to innovate is enormous. Here we mean not just product innovation, though that's of particular interest to us. Businesses have to create new business models, new financial strategies, new organizational structures, and even new institutional frameworks to deal in these new markets. For all of these, the artful deployment of knowledge is at a high premium. Yet many of the organizational factors involved in innovation and the deployment of knowledge are not easy to understand, as even the "experts" find.

KNOWLEDGE CONUNDRUM

A couple of years ago, we had the good fortune to attend the first "Knowledge Forum" at Berkeley's Haas School of Business. Some of the most experienced knowledge managers and theorists spoke with remarkable frankness about their concerns—the transformation of the economy, the kaleidoscopic character of modern markets, and the failure of old business models and organizational theory. Yet, as people expressed sympathy for each other's dilemmas, we found the room mysteriously dividing into two diametrically opposed camps, each in warm agreement with the other.[4]

One party stressed the critical difficulty of moving knowledge. (The comment "if only HP knew what HP knows" was often quoted, and heads nodded in agreement.) People expressed the belief that much of the knowledge needed to stay ahead of competitors existed in their firms—indeed, it provided the firm's critical competitive advantage. Yet, they continued, this knowledge could not always be found, and when it was, it could not be moved to where it was needed.

The other party offered a strikingly different picture. Again they saw knowledge as critical, and again the central problem concerned its movement. But these people did not say that they couldn't move knowledge. Instead they reported how they couldn't stop it moving. Knowledge, from their viewpoint, was like water, constantly flowing and difficult to dam. But it was not flowing across the firm. It was flowing—or more appropriately leaking—out of the organization, and intellectual property laws were powerless to stop it.

In the end, despite optimistic pictures of the firm as a "knowledge generator" or "innovative system," from the perspective of the Berkeley Knowledge Forum knowledge, innovation, and the firm seemed almost incompatible. What knowledge the firm can hold on to, it can't use. And what it might use, it can't hold on to.

FUMBLING THE FUTURE

In some of the cases discussed at the Forum, it became clear that the same knowledge that would clot within a firm would nonetheless hemorrhage out. Knowledge that appeared "sticky" to some was "leaky" to others. So sticky and leaky knowledge were not always separate kinds or instances of knowledge. One of the best examples of this contradictory character turned out to involve Xerox and its notorious "fumbling" of the future.[5]

At Xerox PARC in the 1970s, pioneering scientists developed the elements of the personal computer. They produced not only much of the technology that sits under the desk but also the stuff on the screen "desktop" that makes up the "graphical user interface" (GUI). This includes the digital documents, files, folders, and menus through which people maneuver by pointing, clicking, and scrolling. These are now standard components of Macintosh, Windows, and the World Wide Web—components that propelled information technology from the preserve of experts to the realm of ordinary users.

Yet most of the extraordinary knowledge generated at PARC never crossed the boundary between the scientists in Palo Alto and the development engineers in Dallas or the management in Stamford. The engineers found the scientists arrogant and almost unintelligible. Management found them naïve and unrealistic. The scientists, for their part, regarded almost everyone in the corporation outside their own community as "toner heads"—unable to think of the world beyond photocopiers.

The story and the knowledge, as everyone knows, did not end here. For the essence of what had been invented by Xerox in Palo Alto ended up being put into production by Apple down the road in Cupertino. In 1979, Xerox managers invited Steve Jobs, one of Apple's founders, to PARC. Once inside, Jobs was able to see what Xerox management could not, the potential of what PARC had generated. So Apple licensed what it could and replicated what it could not. The knowledge that stuck within Xerox leaked readily through its front door.

UNITED IN THEORY,
DIVIDED IN PRACTICE

That knowledge sticks within organizations should surprise no one. In practice, whether as members from within or as clients or customers from without, we all know how impenetrable the divisions within organizations can be. Yet, as we noted in chapter 5, in theory, these divisions may disappear. Discussions of business organization, that is, sometimes take these divisions, which we see as profoundly important, to be little more than by-products of the organizational chart. Wipe the chart off the chalkboard, it's then assumed, and you wipe away the divisions. Business process reengineering, as we noted, claims to dismiss the division of labor as mere economic history. Consultants talk about "cross-functional teams" as a ready cure. And organizational theory, despite major shifts in perspective, generally assumes that firms are essentially homogeneous.

In the 1930s, for example, the early organizational theorists offered the homogeneity of business as a cure for society's divisions. As Eileen O'Connor of Stanford University has shown, these theorists presented business organizations as a great civilizing enterprise. The firm, in their view, was engine for the nation's "melting pot." It would be capable of dissolving the cultural differences of a largely immigrant population.[6]

The 1950s saw a reaction to this cheerful view of the firm both in novels like *The Man in the Gray Flannel Suit* and in studies such as William Whyte's dissection of "organization man."[7] These explored the tension between the individual and organization. Yet even here firms appeared as internally more or less uniform. What the '30s had admired, however, the '50s criticized. Today, uniformity has become a virtue again. There is probably not an employee—no matter how large the employer—that hasn't been encouraged to think of him- or herself as a member of a single "community." Management nostrums encourage everyone to get on board, become part of the team, pull in the same direction, and so on.[8]

In a similar vein, there's been a lot of talk about organizational "culture" and members' "identity" as if these were uniform, too. As we argued in chapter 5, both culture and identity are significant aspects of learning and knowledge. So we need to take such talk seriously. Moreover, members of an organization often do reveal shared, identifiable features. Groups from a particular company— IBM programmers, AT&T sales representatives, or Xerox technical reps, for example—often stand out from people holding similar jobs in other firms.

Yet it's easy to overestimate the significance of these features of identity. For identity is itself not uniform. All of us compose our identities out of the many different groups of which we are members. Moreover, what Jerome Bruner describes as "learning to be," forging an identity, occurs principally through shared practice (see chapter 5). So a work identity, even in multinational firms, is to a significant degree formed locally, where practitioners work together and practice is interdependent. Large organizations stand little chance of forging much of a common identity. Its members are too diverse, too deeply engaged in different practices, and located in too many places. Employees, then, don't simply become members of the Xerox Corporation. They become members of its different communities of practice—technical representatives, engineers, research managers, or sales analysts.[9]

In contrast to these images of business homogeneity, Adam Smith emphasized the importance of the division of labor. He showed, as most people remember, a powerful way to increase productivity.[10] But he also showed that division of labor also produces useful, local knowledge. People dedicated to particular tasks soon find ways to make productive improvements, coming up with new ideas and insights.

Such local knowledge, however, can also reinforce the divisions that help create it. As any one group develops in the direction of its unique practice, insights, and knowledge, it may develop away from the other groups with which it must work (which will no doubt be developing along the lines of their own practices).[11] The creation of local knowledge, then, is likely to create simultaneously problems for coordination. In general, the formal requirements of process and a little creative "processing" (see chapter 4) smoothes over such problems. As a result, they are likely to dampen (or at least make invisible) creativity.

LOOSENING TIES

As tightening the ties of formal coordination inevitably inhibits creativity, firms often loosen them to encourage it. Loosening ties this way is a well-established business practice. Lockheed did it with its "skunk works." Xerox did it with PARC. GM did it with an entire division when it set up the Saturn project. IBM did it with its PC division in Boca Raton. Apple did it with the small groups set up to develop the Macintosh, the PowerBook, and its multimedia QuickTime software. Even in much smaller organizations with no R&D budget, groups are occasionally sent away for short periods to "think outside the box."

Decoupling organizational links in this way does more than provide room for new ways of thinking outside the old prescriptions. It also keeps exploration safe from those organizational antibodies that flock to protect the corporate body from invasions of the new. Power struggles between old ideas and new inevitably favor the old and established, which have a proven track record, over the new, which by definition has none. So fledgling ideas are easily pushed from the nest. The defenders of the old copier business within Xerox, for example, had much more collateral (epitomized principally by an established revenue stream) than the champions of the new digital technology when the struggle developed for resources. Without the means to fight directly, new research usually relies on its obscurity and isolation to resist attack.

BECOMING UNTIED

Separation that advances invention, however, creates problems for innovation, which is the implementation of invention. Invention produces new ideas. It requires innovation and organizational coordination, however, to turn these ideas into new products and processes. But the distance that supports initial invention can hobble its transformation into organized innovation. People who have gone away to think outside old paradigms may return sounding to those within the old paradigm like Mark Twain's Connecticut Yankee at King Arthur's Court, babbling of unheard and unintelligible wonders.

Work on new imaging processes (NIP) at PARC in the 1990s recently reminded us of the difficulty of reconnecting community knowledge. The NIP researchers developed an imaging technique of some potential. The next step required presenting this to the production engineers who would actually have to build it into printers.

The NIP researchers had definitely thought outside the box. In the process, they had become cut off from the standard box. They had developed a technique whose critical parameters were radically different from those used in conventional printing. The end result, the image, was much the same as before. So the engineers, used to dealing with standard print technology, assumed that their conventional understanding and measures still applied. But the new route to that image was radically different. Consequently, when tested with conventional measures, the new device produced incoherent results. Understandably, the engineers rejected it.

It's easy, this case reminds us, to believe that scientific results provide objective measures that can show one technology to be "superior" to another. All that's needed for ideas to flow, from this perspective, is the right information. In fact, such judgments rely on subjective understanding, intuition, and envisioning that varies from community to community and practice to practice. These variations are much harder to deal with.

The meeting point between the scientists and the engineers is, of course, the hurdle at which the GUI fell. So this time, Xerox worked hard to keep these two groups talking. Over time and with care, it was possible to broker understanding and agreement around shared commitment. But to do this first required acknowledging the nature of the gulf between the two—a practice-based, cultural gulf that, as we have said, organizational theory often assumes does not exist.

In case of the GUI, however, when the researchers, with their new criteria, met the engineers, each side accused the other of arrogance or stupidity (or both). It's easy to blame the corporate side of such exchanges, particularly when the invention goes on to be a success. But where the GUI researchers had had the opportunity to develop their understanding incrementally in practice, the engineers had to make a large conceptual leap in one go. Nature, it's said, doesn't make leaps. And it isn't in the nature of corporations, either.

In this case, ties had not simply been loosened. They had broken. As one of the engineers who tried to work with the GUI developers noted:

> *I just couldn't get anything out of them. I even told them I was their savviest, best customer in the corporation. But they were only interested in their own thing. They thought they were four feet above anything else.*[12]

The sense of unbelonging went both ways. The scientists saw themselves as members of a computer avant garde that went unappreciated in a corporation biased toward the copier business. And they were right. A firm building large, heavy-duty, commercial machines (and at the time struggling with competition from IBM, then Canon and Kodak as its patents expired, and with a formal complaint from the Federal Trade Commission for antitrust violations) was in exactly the wrong position to understand personal, digital technologies and their implications.[13] So neither side appreciated what it would require to move these ideas in such circumstances. Instead, the antibodies swarmed.

COMPUTER NETWORKS

With the PC, of course, all was not lost (though a good deal was lost from Xerox's point of view). The knowledge that stuck so firmly within, leaked rapidly out and down the road to Apple, and from there to Microsoft and a thousand other software developers.

It's a mistake to understand this change of direction solely in terms of the obtuseness of corporate managers or the limited "absorptive capacity" of engineers. Certainly there were bright people at Apple. But there were bright people at Xerox too. It's more revealing to think in terms of communities and networks of practice.

First, however, we need to get rid of a little Monday morning quarterbacking. Xerox, in its blindness to the PC was not alone. People who felt they knew the industry talked of "toy computers."[14] Gordon Moore, co-founder of Intel, whose Law reveals a good deal of foresight, candidly admits "I personally didn't see anything useful in [the PC], so [Intel] never gave it another thought."[15] Rejected by Xerox, the ideas behind the PC didn't flow into an otherwise receptive world. Rather, they found their way to one of the few organizations at the time that did have a strong vision of the PC and where it was going. This wasn't pure chance. The ideas traveled there along rails laid by practice.

The community of practice in which the ideas developed was cut off by its distinctive practices from the rest of the corporation.[16] As a result, communication as well as coordination had broken down. But those same practices connected this community to others whose similar interests and related practices gave them a more receptive worldview. Here we have an example of the "networks of practice" that we described earlier and in which communities of practice form subsets.

Almost everyone who works in an organization is also a member of such cross-cutting networks. These join people in one organization to people in similar positions with similar practices in other organizations. For well-established practices, professions and professional associations form the basis of such networks. They embrace people who not only do similar work, but go to the same conferences, read the same journals and magazines, and recognize one another as part of a field. Though based in separate organizations, common practice allows members of your network to provide an understanding shoulder to cry on when no one in your own corporation understands you.

It's along these networks of practice that knowledge leaks while sticking between practices within an organization. Accounts of the GUI leak still conflict, but it is generally agreed that informal links between Apple and PARC were well established by the time Jobs came to visit. These may have helped him to look beyond what Xerox intended to show. Certainly, between common practice and informal links, scientists at PARC finally felt they were dealing with people who understood them as their corporation did not. The people from

Apple, they found, looked at the world in a similar way. As one of the PARC scientists reported of the first formal discussions with developers from Apple, "It was almost like talking to someone in the [PARC] group."[17]

EXCHANGING COMPLEMENTS

The evident failure of the Xerox Corporation to make use of the knowledge developed at PARC has well-known parallels, even in Xerox's own history. Chester Carlson, who invented the xerographic process, offered several corporations, including IBM and A.B. Dick, his idea. None would buy it, for none could imagine how a photocopier could justify its expense when carbon paper was so cheap. The copier did not merely replace carbon paper, however. It transformed the way people used documents to organize work—as the Web is doing once again. Even innovative organizations are often quite unable to understand such transformations. Their failures, then, might appear to advance attacks on formal organization and to favor the "marketplace of ideas" as a more receptive alternative.

We need to remember, however, that the knowledge didn't simply flow out of PARC into the marketplace. It flowed into another organization. It was within Apple, not in the marketplace, that invention turned into innovation. Here the knowledge that stuck within Xerox found the insight, the capacity, and the organizational commitments required (after a couple of false starts) to bring it to market.

Moreover, while Apple did "gleefully recover" what Xerox fumbled, it too juggled for a painfully long time (1979 to 1984) before it made the catch secure. This is not a criticism of Apple. Rather, it is an acknowledgment of the organization required to take even something as appealing as the GUI to the marketplace. Within Apple there were many bridges between communities and practices to build. The Macintosh was for a while something of a pariah. The larger Lisa and the older Apple II drew most resources. There are accounts of pitched battles between the old and the new, where the lines of confrontation resemble those between the photocopier stalwarts and PC visionaries within Xerox.[18]

In these conditions, the journey from new invention to robust innovation required hard work, tough decisions, contentious resource allocation, power struggles, hard-won organizational commitment, leadership, and a great deal of trust. It took an organizational leap of faith to build the multidirectional, cross-communal links from R&D, through engineering, manufacturing, sales and marketing, to the market itself. Nothing was preordained.[19] Indeed, the organizational effort was significant enough that developing the knowledge redeveloped the corporation.[20] In all, moving from the initial idea to the market involved much more than taking it from PARC to Cupertino.

To understand the success, despite the difficulties, it helps to see the other side of corporate divisions. We need to appreciate not their divisiveness (which we saw in Xerox), but their synergistic, complementary character (found, by contrast, in Apple at that time). Organizations are the ultimate cross-functional team. They may indeed spend a good deal of time at cross-purposes, but when they are working well, the different practices work as a system to build a larger whole. This complementarity is certainly important to the normal work of organizations, taking productive advantage of the division of labor. But it is also essential for dealing with the demands of innovation.[21]

Many inventions, as Nathan Rosenberg of Stanford University argues, require complementary invention to produce innovation.

The laser, he notes for example, needed "essential complementary technology" before it could be usefully deployed.[22] Similarly, for the GUI to become useful, several advances in hardware and software design were needed.

Complementary innovation often involves more than the products of R&D labs, however. It requires innovation elsewhere in the organization. The mechanical inventions of the nineteenth century required, as the business historian Alfred Chandler suggests, complementary administrative invention to come to fruition.[23] The railroad needed inventions in information systems and documentation to become a safe and efficient network.[24] Carlson's photocopier waited on complementary inventions in marketing, sales, and leasing to become a success. Thus the challenge in moving systemically from an initial invention through complementarity to innovation is the challenge of coordinating diverse, disparate, and often diverging, but ultimately complementary, communities of practice. In going from Xerox to Apple, the GUI was in effect going from a corporation unable to manage this complementarity to one able to manage it.

CLUSTERING

The picture we have drawn of sticky and leaky knowledge, communities and networks of practice, and parallel firms with different sets of complementarities reflects the loose matrix structure found in places like Silicon Valley. This is not the familiar matrix model of organizations, which deals with their internal structure. Our matrix of organizations and networks of practice, by contrast, connects an organization's internal structure to the structure of the world around it.[25]

This matrix is difficult to describe. But we try with the help of a highly schematic diagram. A firm may be thought of as one of the vertical lines (A through E) in the figure. It will comprise a variety of complementary communities of practice. Any one of these communities of practice thus maintains links to the other communities within its organization. The vertical lines in our diagram represent these links. The firm holds these communities together as a system made up of distinct but related parts.

But each community is also linked to similar communities in other firms. So, while they are linked to other communities in the same firm through a relationship of *complementary* practices, they link to communities in other firms through *common* or shared practices. These horizontal relationships make up what we have called *networks of practice* and are represented by lines 1 through 4 in our diagram.

A firm, then, will almost always intersect multiple networks of practice. In Silicon Valley, for example, some firms will have crosscutting networks of engineering, manufacturing, sales and marketing, and customer service. Networks of practice, then, will run through multiple firms. Networks of computer engineers, for example, will run through all the firms manufacturing computers.

Of course, not all firms, however similar, intersect all the same practices. As we have suggested, firms distinguish themselves by their different sets of complementarities. We have tried to indicate this with broken lines B and C. B might, for example, represent a firm with research and design, but no engineering. That firm, then, would not intersect directly with the network of practice made up of engineers. An engineering firm might then fill the gap with its complementary capabilities. Consequently, while A, D, and E represent single firms that join the same set of diverse communities, similar capabilities might

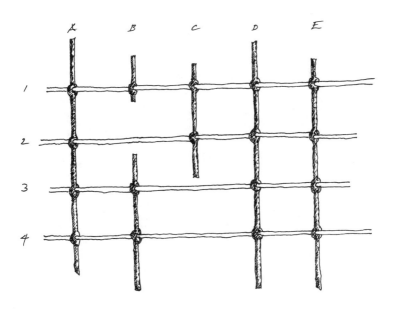

Sketch of a Cluster Matrix

also be achieved through joint ventures if, for example, B and C formed an alliance. These networks, which in reality are far more complex than a simple two-dimensional diagram allows, enables knowledge to flow between firms, as it did between Xerox and Apple. Thus the networks open the boundaries of firms and create links between them.

Knowledge seems to flow with particular ease where the firms involved are geographically close together. Being in the same area allowed the Apple and PARC scientists to meet and exchange ideas informally, paving the way for more formal links. Relations between the PARC scientists and the Dallas engineers were in every sense far more distant.

In Silicon Valley the parallel vertical strands (represented by the lettered lines) might represent Hewlett-Packard, Apple, Sun, Oracle, Xerox PARC, Intel, Cypress, Netscape, Yahoo!, and so on. The numbered lines could represent R&D, software engineers, chip designers, financial managers, accounting, librarians, legal services, and catering. Such links become specially interesting where several, similar firms group tightly together. Then the lines between them are relatively short and the links dense.

CLUSTERED ECOLOGIES

Clusters like the one that makes up Silicon Valley have a long history. The great economist Alfred Marshall studied them in industrial England. He noted how industries might cluster for geographical reasons. The coal industry inevitably grew near coalfields, but so, too, did industries that consumed a lot of coal. But Marshall noted other, serendipitous reasons for clustering. He traced, for example, the roots of the iron and steel clusters of south Lancashire, driving forces in the industrial revolution, to "Norman smiths who were settled at Warrington . . . during the time of William the Conqueror."[26]

More recent studies have considered such things as the fashion cluster in the "Third" Italy, the Formula 1 cluster of racing engine designers outside London, and even the golf-club cluster outside Los Angeles as well as Route 128, the high-technology corridor outside Boston, and Silicon Valley itself.[27] Within clusters, there is a shared high-level understanding of the demands and possibilities of a particular sector. As Marshall put it, "[t]he mysteries of the trade become no mysteries; but are as it were in the air." There is also, Marshall noted, a "constant market for skill," which draws qualified labor looking for work and equally new businesses looking for qualified workers. Here, too, "subsidiary" trades will develop to service the dominant ones.[28]

Marshall showed that these clusters can have significant economic effects. They produce, at the level of the region and among competing firms, economies of scale greater than those that any one firm can develop on its own. Regional advantage (in the words of AnnaLee Saxenian, a professor of city and regional planning at Berkeley) may then accrue, allowing a region and the firms within it to outperform other regions.[29] This advantage is cumulative. A leading region will attract more investment and jobs, allowing it to maintain or increase its advantage.

Despite the rather inorganic appearance of our cluster sketch, we tend to think of these dense, cross-hatched relationships of practices and processes as "ecologies" of knowledge. These are fertile for the growth of knowledge because they dispose of that knowledge effectively. Knowledge that sticks within firms quickly finds ways to flow between them, as if seeking out the firm with the most suitable complementarity. In such circumstances, as firms keep a constant benchmarking eye on each other, the ecology develops as a whole. Both invention and innovation develop rapidly and together, turbocharged by feedback loops that run both within and between firms.

These interfirm relations encourage an ecological perspective that, like Marshall's view, considers the region or the cluster as a whole. From the point of view of an individual firm, knowledge that leaks to another is lost. From the perspective of the ecology as a whole, however, it is much more productively used. Similarly, while failure is undoubtedly hard on a particular firm and its employees, it too may be beneficial for the ecology as a whole, providing useful insight into market conditions. Hence, as Urs von Burg and Martin Kenney argue in their study of the development of local area network (LAN) technology, the firm "Zilog, an innovative failure, seeded the Silicon Valley with LAN entrepreneurs."[30]

Consequently, firms in an ecology produce synergistic effects which isolated firms find hard to imitate. Within such ecologies, the health and innovative ability of firms is not an isolated matter. Firms that feed into also feed off the ecology. The same networks that allow knowledge to flow out, allow other knowledge to flow in. Reciprocity is important to survival in the region and to regional survival.

This reciprocity takes various forms. There are many formal ties. These include subcontracting and joint-venture agreements. They also include increasingly inventive ways to deal with intellectual property, from simple fees and royalties on copyrights and patents to more intricate licensing, cross-licensing, portfolio sharing, and joint research projects. But these formal ties are often preceded by informal relationships that develop across networks. Apple's relationship with PARC developed this way. Informal ties can form rapidly, running directly along networks of practice, speeding well ahead of the slow pace of formal contacts and negotiations between organizations.

Marshall pointed out how in clusters, "[s]ocial forces cooperate with economic ones." And in a similar vein, Saxenian draws attention to the importance of social forces to the development of Silicon Valley, contrasting its "culture" to that of Route 128.[31] In explaining the success of the former, she notes such things as the remarkably permissive attitude in Silicon Valley that both encourages and is encouraged by the networks of practice that run between companies. By contrast, the companies of

Route 128 discouraged fraternization between firms. This insularity not only cut firms off from their ecology but also prevented the ecology as a whole from developing. As a result, that region showed much less agility when its core, the minicomputer industry, was attacked by the PC.[32]

REVIVALS

This ecological view of knowledge not only highlights routes of innovation in the information age, it also challenges a couple of related "endisms" that infoenthusiasts have championed. The first is what has been talked of as the "death" of distance. The second, the death of the firm. Rumors of their death have certainly been exaggerated.

Death of Distance

Despite our various mixed metaphors, when we talk about the region and related notions of *place* and *locality*, we mean these terms quite literally. Even for information technology firms, neighborhoods and regions remain significant. The names—not only Silicon Valley, but less-familiar names from the Silicon family ("Silicon Glen" (Scotland), "Silicon Alley" (New York), "Silicon Forest" (Oregon), and many more) as well as others such as "Multimedia Gulch" and "Audio Alley"—suggest the continuing formation (and imitation) of clusters.

Like firms, ecologies need a range of overlapping but also complementary practices and organizations. From its origins in semiconductors, Silicon Valley has developed rich related expertise in disk drives (IBM), networking (3Com, Cisco Systems), operating systems (Apple, Bee, NeXt), high-end workstations

(Sun, HP, Silicon Graphics), and database management (Oracle). The region's venture capitalists have also long played a critical role, understanding issues involved in ways that venture capitalists based elsewhere have not.

The region's ecological diversity extends to its universities and colleges, notably Stanford and Berkeley, but also San Jose State and Santa Clara Community College. These are an integral part of the ecology. The diversity these represent has allowed the Valley collectively to turn toward new areas of opportunity and expansion such as the Internet with remarkable speed, as the high-speed development of firms like Netscape and Yahoo! showed.[33]

The complementary character of these firms allows the vertical lines in our drawing to be made up not only by single firms, as we suggested, but by joint ventures and subcontracting, as firms chain their complementary strengths together. For the same reason, it allows symbiotic relationships between large and small, with large firms fostering start-ups and using them to test new markets and products.[34] Claims that in the era of the small start-up the large firm is dead overlook these exploratory and risk-distributing relationships.[35] Start-ups need to be understood not in isolation, but in relation to openings created and opportunities missed by larger firms.

For the ecology to flourish, however, it evidently needs not just a range of capabilities, but a close range. The informal links that we mentioned earlier develop directly and in close quarters. In the Valley, people live in and out of each other's pockets, and this helps them see what's doing, what's doable, and what's not being done. This close proximity not only shows how to attack a particular niche, it provides the ability to see a niche before it is visible to most eyes. Thus, for example, when 3Com developed as a networking firm, its obvious market was minicomputers, which needed good networking capabilities. But from its position in the Valley, the firm understood that the future was likely to be in personal computers. Thus it bypassed the obvious, lucrative, but soon-to-be-dying market, positioning itself for a not-yet-visible but far more lucrative and enduring one.[36]

Density of firms, practices, and practitioners also promotes reliable risk- and trust-assessment. The Valley forms what might be thought of as a "knowable community."[37] Not that everybody knows everybody else, but the degrees of separation between people are few, and it's usually possible to find out about potential employers, employees, or partners. Because people can and do look beyond the conventional signs of public reputation, entrepreneurs can take greater risks. Public failure will not damn them for life.

It has long been predicted that information technology would disperse these clusters. "Every cheapening of the means of communication," Marshall argued at the end of the nineteenth century, "alters the action of the forces that tend to localize industries."[38] Yet, in Silicon Valley, at the heart of the information industry, we see this localization or clustering thrive. For while, as we argued earlier, information technology is very good at reach, it is less good at the sort of dense reciprocity needed to make and maintain such strong and informative informal links. And it is these informal links running along networks of practice that allow knowledge to flow to where, from an ecological perspective, it belongs. So distance is far from dead, even where distance technology is at its most advanced.

In 1999, for example, after years of looking on from Redmond, Washington, Microsoft, whose ads suggest travel is near irrelevant (see chapter 1), moved part of its research operation

to Silicon Valley. Physical presence and proximity still mean
something. Microsoft evidently fears that silicon inventiveness
might stick in the Valley.

Death of the Firm

More than localization appears threatened by information technology. As the information economy steamrollers along, flatten-
ing, stretching, and smashing as it goes, the firm stands clearly in
its path. Encouraged by the 6-Ds (see chapter 1), people predict
that this nineteenth-century institution may have an increasingly virtual presence in the twenty-first. Once the firm is gone,
such arguments assume, the individual entrepreneur and inventor will be liberated and innovation will be unleashed.

Arguments against the structure of organizations and for the
spontaneity of the market are enticing. Since the collapse of the
"command economies" of the old Eastern Bloc, much attention
has been paid to the unplanned or spontaneous character of markets. They can, it seems, arrange themselves like a flock of birds in
flight, where order emerges from each bird acting individually
and instinctively. (As result of examples like this, people who talk
about self-organizing markets occasionally sound less like economists or technologists than like entomologists. Ants and termites,
as well as birds, bats, and other small mammals, provide much of
the evidence.[39] Others draw examples from "artificial life."[40])

Yet while it's clear that self-organization is extraordinarily
productive, so too is formal organization. Indeed, the two perform an intricate (and dynamic) balancing act, each compensat-
ing for the other's failings. Self-organization overcomes formal
organizing's rigidity. Formal organization keeps at bay self-organization's tendency to self-destruct. Markets help society escape

the rigidities of planning. Planning, meanwhile, preserves markets, providing the regulation to maintain competition and prevent monopolies. As Carl Shapiro and Hal Varian, two economists at Berkeley, argue in their book *Information Rules*, even an information economy needs some formal institutions to guard against monopolies.[41]

The use of deliberate structure to preserve the spontaneity of self-organization may be one of humanity's most productive assets. Since the nineteenth century, when the economist Thomas Malthus gloomily predicted that the geometric growth of population would outstrip the arithmetic growth in resources, predictions appear regularly that humanity is on the edge of destroying itself.[42]

Most of these predictions take humans to be, like insects, relatively passive in the face of such problems. Whereas, of course, humans are capable of reflecting on such problems and taking collective action against them.[43] By organizing together, by researching and planning, by directing investment and restricting destructive behavior, and by developing institutions to unleash and protect individual creativity, people have found ways to increase productivity at a greater pace than population. Organizing knowledge, they have produced more food out of the same areas of land, extended known energy resources and searched for new ones, established new regions for human endeavor, held natural forces at bay, and even designed the very technologies that are now paradoxically invoked as the end of organization.

In all such cases, organization has helped to foster and focus humanity's most valuable resource: its infinitely renewable knowledge base. As we have tried to show, organizations play a critical part in the step from invention to innovation, the transformation of ideas into products and processes. Once you have a well-defined product or process, markets take over. But before that, organizations, large and small, play a vital role in organizing knowledge, practice, and practitioners.

Ecologies, then, rely on a balance between the formal and the informal, the spontaneity of practice and the structure of organization. In a discussion of knowledge and the firm, the organizational theorist J-C. Spender talks of the "husbanding" role of the firm.[44] This farming image helps illustrate our notion of the relationship between an organization and ecology. The ecology at large is an enormously powerful, significantly self-organizing ecosystem developing new ideas ubiquitously. Firms, like *farms in a natural ecology*, play their part by taming certain regions, introducing methods to enhance growth and productivity, and turning the seeds of invention into the produce of innovation.

7

Reading the Background

I was working in an archive of a 250-year-old business, reading correspondence from about the time of the American Revolution. Incoming letters were stored in wooden boxes about the size of a standard Styrofoam picnic cooler, each containing a fair portion of dust as old as the letters. As opening a letter triggered a brief asthmatic attack, I wore a scarf tied over my nose and mouth. Despite my bandit's attire, my nose ran, my eyes wept, and I coughed, wheezed, and snorted. I longed for a digital system that would hold the information from the letters and leave paper and dust behind.

One afternoon, another historian came to work on a similar box. He read barely a word. Instead, he picked out bundles of letters and, in a move that sent my sinuses into shock, ran each letter beneath his nose and took a deep breath, at times almost inhaling the letter itself but always getting a good dose of dust. Sometimes, after a particularly profound sniff, he would open the letter, glance at it briefly, make a note and move on.

Choking behind my mask, I asked him what he was doing. He was, he told me, a medical historian. (A profession to avoid if you

*have asthma.) He was documenting outbreaks of cholera. When
that disease occurred in a town in the eighteenth century, all letters
from that town were disinfected with vinegar to prevent the disease
from spreading. By sniffing for the faint traces of vinegar that survived 250 years and noting the date and source of the letters, he was
able to chart the progress of cholera outbreaks.*

*His research threw new light on the letters I was reading. Now
cheery letters telling customers and creditors that all was well, business thriving, and the future rosy read a little differently if a whiff
of vinegar came off the page. Then the correspondent's cheeriness
might be an act to prevent a collapse of business confidence—
unaware that he or she would be betrayed by a scent of vinegar.*

—PAUL DUGUID, Trip Report from Portugal

UNDER THE HAMMER

Infoenthusiasts have thrust nothing under the hammer with quite
so much enthusiasm as the paper document. Ideas of pure information traversing digital networks lead, as we noted in chapter 1,
to outbursts of "endism," and in particular to prophecies about
the departure of paper and the arrival of such things as the paperless office, the electronic newspaper, and the digital library.

Like the home office, the paperless world seems not only
feasible but, for environmental reasons, highly desirable. The
home office promises to reduce pollution by reducing com-
muting. Paperless work and communication, for their part,
would restrain deforestation, limit the damaging effluent from
paper plants, and cut between 35 and 40 percent of the solid
waste currently pouring into landfills.[1]

Yet, despite both the means and the desire, paper remains. As
digital communication grew over the past decade, so did paper

consumption—from 87 million to 99 million tons per year. Over roughly the same period, many offices in particular have attempted to reduce their printing needs. Aetna, for example, claims to have shed 100 million pages annually. Nonetheless, the amount of paper consumed in offices actually outstripped the general growth in paper, increasing by 33 percent. It's not surprising, then, that despite digitization, paper stocks offer significant paper profits. In the boom year of 1998, paper companies outperformed the high-performance Dow by about 40 percent. Prophets clamor, environmentalists hope, and technophobes lament, but no one seems to be putting their money on paper disappearing any time soon.[2]

It therefore seems worthwhile to try to understand why paper has held on in the face of direct, well-financed, and impressive attacks. Like other technological attacks on conventional tools, these attacks fail primarily because they have underestimated their opponent. Digital champions generally misunderstand (or miss entirely) the remarkable resourcefulness of paper documents. In yet another case of redefinition, documents appear as mere carriers of information, a shell to be cast off now that information has reached maturity. Because documents are more than that, the assaults fail. To make better progress against paper, to make better document technologies, designers of alternatives need to understand paper better. More generally, the robust and efficient ways documents handle information still have, we believe, a lot to teach about how to socialize a technology. (Books have been so well socialized that people barely even think of them as a technology.)[3]

GOING, GOING . . .

There is no doubt that many paper-based artifacts are disappearing. The black-edged letter, the social security check, the Rolodex, the pink slip, the airline timetable, and the library catalogue are all fading into oblivion (not always without a fight).[4] And many other catalogues and manuals that were always ill suited for paper-based documents have gone the way of Aetna's 100 million pages. As examples of paper holding its ground, however, consider the three futuristic categories we mentioned above, the paperless office, electronic newspaper, and digital library.

Paperless Office

As we noted in chapter 1, *Business Week* confidently foresaw the paperless office in 1975. The phrase quickly settled into the language as a vision of a fast-approaching future. Twenty-five years on, despite extraordinary advances in communications technology, quite unforeseen in 1975, still that goal remains just that, fast approaching. Meanwhile, the volume of paper used in the office grows. In 1975, offices consumed less than 100 pounds of paper per head; now they consume more than 200. The appearance of information technology seems to have accelerated the use of paper, not diminished it.

Surprisingly, this curious symbiosis was marked early in the history of PARC. There, more than anywhere, a paperless future was an act of faith. And in the late 1970s, the personal computer, the Ethernet and local networks, and word-processing software were all under development in service of that faith.

Yet even within PARC, none of these tools, startlingly innovative though each was, was quite the "killer" it was expected to be. That came with another PARC invention, one that transformed all these inventions into the indispensable office tools we know them to be today. Bob Metcalfe, one of the Ethernet's designers, got a clear sighting of the critical addition early on.

Metcalfe would regularly take down the Ethernet links connecting researchers' workstations to one another so that he could work on the system. The traffic along the network was so light that no one bothered about the irregular downtime. Until one particular day. On this occasion, Metcalfe took the network down, and doors opened all along the corridor. His colleagues had noticed immediately that their connections had been interrupted and came straight out to see why. The difference, Metcalfe realized, was the latest PARC invention to be added to the network, the laser printer.[5]

Time has only confirmed this early indication of paper's importance in the digital office. While other print technologies have come to compete with it, laser printer sales have increased twelve-fold in the past decade. If the digital office from PARC to the present is anything to go by, bits and atoms, the digital and the material, don't seem so much in opposition as in tandem. Despite confident claims that their only relationship is one of replacement and dismissal, the two look much more like complementary resources.[6]

Electronic Newspaper

The bulky newspaper, with its high production and transportation costs and quick journey from commodity to trash, has long presented a red rag to technological bulls. From the telegraph to the on-line database, people have widely assumed that *now* the paper newspaper would shrink into irrelevance.

Some fifty years ago, adventurous publishers tried to replace it with a forerunner of the fax machine. Later, others offered a daily microfiche, complete with handheld readers. Advanced labs at MIT and BBN developed alternatives, and major publishers brought them to market. Knight-Ridder lost some $50 million with its Viewtron experiment. Others—including Gateway (Times Mirror Newspapers), Keyfax (Field Communications), and Covidea (AT&T)—have all come and gone, taking a good deal of money along with them. The World Wide Web offers the latest and most serious threat, but electronic books are also muscling in.[7]

Yet still, to the surprise of even their editors and proprietors, the inefficient and outmoded newspaper hangs on. Meanwhile, even the flagships of the digital age lean toward print. *Wired*, with its flashy color, paper, and layout, is inescapably a hard-copy magazine. And when Microsoft's *Slate*, one of the most heavily backed attempts to produce a mass-circulation on-line magazine, found itself sinking, it turned to a paper edition for temporary buoyancy.

Undoubtedly, there's much movement in the other direction. All major newspapers now have Web sites. The *New York Times*, the *Wall Street Journal*, and the *San Jose Mercury News* (Silicon Valley's local newspaper) have each taken aggressive positions on the Web. Exactly what is the best position to take, however, remains unclear. Many newspapers have redesigned their sites several times, throwing money away in quantities that usually measure bits, and changed business models repeatedly. Some sites are open to all. Most give access only to the current edition. Some require users to register. Others are purely pay-per-view. A few allow subscribers to the print edition access to their archives. Some charge a separate on-line fee. Others a fee per item accessed.

Some, like the *San Francisco Chronicle* or the *Guardian* in England, also provide a route to many resources beyond their own site but of local interest to their readers. These ventures may even be edging toward the vaunted role of Web portal. Here the complementarity between the print and the digital world may give them an edge over purely digital sites. Certainly, newspapers have a strong institutional identity and a well-honed sense of audience. And to their experience with immediacy (which the Web favors) they can add experience with archiving and access to deep archives (which the Web has tended to ignore) to position themselves.[8]

In the confusion, as newspapers pour cash into different models for modest return (and some significant losses), one thing remains curiously secure. Paper. No one seems willing to give up the material paper itself. Building a digital extension is clearly viable. Extracting the paper from the news, by contrast, has turned out to be much harder than expected, for reasons we'll look at in a moment.

Digitized Libraries

The conventional library, with its massive weight of paper gathering dust and resisting efficient searches, is another paper-based institution that sets fingers itching at the keyboard. The sense that the information is "there" somewhere, but can't be found can drive anyone to digitize. It motivated Vannevar Bush, a pioneer in computer design and grandfather of the U.S. National Science Foundation, which has proved a generous funder of much digital library research. In a famous article in the *Atlantic*, Bush suggested that the difficulty scientists had in getting access to each other's work seriously damaged scientific progress. As a solution, he envisaged a system, Memex, which would compress and store documents in such a form that scientists could have access to a database of scientific knowledge from their desks through "a sort of mechanized private file and library."[9] Memex, as many people have pointed out, looks like a prototype for the World Wide Web.

The idea of a mechanized (now digitized) library has held out a popular promise that what people now find in conventional libraries will eventually be available on-line. Yet the dream of making all printed material digitally accessible—even all the books in your local library, let alone all the books in the Library of Congress—died not long after it was born. Project Gutenberg, a well-established attempt to put the texts of books on-line helps illustrate one difficulty. It is currently approaching 30 years of work and 10,000 titles on-line. A significant number. Unfortunately, in the United Kingdom alone, some 100,000 new titles appeared last year (an increase of 50 percent over 1990's output).[10]

Research has now shifted attention to digital (rather than digitized) libraries. These look far beyond digitized versions of conventional documents. Their relation to what most of us think of as libraries is hard to fix. Some researchers see the two as complementary. Others find even the name *library* an embarrassment and encumbrance on their work.[11] Consequently two different schools of research are developing. One, predominantly British and calling itself *e-lib research*, retains connections to the conventional library, which it sees as its mission to support. The other, predominantly in the United States and calling itself *d-lib research*, has severed many connections to the conventional library. One seeks to complement paper resources; the other, primarily to ignore them. In both cases, pursuit of a head-on collision between the paper and the digital worlds has been left to the visionaries.

As visions, plans, and targets have shifted, perhaps the most significant change has been a growing awareness of the complexity and diversity of libraries, their holdings, and their users.

Early in the digital age, the vision of collecting "all knowledge" in a single place revived. (We say *revived* because the idea is at least as old as libraries and probably as old as documents.) But as these visions have confronted reality more directly, it has become increasingly clear that libraries are less "collections," than useful selections that gain usefulness from what they exclude as much as what they hold. They are also reflections of particular groups of users and their needs. As such, it's very hard to see one technology (atom-based or bit-based) or one solution fitting all.[12]

Sticking Around

As these brief examples suggest, paper documents have proved more resistant than many of their antagonists (or defenders) expected. Paper is not, moreover, simply hanging on. New avenues for paper documents continue to develop, while its resourcefulness and complementary properties, though previously dismissed, are now becoming an asset for digital technologies.[13]

The startling rise of the fax in the lifetime of the office computer, which we noted in chapter 1, is one recently developed avenue. Faxes mix the rapid circulation of information technology with many of the advantages of paper documents, including the ability to mix manuscript and typescript. Annotations can be made easily but circulated rapidly. You can scribble "No!" beside a point of disagreement and slap it back on the fax, instead of having to write "I don't agree with line 3, para 17 of section 5." It's so much easier to point than to describe.

The usefulness of pointing points itself to another paper phenomenon in the age of paperlessness, the Post-it. At the height of digitization, this paper tool came from nowhere to be found everywhere. The Post-it, too, helps annotate. It also efficiently attaches information to things, bridging the world of information and material objects. Again, it's much easier to write, "Take this" and stick it on a chair than to leave a list describing the chairs to be taken and the chairs to be left.

The digital world continues to acknowledge this sort of usefulness, if on occasion grudgingly. Computer faxes, though still buggy as if to register the digerati's disapproval, are now commonplace. So are digital Post-its (though you can't yet attach these to the furniture). Word-processing systems also offer annotation. All these, however, still leave plenty of reasons for printing and hand annotating.

Elsewhere, attempts at replacement are curiously turning into tributes. In their slow search for viability, electronic books slavishly copy features of the conventional book. Indeed, one company is projecting itself as the true heir to the "book" because it opens to a two-page spread. Single-page competitors, it insists, offer merely "tablets."[14]

But nothing has paid as strong a compliment to documents as the World Wide Web. The Web made the informationally dense and inscrutable Internet intelligible, in the process turning it into the extraordinary phenomenon it has become. Somewhat like the "Windows" interface, from the user's point of view, it did this by relinquishing the mystique of information for the language of the document. Pages structure the Web. Bookmarks help us find our way back to where we have been. Indexes and tables of contents organize it. "Libraries" are built on top of it. And now ThirdVoice.com provides software that allows people to stick annotations on others' Web sites (much to the distress of some disgruntled Web site administrators, who view this more as graffiti than annotation.)

Of course, we need to ask how much this sort of talk has to do with the old-fashioned paper document. The airplane, after all, took over much of the language of the ship. It has captains and crew, galleys, cabins, gangways, and flight decks. Beyond that, there isn't much similarity between the two except that both carry passengers. So perhaps the similarity between the old document and the new is simply that both carry information. Now, it might seem, fiber optics, video terminals, magnetic storage, and search engines offer a cheaper, faster, and more resourceful means to deal with the same payload.

It seems to us, however, that this information-payload view is the source of many wrongheaded confrontations between paper and information technology. The emerging, more sophisticated view of paper documents, revealing both how they structure information and even how they structure society, is making the old war on paper and paper-based institutions appear not only futile, but wasteful. Complementarity and compliments rather than confrontation and abuse seem more appropriate. In pursuit of better understanding and hence better technology, setting aside the view of documents as no more than information carriers is an important step.[15]

DOCUMENTS AS DARTS

It's hard, however, to set that view aside. Things such as the five-paragraph essay that most of us painfully wrote in childhood simultaneously carved the idea of documents as carriers into our subconscious. But we suspect that, like us, other learners were profoundly influenced by the magical moment when one braver kid folded his five paragraphs into a paper dart and send it skimming across the room. It was a misleading lesson, but one that has taken a long time to shake off.

From both the proper and improper classroom activity, the lesson was much the same. Documents appear like planes or some other form of transport onto which information is loaded. With its freight, the document makes its way from writer to reader to be unpacked at the other end. If a little is lost on the journey, it is of no more significance than the odd package lost in transit.

The English language also reflects this view. Documents are said, for example, to *contain, hold, carry,* and *convey* information. For those who remember them, this way of talking recalls the old-fashioned telegram (or ransom note) where strips of text were pasted down on a backing sheet. Ted Nelson, one of the early champions of hypertext, was no doubt thinking in much the same way when he dismissively described paper documents as just "an object that information has been sprayed onto in the past."[16]

All these usages are instances of what the linguist Michael Reddy has called "conduit" metaphors. Reddy notes how people talk about *getting, delivering, passing along,* or *circulating* ideas. The metaphor takes information as an object that passes back and forth between people along a conduit. From this point of view, documents are simply one type of conduit or delivery vehicle that helps carry information from *A* to *B*.

Basic ideas of sending and receiving make digitization, for example, seem easy. You distill the information out of books or articles and leave the paper residue behind. Paul's experience in the archives, recounted at the opening of this chapter, questions this view. Digitization could have distilled out the text of those letters. It would, though, have left behind that other interesting distillate, vinegar. Yet the whiff of vinegar contributed to the understanding of the letters, for historians and contemporaries. Getting ideas across, as everyone knows, can be a tricky process.

Human inventiveness draws on all available resources—down to the look, the feel, and even the smell coming off a document.

The vinegar-scented letters draw attention to the way in which people read beyond a text and between the lines, finding other means to make sense and corroborate (or undermine) what the text itself says. It's not pure information alone, but the way the information was produced that supports interpretation. In this light, paper documents perform less like a cable carrying a stream of bits and more like a program to help interpret those bits. As a consequence, separating the delivery vehicle from the communication delivered isn't quite the same as waving away the UPS van that delivered a packet. Unlike the UPS van, documents are not indifferent to the information they carry. They help shape it and, in the process, help shape its readership.

MAKING NEWS

The conduit metaphor suggests that information sits around in discrete lumps waiting to be loaded onto a carrier. Newspapers, for example, appear to be freighted with news that they carry out to readers. But, as we suggested in chapter 1, news is not some naturally occurring object that journalists pick up and stick on paper. It is made and shaped by journalists in the context of the medium and the audience. There's no need to go as far as Marshall McLuhan's claim that the "medium is the message" to see that the medium is not an indifferent carrier here.[17]

The newspaper, then, is rather like the library—not simply a collection of news, but a selection and a reflection. And the selection process doesn't just "gather news," but weaves and shapes, developing stories in accordance with available space and priorities. Properties of the newspaper inherently convey these priorities to readers. Is it on the front page? Above or below the fold? Where does it jump to? What does it appear next to? For most newspaper readers, it's possible to gauge most stories by combining the position in the paper, the headline, accompanying graphics and their captions, and highlighted text. Along with the kind of paper—does it look or feel like a tabloid or a broadsheet?—these characteristics indicate to an experienced reader whether to read on and also how to read on.[18]

By contrast, pick up these stories from a standard on-line database, where the picture and position and highlights are missing, where length no longer carries significance, and it is much harder to do this sort of efficient personal indexing. Trying to keep the news but lose the paper proves trickier than it at first seems. Indeed, even the databases rely on the implicit assumption that what they carry appeared first in paper form.

The idea that documents merely gather information gets support from the way in which it does seem possible to pull information out of documents. But the assumption that what comes out is no more than what went in is misleading, as everyone involved in production processes, from cooks to chemists, knows. It might be said that soldiers come out of the army. But it isn't soldiers that go in. What go in are raw recruits. The process of joining the army turns them into soldiers. So, while we may indeed get facts out of documents, it's a mistake to assume that that is what is put in. Making news, making the sort of information that papers carry, is an intricate process. There is more involved than just packing and carrying. You can see this in the way the word *media* (like the word *press*) conventionally spans technology and social institutions. For both are involved in the process of making news. By contrast, in the digital world *media* has been reserved almost wholly for technology. Institutional processes here are still much harder to detect.

UNRELIABLE WITNESSES

Documents not only serve to make information but also to warrant it—to give it validity. Here again, the material side of documents plays a useful part. For information has trouble, as we all do, testifying on its own behalf. Its only recourse in the face of doubt is to add more information. Yet people do not add much to their credibility by insisting "I'm telling the truth." Nor does it help much to write "good" on the face of a check. Piling up information from the same source doesn't increase reliability.[19]

In general, people look beyond information to triangulate reliability. People look past what others say, for example, to gauge trustworthiness. Some clues might be formal and institutional: Who does a prospective client work for? What is her credit rating? Others are informal, such as dress, address, and cars.[20]

In a similar way, readers look beyond the information in documents. Published documents, for example, often embody the institutional authority of the publisher. The investment evident in a document's material content is often a good indicator of the investment in its informational content. Physical heft lends institutional weight to what it says.[21]

Readers rely on more informal warrants, too. For example, they may examine a report to see whose handwriting appears in the margin, whether the spine is broken, how well the pages are thumbed, where the highlights fall, or whose names are on the routing slip. (The Irish writer Flann O'Brien imagined a book-handling service for the culturally insecure. For a fee, book handlers would crease the spines of your books, turn down pages, mark passages, put intelligent comments in the margins, or, for a slightly greater sum, insert tickets from operas or classic plays as bookmarks.)[22] Material objects are good at picking up such incidental traces, and people are good at making the incidental significant.

HAMLET IN CYBERSPACE

Because people rely on these indicators almost without noticing, the question of warrants has been a difficult one for documents in a world of information. Though digital documents may look the same, lacking physical embodiment, they pick up fewer institutional and material traces along the way. Consequently, it's easy to feel like Hamlet in cyberspace, receiving disturbing tales from ghostly figures without any form of corroboration except for yet more information. For the paranoid, spooky tales alone are often enough to get a good conspiracy theory going. It can be enough for the innocent, too, as the former Kennedy press secretary Pierre Salinger showed when he slapped his personal warrant on a 'Net-borne conspiracy theory about flight TWA 800.

More experienced users have learned to triangulate what comes across the 'Net in other ways. The celebrated "virtual community" that Howard Rheingold wrote about, for example, was backed up by a good deal of old-fashioned telephone calling, meeting, and conventional neighborliness.[23] Many people buy only from companies with an established off-line existence. On-line auction houses suggest that bidders get in touch with suppliers to judge their reliability for themselves. Services such as Alexa.com try to provide the equivalent of wear and tear, by indicating how often a Web site is "hit" and how often updated.[24]

Nevertheless, the comparative ease with which conventional documents provide institutional and personal warrants, carrying these with them wherever they go, indicates why paper may not disappear as readily as the logic of information suggests. It also points to the uncertainty that may come as information shifts between contexts. "Translation" between "platforms" (digitizing book text, for example) inevitably makes decisions about where the information ends and the residue (which may include such things as the scent of vinegar) begins.[25]

Microsoft executives have confronted problems of translation as digital e-mail messages have been entered as paper evidence in the antitrust suit against the company. When electronic messages are turned into paper ones, whispers can turn into broadcasts. The informality of a hint or a guess suddenly looks like a firm decision cast in ink. The defensive claim that a particular statement was taken "out of context" only testifies to how important context is to content.

NETWORKING

So documents do not merely carry information, they help make it, structure it, and validate it. More intriguing, perhaps, documents also help structure society, enabling social groups to form, develop, and maintain a sense of shared identity. Viewing documents as mere information carriers overlooks this social role.

In many ways, the neglect of this social aspect of documents is surprising. The community-forming character of the 'Net has drawn significant attention. Books, scholarly dissertations, and miles of newsprint have considered these "virtual communities." Roger Fidler's *Mediamorphosis* noted how in France, enterprising freelancers turned the Minitel system, designed by the post office to serve principally as an electronic phone book, into a messaging system and in the process created innumerable interest groups. Howard Rheingold's *The Virtual Community* described the friendships and even marriages that sprang out of an early West Coast messaging system called the WELL (Whole Earth 'Lectronic Link), while Julian Dibbell's *My Tiny Life* has made public his account of a digital community that developed through a computer running at PARC that anyone could reach from an Internet connection. (In all these cases, sexual shenanigans make up the lead, but there was a great deal more to these stories than the sex.)[26]

Though histories of the 'Net often assume that the past was another world entirely, these 'Net communities extend a long tradition of communities forming around documents. Anselm Strauss, a sociologist, described such communities as "social worlds." Well before the 'Net appeared, Strauss was interested in the ways that his fellow academics, though spread out around the country and even across the world, developed a sense of their colleagues, their field, and their position in it through the constant circuit of communications. The shared texts as much as anything else gave texture to the notion of a discipline, a profession, or an interest group, though most of the people in these "worlds" knew little of one another directly.[27]

Strauss's worlds, too, have roots that go much further back. Communities bound together by texts and a shared disposition toward those texts, as ancient philosophical and religious communities remind us, predate not only the 'Net and the telephone, but even the printing press. Textual communities may be as old as texts themselves. Shared and circulating documents, it seems, have long provided interesting social glue.

INVISIBLE COLLEGES

The printing press, however, played a critical part, particularly in the development of modern scientific communities. The early postal service deserves some of the credit, too.[28] For not only documents, but letters circulating and recirculating, copied and recopied, among individuals throughout Europe helped to create what have been called "invisible colleges," with members spread across continents and beyond. [29]

One of the most influential local groups, forming a subsection in this larger network, was the British "Royal Society." The Society included some eminent figures, among them Isaac Newton (who produced Newton's laws of physics), Robert Boyle (who produced Boyle's law of gases), Robert Hooke (who produced Hooke's law of springs), and Christopher Wren (who produced St. Paul's Cathedral). Circulating documents played a critical role in binding together the members of this group. They also helped to link the group to others in continental Europe. These documents included not only private letters, but semipublic "erudite letters" (which were private letters copied for public use) and more public "news-letters."[30]

So important was this communication to the development of the Society, that, while it maintained no labs or researchers or equipment and sponsored no research, it did maintain a corresponding secretary whose job was to oversee this vital correspondence.[31] This way of proceeding forms the sharpest contrast between what are thought of today as the early scientists and those who are dismissed as "alchemists." The interests and actions of these two groups often look indistinguishable. But the Royal Society categorically rejected the instinctive secrecy of their predecessors. Boyle's first publication was, quite aptly, a plea for open publication and commentary.[32]

In 1665, the Royal Society took another step toward scientific practice as it is recognized today by adding the printed scientific journal to scientific communication. That year, the *Philosophical Transactions* started publishing on the first Monday of every month.[33] Printed journals provided members of the community with more-or-less identical documents to analyze. But they also consolidated the sense of a public scientific community among a body of people who did not know each other or communicate directly with one another. It took time for a sense of what was important—and what was not—to develop.[34] The sense of common membership and pursuits seems to have occurred first; the scientific information followed later.

OTHER WORLDS

In a way, then, the world of science developed around the documents of science, each shaping the other. The process wasn't restricted to science. The historian Brian Stock has shown how, from the eleventh century on, the spread of the written word and literacy together allowed "textual communities," particularly religious communities, to organize themselves. The most distinctive of these were groups of heretics or reformers who organized around new interpretations of sacred text, developing new ideas of how to live. These new groups, Stock argues, were important "laboratories of social organization."[35]

If we skip a millennium to the borders of the twenty-first century, we can see similar community formation still at work. Letters passed from hand to hand, handwritten circulars, ink-leaking stencils, and more recently photocopies, faxes, and other cheap reproductions have helped uncountable groups of people with shared interests form a social world with relative ease and autonomy. From political undergrounds connected only by *samizdat* journals to windsurfers, DeLorean owners, and beekeepers, people with shared interests have organized around shared documents, while in turn such documents have helped develop new interests. Many of these groups have been served by *zines*—cheaply produced newsletters. Zines (at first called "fan-zines") emerged in the sixties as fans of particular television programs and rock bands used typewriters, stencils, staplers, and the post office to create small groups around shared interests. An estimate in 1995 reckoned that some 20,000 titles had appeared in the past couple of decades. And this "cottage" industry was then still growing at 20 percent per year.

Though off-line in origin, documents like these help to explain the enthusiasm of small, widely scattered interest groups for the Internet, where electronic zine publishing, which is even cheaper than conventional zines, has developed rapidly. The Internet now has thousands of e-zine titles (from *The Abraxus Reader* and *Abyssinian Prince* to *Zen Anarchy*, *ZIPZAP*, and *Zmagazine*). And these are little different from many newsgroups and on-line newsletters, whose growth well outstrips the 20 percent of the paper form.

As these groups grow, their own reformers or heretics may emerge, changing the main community or splitting off to form a new faction. (The Internet proves particularly volatile in this regard.) Documents then contribute not only to forming and stabilizing the worlds but also, as Stock's heretics did, to reforming, destabilizing, and transforming them. The presence of heretics reminds us that the "information" is not the sole contributor here. The orthodox and the heretics both form around the same information or content. They are distinguished from one another by their unique disposition toward that information. Their documents—whether manuscript, typescript, or digital—are not simply darts.

THE PRESS, THE PEOPLE, AND THE REPUBLIC

The political scientist Benedict Anderson provides yet another example of the way groups form around documents. He considered networks so large, so diverse, and so spread out that individual members could not possibly know one another. They nonetheless may develop a sense of membership and belonging if they can create an image of the group as a single community with a single identity. Anderson described the communities that developed as "imagined" and claimed that shared documents play an essential part in this imagining.[36]

Anderson argues that such a document culture made a key contribution to the creation of independent nations. The United States forms his chief example. Printed documents, Anderson maintains, helped replace the ideology of sovereigns and subjects with the idea of a self-constructed society built around shared ideals, shared interests, and shared practices.

The first documents to spring to mind in the formation of the United States would usually include such revered works as the *Declaration of Independence*, the *Articles of Confederation*, the *Federalist Papers*, and the *Constitution*. But Anderson suggests that popular cultural items, such as journals, novels, newsletters, pamphlets, lampoons, ballad sheets, and so forth were just as important in creating the sense of a common nation that could stretch from Maine to South Carolina. The emergent common sense of community provided by these documents probably contributed as much to the formation of nationhood as the rational arguments of Tom Paine's *Common Sense*. Indeed, the former helped create the audience for the latter.[37]

AMERICAN IMPRESSIONS

In the United States' development of a national consciousness, newspapers played a central role. Once the daily newspaper arrived on the scene in the early nineteenth century, the streets of towns and cities, the carriages of railways, and the public rooms of hotels and saloons were submerged in cheap papers. These were picked up, passed around, clipped, and forwarded with abandon. The proliferation of newspapers was one of the first things that visitors to the new country noticed.[38]

Not only readers but also editors cut and pasted copy. With lax copyright laws, stories traveled quickly from one paper to another or from books to papers. Mingling old news, new news, ads, and extracts from novels, newspapers resembled today's Web as they desperately sought novel copy to support the ads that ran around it and paid for the paper. Sounding like a modern Web manager, the great editor Horace Greeley of the *New York Tribune* was sanguine in the face of mounting losses. "We lose money on our circulation by itself considered," he reported, "but with 20,000 subscribers we can command such Advertising and such prices for it as will render our enterprise a remunerating one."[39]

Clearly, these old technologies could not imitate the speed of digital technology. They were no slouches when it came to keeping pace with a breaking story, however. When pirated sheets of Charles Dickens's book on America, *American Notes*, arrived in New York in 1842, the *New York Herald* had its own edition of the 100,000-word book out on the street in nineteen hours—a speed that many who have attempted to assemble a Web page would envy. Once that edition was out, other papers inevitably picked it up and copied chunks large and small for their readers. (The poet Longfellow noted wryly that the piratical press made so much money out of it that they might almost consider supporting copyright.)[40]

Many (Dickens included) were disdainful of the bulk of the copy these papers used to sustain an audience. Certainly "information" is not a word that comes readily to mind. Then as now, much of the fast-breaking news was little more than gossip and scandal dressed as public interest and surrounded by ads. Thomas Jefferson once stated, "A man who never looks into a newspaper is better informed than he who reads them."[41] But the content, the information, was not key to the way these documents helped to make and maintain a sense of community across the nation. As the philosopher George Santayana summed it up: "It doesn't matter what, so long as they all read the same thing."[42] And the endless cutting, pasting, forwarding, reading aloud, and discussing meant that, to a surprising degree, Americans were—or felt they were—reading much the same thing.

The blizzard of newspapers, pamphlets, journals, and tracts allowed each reader to feel that what he or she was doing, thousands and possibly tens of thousands of others with the same interests were doing at the same time. "Nothing but a newspaper," the great French sociologist Alexis de Tocqueville wrote in 1835, "can drop the same thought into a thousand minds at the same moment." "They maintain civilization," he went on. "If there were no newspapers, there would be no common activity."[43] One hundred years later, the U.S. newspaper still suggested participation in a collective ritual to the Dutch historian Johan Huizinga. After his tour of the States in 1926, he wrote that the newspaper

> *Fulfills in America the cultural function of the drama of Aeschylus. I mean that it is the expression through which a people—a people numbering many millions—becomes aware of its spiritual unity. The millions, as they do their careless reading every day at breakfast, in the subway, on the train and the elevated, are performing a . . . ritual. The mirror of their culture is held up to them in their newspapers.*[44]

These accounts make newspapers, however informative, more than simple information carriers. They illustrate the power of shared documents to bind people together into communities, large and small, creating a common sense of purpose and social identity, ideas obscured by infocentricity.

FIXED OR FLUID?[45]

The idea of textual communities, from de Tocqueville to Anderson or from Brian Stock to Anselm Strauss, takes for granted the fixity of documents. Indeed, the path to publication looks as though information is being weighted down with a series of material objects to hold it in place. A manuscript acquires type, binding, a cover, embossing, and a jacket before being pushed out into the world. From the perspective of freedom-seeking information, the conventional publishing term *released* seems inappropriate given all the shackles documents must carry.

Contrasting views of the fixity of documents and the fluidity of information get to a tension that is inherent in conventional documents, which, in a suitably academic mouthful, the French sociologist Bruno Latour describes as "immutable mobiles."[46] One quality of documents, then, is their mobility—the ability to circulate, unlike, for example, cave walls, on which humanity made its mark long before paper was around. The other is their immutability. We expect this book to travel unchanged, so that what reaches you is the same as what left the publisher.[47]

These two qualities tend to pull against one another. Clay, wax, and paper were more portable but also more mutable than rock walls. Paper and ink established a useful balance—light enough to be portable, but fixed enough to be immutable. Printing maintained that balance. The telegraph, radio, and telephone pulled against immutability. Only a small portion remains, for example, of the programming broadcast since radio began.

The digital world, too, pulls against immutability, while simultaneously adding a layer of confusion. For digital documents in other ways resemble paper ones. Yet with the digital, while transportation and mobility are enhanced, immutability is diminished. Some documents, such as Web pages, are constantly changing. On the Web it can be very hard to know what the "same document" might mean.[48]

So some people argue that the old balancing act is over: Fixity has given way to fluidity. And others add, don't worry. John Perry Barlow, for example, argues that with information technology, the economy is shifting over to a service economy of fluid practices, not fixed products.[49] A songwriter himself, Barlow claims that musicians must shift their income streams from products and copyrights (that rely on fixity) to performance (which is fluid).[50] In a similar vein though a different context, Davenport and Prusak point the same way: "Firms," they argue, "need to shift their attention from documents to discussion."[51]

Firms, as Davenport and Prusak are well aware, should only

shift some of their attention in this direction. Those who call for shifting it all fall for the linear arguments we discussed in chapter 1. They look beyond a recent trend to its logical (but not necessarily likely) conclusion, then celebrate its arrival. For all the advantages of fluidity, we should not forget that fixity still has its charms. Most of us prefer the checks we receive and the contracts we write to remain stable.

Fixity also plays a critical part in the power of the newspaper. A sense of community arises from reading the same text. For this reason, the personalized newspaper does not function in the same way as a conventional newspaper. It does not bind people together. You cannot ask someone "Did you read this story about *x*?" if your paper was created personally for you. Indeed, a world of personalized entertainment and news may make it hard to find common ground.

And yet, the need for shared cultural objects lives on. Today some people pass around URLs (Web site addresses) as a way of sharing experiences.[52] In doing so, they expect the site to be more or less the same when visited next. Even in the new fluid world of music, concertgoers expect the songs to be the same. (Though performers such as Bob Dylan test this idea of sameness to extremes.)

New, comparatively fluid communications technologies make it easy to deprecate older, more fixed ones as if the latter were simply failed attempts to be fluid. From the same perspective, it can seem as though all types of comunication are merely inadequate conversations. But different technologies are not all simply rivals. They may offer complementary or contrasting capabilities. The telephone, after all, did not annihilate the letter or the memo. In many situations, fixity is more important than fluidity. Indeed, technologies associated with fluid comunications are often as useful for the fixity they may provide. So while people use e-mail and faxes in part to overcome the limited mobility of "snail mail," they also use them to provide some capture in place of conversation's escapism. People will call to talk to an answering machine rather than a person or will send e-mail rather than calling.[53]

BINDING ISSUES

These local fixes to the fluidity of modern communication reflect some larger issues raised by fluid technologies. Societies rely on repeated access to many of their communications for both legal and cultural reasons. Indeed, one of the essential distinctions between a performance and a document is that the latter can be revisited. In the excitement and immediacy of the 'Net's fluidity, it's easy to miss the social significance of this aspect of fixity.

Harold Innis, an early communication theorist (and an important influence on Marshall McLuhan) suggested that communications technologies tend to favor one of two contrasting characteristics: "time binding" or "space binding."[54] Some, that is, tend to immutability (preserving communications across time); others to mobility (delivering communications across ever greater spaces).

Society's attention generally follows the latest shift in technology. So at the moment, the speed of modern communications dazzles. Its lack of time binding gets far less attention. As a result of this inattention, the most threatened records in modern archives are usually not the oldest ones, but the newest. The letters Paul read in Portugal may well be around in another 250 years. The files on which he recorded their text are unlikely to last twenty five.

Early in their history, too, books were treated with as little care. The sixteenth-century scholar John Dee petitioned the queen of England to set up a library to preserve books and manuscripts in 1556—some 75 years after the spread of printing. It took 250 more years to establish a national library as part of the British Museum. During that time, the inherent immutability of print documents preserved these despite neglect. Later products have not been so lucky. For all their cultural impact, much of the output of television and film has simply been lost in the ether.

Now comes the 'Net. Again, the lure of space binding has made time binding seem irrelevant. Despite some efforts to capture the content of the Web, huge amounts are lost everyday as sites come down and links "rot."[55] Enthusiasts will tell you that the World Wide Web is the most exciting cultural phenomenon since the printing press. Its output, however, resembles less the books the first presses produced than the type in which those books were set, most of which was broken up as soon as the printing finished. (Of course, one of the easiest and cheapest ways to preserve such transient modern records is to make a paper copy of them.)

MATTER OF DESIGN

There are good cultural reasons to worry about the emphasis on fluidity at the price of fixity. But fixity serves other purposes. As we have tried to indicate, it frames information. The way a writer and publisher physically present information, relying on resources outside the information itself, conveys to the reader much more than information alone. Context not only gives people what to read, it tells them how to read, where to read, what it means, what it's worth, and why it matters.

Though text runs through books from front to back, only the most naïve reader starts at the front, reads it all, and ends at the back. In general, readers know to skip the copyright data on the back of the title page, the page numbers on each page, and so forth. Many choose to skip footnotes or references. Experienced readers of nonfiction skip much more—rarely reading a whole book, but skimming and jumping. Some start certain books at the back, working in from the index. Similarly, people read historical novels differently from historical treaties, detective novels differently from forensic science manuals. All the time this efficient engagement with the text is shaped, directed, nudged, and hinted at by the design of the book—the weight, the binding, the cover, the size and arrangement of the type. In effect, people take a reading of the physical book in order to read its information. The periphery of the text guides us to what's central. Context shapes content.

The word *context* comes from the Latin *cum* (with) and *texere* (to weave) and etymologically suggests a process of weaving together. And document design weaves together the clues we have talked about to help readers read. No information comes without a context, but writers and designers always face the challenge of what to leave to context, what to information. The ease, availability, and enthusiasm for information often shifts this balancing act in favor of information. So, as noted in chapter 1, when there are problems with information, the solution offered is usually add more. The history of documents and communities points in the other direction—toward less information, more context.

To consider the difference, take a conventional Web page. The source of a Web design is almost pure text, which stands in for context. You don't see the distinction between head and body text; you simply get more text on the matter. A portion of a simple page generally looks something like the following lines:

‹HTML›

‹HEAD›

‹TITLE›John Seely Brown‹/TITLE›

‹META NAME="GENERATOR" CONTENT="Mozilla/3.01Gold (X11; I; SunOS 4.1.4 sun4m) [Netscape]"›

‹/HEAD›

‹BODY TEXT="#000000" BGCOLOR="#FFFFFF" LINK="#0000FF" VLINK="#52188C" ALINK="#FF0000"›

‹CENTER›‹TABLE CELLSPACING=2 CELLPADDING=10 WIDTH="550" HEIGHT="60" ›

‹CENTER›‹P›‹!--‹td width=550 align=center valign=middle›‹img src="images/wip2-banner.gif"›‹/td›--›

‹/P›‹/CENTER›

‹/TABLE›‹/CENTER›

‹CENTER›‹TABLE CELLSPACING=2 CELLPADDING=10 WIDTH="550" ›

‹TD width=550 align=center›‹!--| ‹a href="home.html"›Home‹/a› --›‹B›‹FONT SIZE=-1›|

‹A HREF="index.html"›Index‹/A› | ‹FONT COLOR="#FF0000"›John Seely Brown‹/FONT›

| ‹A HREF="pduguid.html"›Paul Duguid ‹/A›| ‹A HREF="credits.html"›Credits‹/A›

| ‹/FONT›‹/B›‹/TD›

‹/TR›

‹/TABLE›‹/CENTER›

‹CENTER›‹TABLE CELLSPACING=2 CELLPADDING=10 WIDTH="550" HEIGHT="75" ›

‹TR›

‹TD width=550›‹IMG SRC="images/john-guy2.gif" HEIGHT=108 WIDTH=83›‹/TD›

John Seely Brown

John Seely Brown (also known as JSB) is the Chief Scientist of Xerox Corporation and the Director of its Palo Alto Research Center (PARC). At Xerox, he has been deeply involved in corporate strategy and in expanding the role of corporate research to include such topics as organizational learning, ethnographies of the workplace, complex adaptive systems and techniques for unfreezing the corporate mind. His personal research interests include digital culture, ubiquitous computing, user-centering design, organizational and individual learning. A major focus of JSB's research over the years has been in human learning and in the creation of knowledge ecologies for creating radical innovation.

JSB is a co-founder of the Institute for Research on Learning, a non-profit institute for addressing the problems of lifelong learning. He is a member of the National Academy of Education and a Fellow of the American Association for Artificial Intelligence. He also serves on numerous advisory boards and boards of directors. He has published over 95 papers in scientific journals and was awarded the Harvard Business Review's 1991 McKinsey Award for his article, "Research that Reinvents the Corporation." In 1997 John published the book "Seeing Differently: Insights on Innovation" by Harvard Business School Press. He was an executive producer for the award winning film "Art : Lunch : Internet : Dinner" which won a bronze at Worldfest '94, the Charleston International Film Festival. More recently, he has been awarded the 1998 Industrial Research Institute Medal for outstanding accomplishments in technological innovation and the 1999 Holland Award in recognition of the best paper published in Research Technology Management in 1998.

He has a B.S. in Mathematics and Physics from Brown University and an M.S. in Mathematics and a Ph.D. in Computer and Communication Sciences from the University of Michigan.

Last edited on November 8, 1999.

From John's Actual Web Page

What readers see, of course, is quite different. The page that appears in a browser makes more subtle distinctions. And from those distinctions, readers have a good sense of how to read, what to skip, where to scan, or where to go next. The design of pages like this draws not only on modern information and information technology but also on centuries of document design and use. The latter reflects the implicit understanding that writers and readers have developed that allows much to be taken for granted.

In all, books and paper documents set a useful precedent not only for document design, but for information technology design in general. In a time of abundant and even superabundant raw information, they suggest that the better path in creating social documents (and social communities) lies not in the direction of increasing amounts of information and increasingly full representation, but rather in leaving increasing amounts un- or underrepresented. Efficient communication relies not on how much can be said, but on how much can be left unsaid—and even unread—in the background. And a certain amount of fixity, both in material documents and in social conventions of interpretation, contributes a great deal to this sort of efficiency.

In pointing to these various interests in fixity, we are not attempting to minimize the significance of the new fluid technologies. We are suggesting, however, that social and institutional pressures that favor fixity will also have a say in the outcome of current transformations.

8

Re-education

We're deep in the heart of the Apennine Mountains in Italy. It's dusk; the sun is setting over a farmhouse tucked away by itself at the end of a road. There we spy the farmer, a retired man in his late 60's, walking with his 25 year old granddaughter. In this particular corner of the world, it seems like things haven't changed that much in the last 100 years. We move in closer so we can eavesdrop on their Italian conversation.

GRANDFATHER: Well, I finally finished my doctoral thesis.
WOMAN: Way to go, Gramps!
GRANDFATHER: Did my research at Indiana University.
WOMAN: Indiana?
GRANDFATHER: Yup. IBM took the school's library ... and digitized it. So I could access it over the Internet.

She cocks her ear to take this all in.

GRANDFATHER: You know ... It's a great time to be alive.

—*IBM "Solutions for a Small Planet" advertisement*[1]

Like these sleepy corners of the Apennines, it can seem that in the university, too, "things haven't changed that much in the last 100 years"—and that they don't want to change. As one English academic said to us when we suggested a new approach, "We've done things this way for the past 500 years; why should we change now?" The remark reminds us that universities are one of the few institutions that have been around throughout the last millennium. It also indicates why some doubt whether they will make it very far into the next. Peter Drucker, the management theorist, has given them thirty years.

Yet, in the late 1990s and under strong pressure, universities and colleges (we use the terms interchangeably in this chapter) have started to move quite rapidly. Whether in the direction of extinction or, as the name of the new University of Phoenix perhaps suggests (see below), to escape it remains unclear.

PRESSURES

The pressures, though, are clear. First, there have been significant changes in the student body. The once typical 18- to 22-year-old undergraduate going through school on a parent's paycheck in four consecutive years is becoming increasingly rare and unconventional. People are taking up their degrees later and over longer periods, assembling them out of one course here and a few credit hours there, snatched between jobs and bank loans, as time, money, interest, and opportunity arise. Their desire for worthwhile education on topics that matter to them in a system that responds to their needs has pushed colleges hard.

Second, there are profound changes in competition. These are changes that, among other things, have pushed universities to think like businesses. It's commonplace now for schools to take seriously notions not only of competition, but also of markets, products, customers, clients, productivity, and above all else, economic survival.[2] New competition comes in a variety of forms. The fiercest arena is probably in the fight for paying students. Here, "mega-universities," which we mentioned in chapter 1, hungry for students and familiar with distance teaching and distance recruitment, have landed next to some ivy towers with the delicacy of Wal-Mart arriving in a small town. They threaten quickly to draw people away from the familiar retail outlets for education. As Britain's Open University, a school with some 160,000 off-campus students, came ashore in the United States, the cry went up that "the British are coming."[3] Many universities will rightly feel that their independence if not their very existence is at stake.

Not all such threats are foreign born. The University of Phoenix, now a major force in U. S. adult education, has grown in twenty years (it was accredited in 1978) to a school with 61,000 students, 77 campus centers, and 450,000 alumni. As a sign of the new competition from the for-profit sector, the University of Phoenix has also charmed the stock market, allowing its parent company to double revenues and split stocks in the four years since its IPO in December 1994.[4] From freelancing professors to the junk bond king Michael Milken, people are realizing that there is serious money to be made in education.

For-profit colleges compete in particular with smaller, less-well-endowed conventional schools that cannot protect themselves with generous scholarships.[5] But their strategy of what might be called "unplug and pay"—offering individual courses at rates cheaper than the conventional college threatens all schools. This strategy lures students from the courses with the highest profit margins and best chance for economies of scale. Taking these away makes it more difficult for established schools to cross-subsidize their more expensive classes as many have traditionally done.

The for-profit sector is not only competing for undergraduates and their courses. Corporate research centers (like Xerox PARC and Microsoft Research) increasingly compete with universities for the same funds, projects, and researchers. The various national academies and foundations, assumed by many universities to be loyal allies and reliable funders, are turning out to be committed primarily to the research being done and not the type of institution in which it is done. Thus, some universities are finding that they cannot compete directly with corporate-funded labs and are struggling to find the right complementarity to take advantage of their distinct institutional form.[6]

The third major pressure on universities to change comes, as the IBM ad with which we opened suggests, from new technologies. These offer new ways to think of producing, distributing, and consuming academic material. As with so many other institutions, new technologies have caused universities to rethink not simply isolated features but their entire mission and how they go about it. As elsewhere, they also make administrators consider not just how to do things differently, but also how to do them more cheaply.[7]

SOLUTIONS

The IBM "solutions" ad reflects many common conceptions of how these various pressures may be resolved with the help of the new information infrastructure. It also captures many of the tendencies of infoenthusiasts that we have encountered at various points in the book. First, there's the 6-D focus on disaggregated institutions, demassified consumption, disintermediation, and so forth. Second, there's redefinition. Books and libraries appear as

little more than containers, education as little more than infode-
livery, learning as infoconsumption. And third, there's a good bit
of endism. The death of distance will apparently produce a global
villagio uniting Indiana and the Apennines.

With the *villagio* in mind, there's much buzz about such things
as an "emerging electronic worldwide university" and the "virtual
university."[8] The latter, according to one group of scholars, "does
not have a traditional campus" because "electronic workspaces
and global libraries . . . provide richer functionality than their
physical analogs." So, these scholars continue, the function of the
university will be met by a system of surveys to find learners'
needs and bots to match these needs with learning providers.[9]
Already, many brick-and-mortar colleges are attempting to build
their place in cyberspace to reflect these visions. Penn State University has a "World Campus" while California has a statewide
"Virtual University," with "more than 1,600 online courses."[10]
The ivy towers, which have always looked a little like gothic
palaces, seem set to become gothic ruins.

RESISTANCE

IBM's vision is, of course, itself part of a tradition, reflecting many
earlier attempts to overcome geographical distance and get
beyond the limits of the conventional face-to-face classroom.
Earlier forms of distance education began if not with traveling
medieval scholars, then with the old correspondence course,
which, relying on regular mail, has been around for a long time.
Radio, television, and particularly video made that system more
flexible and more extensive, though still the demand for campus-
based universities continued to grow. Then came the computer.
In the late 1970s, PLATO, designed by the University of Illinois

for the army but marketed by Control Data Systems, was one of the earliest computer-based distance-teaching systems. Many others, based on a similar model of teaching and learning followed.[11] With the 'Net, such tutoring systems gave way to ftp servers, e-mail and other digital analogues of the correspondence course. And now the Web has advanced things dramatically. The University of Southern California started on-line teaching in the early 1980s. Now, as we have seen, there are at least 1,600 accredited courses in the state.[12]

It's important to note, however, that here as elsewhere in the digital world there is much hype. The California Virtual University, for example, is not quite the replacement for a bricks-and-mortar university that its name might suggest. It's a Web site—one that defiantly tells visitors that the California Virtual University does not "grant degrees or certificates." It doesn't even "answer individual questions about courses." It is, in fact, a site to "help you find out about courses and certificate or degree programs offered at a distance by California's leading institutions of higher education and . . . connect you to the appropriate campus to enroll and find out more information."[13] This "Virtual University," then, is little more than an on-line catalogue for on-line courses. It certainly provides a useful service, but its name is a bit of self-serving redefinition that obscures many distinctions. Here, it's no wiser to confuse the catalogue and the college than it is to mistake the keys for your car.[14]

The Penn State "World Campus" also promises to be useful. At the moment, however, it comprises five courses that can be taken toward the "Turfgrass Management Certificate." (It hopes to have 300 courses by 2002.)[15]

Finally, though an innocent viewer might never know it, the IBM scenario we began with is a fictional "envisioning," not a reflection of fact. The Indiana University Library has not been digitized. There is little prospect that it will be in the granddaughter's lifetime, let alone the grandfather's. IBM did, however, help digitize a part of the music collection at the university. Second, the university does have some on-line courses, but none seem to lead to a doctorate, and most are in the school of education. It might have seemed a little strange to envision an Italian farmer coming to the United States to take a Ph.D. in music, yet it's stranger still that he would come to qualify to teach in a U.S. high school.

So, as with many of the institutions and objects we have discussed so far, one reason that the conventional university may last is that its apparent alternatives are more vapor than virtual.[16] As with newspaper or the home office, however, we suspect that the university also resists attack because those trying to change it are looking through the wrong lenses. They are looking with glasses like IBM's. They see universities as delivering information to comparatively passive learners.

As we hope readers can predict by now, our response is not to say change is wrong or must not happen. We only say again that envisioned change will not happen or will not be fruitful until people look beyond the simplicities of information and individuals to the complexities of learning, knowledge, judgment, communities, organizations, and institutions. That way, it seems more likely that change will reorganize the higher education system, rather than simply disorganizing it.

COMPETING BY DEGREES

The U.S. system of higher education is significantly self-organizing. It embraces more than 11,000 postsecondary institutions of one sort or another, among which are 4,008 accredited colleges.

(The balance offer some sort of diploma for less than two years' work.) Of the 4,008, 1,741 are two-year schools, and 2,267 four-year. Of the latter, 1,862 award only bachelor's degrees, 1,369 include masters, and 488 doctorates. These degree-granting schools enroll about 14.6 million students.[17]

Across such a vast and sprawling system it's hard to say where the essence of these schools lies. Yet, before we can envision change and contemplate alternative types of institutions, it seems important to begin by asking what it is that colleges and universities do. What, in the language of business that has pushed its way into the halls of the academy, is the system's core competence? Why are students, their families, states, and federal agencies willing to invest so much in them? What is it that they want and the system offers? One answer, as the above statistics hint, is that they give degrees.

Describing universities in this way is rarely popular. Many people have much higher goals and don't like to hear universities described in terms of "credentialing." Credentials, they protest, are a crude misrepresentation of what they do. We answer these objections in three ways. First, we don't imagine that giving degrees is all that universities do. But it is a distinguishing and important characteristic. Second, we may describe it simply as credentialing, but credentialing is far from simple, as we hope to show. And third, misrepresentation is, by our account, a critical part of what degrees do and how universities survive.

By their own actions, the people who put themselves through various types of hell to get a degree would seem to place a high value on credentials. They know, and society knows, that coming away with a degree is much better than wearing a T-shirt saying "college of the streets" or "university of hard knocks." It's also better than coming away with 120 credit hours but no degree, even though the experience may be much the same.

Indeed, the degree-granting function of the university is sufficiently important that it underlies almost every scenario for change. It survives, for example, IBM's envisioning. It's also central to the unplug-and-pay model. Raiders may be willing to bite chunks out of the university, but they nonetheless want to be sure that their credits transfer. They know that if there were no university and no degrees, people would be less likely to come to them for a low-cost Calculus 101. Such raiders must always take care that their raids never kill the goose that lays their particular golden egg.

DEGREES OF REPRESENTATION

With the development of a strong for-profit sector and talk about the "marketplace of ideas," "knowledge markets," and "knowledge exchanges," can this degree-granting function survive? Or will the disintermediationists be right? Will the university crumble into individual buyers and sellers? After all, you can buy books brimming with knowledge. (Indeed you can even buy credentials and finished college papers.)[18] Why can't these markets develop to replace the cumbersome university as information provider? Why won't people just buy and sell knowledge across the 'Net?

The answer, of course, is that knowledge doesn't market very easily. As we noted in chapter 5, it's hard to detach and circulate. It's also very hard for buyers to assess. Indeed, people attempting to buy knowledge in one form or another often face a curious dilemma. If they can evaluate it, they probably don't need it. If they need it, they probably can't evaluate it. If, for example, you need the services of an engineer, a lawyer, or a doctor, it's probably because you lack the knowledge that they have. But then you face the question of how to gauge the knowledge that you want to buy. How can you, who know little about engineering, law, or medicine, decide whether what they offer is worth buying? People trying to buy education face a similar dilemma.

Both cases lead to pretty much the same answer. People rely on independent organizations and institutions to provide evaluation. They look, for instance, to the bar association, law schools, and law firms to assess the worth of an individual lawyer. Similarly for academic knowledge, they look to the university and implicitly beyond to accrediting agencies, college ranking, the success of alumni, and so on to see whether an education on offer is worth the investment.[19]

At the center of this process of evaluation, then, the university provides what we have called warranting (chapter 7). In complex institutional ways, it warrants its faculty, its courses, and its degree for the learner. And once a learner has graduated, the university also warrants the learner for future employers and associates, signaling once more to those who cannot assess the knowledge of the graduate directly. The university, then, represents learning to individuals and knowledgeable individuals to society.

MISREPRESENTATION

The representation of most university degrees, as we suggested earlier, includes a certain amount of what we think of as "misrepresentation." We don't mean the sort of misrepresentation that a "doctorate" bought for $200 dollars provides. We mean a more useful kind of misrepresentation.

The degree provides a public front of respectability. Behind its broad facade, students and faculty undertake many activities that society directly values. The broad facade also includes some activities that may be socially valuable but are not easily valued in the market. The ability of the degree to shelter these activities from close scrutiny, immediate justification, and micromanagement helps provide society with more diverse and versatile candidates than it knows to ask for. If every detail of a student's learning were held to public account, a lot of valuable experimentation and improvisation would probably disappear.

A good degree, then, works like a legislative "omnibus package." With broad public support—while, that is, a university maintains public trust and its degree retains value—important but not easily justified amendments can be unobtrusively tacked on unquestioned. Behind the work generally accepted as part of the overall package, other work can be explored before the need is recognized.

This balance of representation and misrepresentation relies heavily on institutional trust. The extent to which education can serve both students and society with more than they know to ask for depends on the extent to which society can trust educational institutions, their judgments, and the certificates they provide for their students' degrees. As the political scientist Martin Trow has pointed out, when universities lose society's trust, micromanaging ensues.[20]

The degree's misrepresentation thus puts slack in a system that might otherwise be too taut. If the degree or the degree-granting institutions lose trust or if the degree as a package disappears, then that slack is likely to disappear as well. It will become harder to tack on any amendments, good or bad. The whole package will, in effect, be opened up to "line-item veto."

Such vetoes will be most difficult to resist when the vote in question no longer concerns a single degree and a single institution, but only a single course from a single provider. The risk of taking an oddball but possibly insightful course as part of a degree is small if the value of the overall degree itself is well supported. The risk is far higher if the value of that course has to stand on its own, and not hide itself in the broader omnibus package. There is, in effect, a warranting cross-subsidy as well as a financial cross-subsidy between courses.

For information technology to lead to such micromanaging would be a paradoxical and unfortunate result. An extraordinary amount of the creative outburst that has generated this technology has come from people who used the slack in a university to explore new avenues. These would include computer scientists who sat up all night pushing too much code into too small microcomputers when they should have been working on problem sets for conventional mainframes. Or business students who followed the potential of 'Net business when they should have been studying the annual reports of Fortune 500 companies. Much digital innovation has come from people who spent their time on campus wandering around in the arts, theater, psychology, and the humanities—areas not well supported in the unplug-and-pay model of education.

That model, like many 'Net visions, is remarkably blinkered. It focuses sharply on clear and well-defined informational and educational needs that technology can readily meet. But in so doing, it may exclude less apparent needs and resources. In a similar vein, the "personalized newspaper" assumes that people are best served if they are given news on topics that they preselect. Such a model neglects how difficult it is for people to know and describe what they want, which we discussed in chapter 2.

It also neglects the importance of serendipitous news—news that people didn't set out to find—to the way people understand the world.[21]

A highly "targeted" view of learning can be equally narrow. We all need to learn things that we didn't set out to learn. "Distribution requirements" are the formal way that conventional education provides this for students and for society. But the collective experience of college and what the German sociologist Karl Jaspers described as the "creative tension" generated by the mingling of people from different fields, different backgrounds, and different expectations makes a critical contribution.[22] Among other things, such experience helps provide not only knowledge and information that people don't know they need, but also the skill to judge the worthwhile from the worthless— an increasingly important skill in an age of ubiquitous and often unreliable information.

LEARNING NOT LADING

Of course, degrees are not usually appreciated for their balance of representation and misrepresentation. Too often, they are seen as little more than an intellectual bill of lading, a receipt for knowledge-on-board much like any other receipt for freight-on-board. Teaching, in this view, is a delivery service, and schools a loading site. No one actually says this, but a delivery view nonetheless underlies much of what is said about schools. Moreover, the delivery view leads people to think of educational technology as a sort of intellectual forklift.

Such a knowledge-delivery view of education overlooks the process of "learning to be" (see chapter 5), which is such an integral part of university life. Learning to be involves *enculturation—*

engaging with communities of practice and of concepts.[23]
Teaching and education, from this perspective, are not simply
matters of putting students in touch with information, as IBM's
ad might suggest. Rather, they are matters of putting students in
touch with particular communities. The university's great
advantage is that it can put learners in touch with communities
that they don't know about, as we have just suggested, or that it
would be hard to access in any other way.

Of course, the type of access needed and the type of community vary with the type and level of students. Undergraduates are prime targets of delivery. They are in a position in
which it is easy to accept that learning is a matter of absorbing
or cramming in information. Yet in good colleges students also
get *extensive* access—access, that is, to a variety of different types
of community. This gives undergraduates a sense that different
communities have distinct understandings of knowledge and
distinct ways of judging what is interesting, valid, significant, and
so on. These differences, they can discover, fall not only between
scientists and humanists, but also between mathematicians and
physicists, and even between theoretical physicists and experimental physicists.

Over the course of an undergraduate degree and through
encounters with an extensive range of different disciplines, students also get some sense, however implicit, of what it takes to
join a particular community. In so doing, they may progress from
learning about to learning to be, from, that is, learning about a
group of different communities toward learning to be a member
of one. This transition is evident as, toward the end of an undergraduate degree, students narrow the extent of their course work
and become more intensively engaged with the fields that interest them and work closer with practitioners from those fields.

Graduate education completes this process, shifting more completely from learning about to learning to be. As their graduate education proceeds, students enter and progress further and further into a particular community. Consequently, as we noted in chapter 5, graduate education usually ends in a form of apprenticeship.

As students shift from learning about several communities to learning to be a member of one, the access they require shifts, too, from extensive to *intensive*. Schools must now offer students opportunities for full, in-depth access.

PEER SUPPORT

One of the most intriguing social aspects of learning is that, despite the metaphor of apprenticeship, the relationships involved in enculturation are not simply ones of novice and expert. Putting learners in contact with "the best in the field" has definite value. Peers turn out to be, however, an equally important resource.

An early attempt at distance teaching by video revealed this quite unexpectedly. Jim Gibbons, former dean of engineering at Stanford, taught an engineering class to Stanford students and engineers from Hewlett-Packard. When it became impractical for the engineers to attend, Gibbons started recording the class and sending the video to the engineers. The engineers would watch these tapes as a group. At regular intervals they would stop the tape and discuss what Gibbons and the class were talking about, coming to some sort of collective understanding before going on.[24]

To Gibbons's surprise, the engineers, though they had lower academic credentials coming into the course, consistently outperformed the classroom students when tested on course material.

This finding has proved remarkably robust, and other courses using this "TVI" method have had similar comparative success.

Gibbons has been careful to note, however, that the success did not simply result from passing videos to learners. The name TVI stands for tutored video instruction, and the method requires viewers to work as a group and one person from that group to act as tutor, helping the group to help itself. This approach shows, then, that productive learning may indeed rely heavily on face-to-face learning, but the faces involved are not just those of master and apprentice. They include fellow apprentices.

The ability of a group to construct their education collectively like this recalls the way in which groups form and develop around documents, as we noted in chapter 7. Together, members construct and negotiate a shared meaning, bringing the group along collectively rather than individually. In the process, they become what the literary critic Stanley Fish calls a "community of interpretation" working toward a shared understanding of the matter under discussion.[25]

TVI is not an easy answer. As Gibbons and his colleagues argue in one discussion, "The logistics of creating videos, organizing training for small groups, finding and training tutors, etc. can be daunting."[26] For many individual learners, of course, the logistics of finding a group—which in Gibbons's approach precedes finding a tutor because the tutor comes from the group—can also be daunting. So colleges and universities play a critical role in providing this sort of access.

Gibbons's results provide positive evidence for the importance of a cohort for learning. There is interesting negative evidence, too. Studies have shown that people doing course work in isolation, though they may do as well on the tests, find the credentials they receive are less valuable than those of their peers who worked in conventional classroom groups. Employers, the research of Stephen Cameron and James Heckman reveals, discriminate between the two. Those who possess all the information of their peers but lack the social experience of school are not valued as highly. This discrimination has led to what Cameron and Heckman call the "nonequivalence of equivalence diplomas."[27] It will be important to see on which side of the equivalence divide the degrees of providers who allow students take their degrees wholly on-line will fall.[28]

In making these distinctions, employers would seem implicitly to distinguish degrees according to the type of access they reflect, access not only to practices and practitioners, but also to peer communities. Stanley Fish once called an essay about communities of interpretation "Is There a Text in this Class?" With distance education, where texts are shipped to individuals, it will become increasingly important to ask, "Is there a class (or community) with this text?"[29]

DEGREES OF DISTANCE

Criteria for access to communities are quite different from criteria for access to information. And they ask new questions about distance and about its death. Undoubtedly, there are many reasons—both in terms of opportunity and need—to put the conquest of distance high on reform agendas for educational reform. The opportunity is clearly here. A rich information technology infrastructure is in place in much of the world and is only getting richer. It would be madness to neglect it.

The need is also inescapable. John Daniel, vice-chancellor of the Open University, maintains that worldwide demand is growing, particularly in the underdeveloped world, so rapidly that were one conventional campus a week to open for the next several years it would not meet demand. Information technology offers the opportunity to address a large and diverse population much more quickly.

Thinking of distance in technological terms, however, easily confuses two kinds of distance. The first is principally geographical distance. There are many places where it is simply a long way to the nearest university. Open Learning Australia, for example, is designed to address a population roughly the size of New York State's in an area about the size of the United States. Similarly, the University of the South Pacific has students spread out over one million square kilometers. For these institutions, geographical distance is a primary issue.

But potential candidates for university also have to overcome another kind of distance, social distance. Minorities, women, and the poor have all had to struggle across this distance for access. For the inhabitants of Morningside Heights (next to Columbia), East Palo Alto (down the road from Stanford), and West Oakland (next door to Berkeley), geographical distance has not been the primary reason for missing out on higher education. In this regard, the British Open University (OU) forms an interesting contrast to Open Learning Australia. In the United Kingdom, geographical distance is not a major problem. For the OU as for the underserved residents of Morningside Heights, East Palo Alto, and West Oakland, social distance has been the central issue.

For all technology's prowess, social distance is not overcome by "a few strokes of the keyboard." Indeed, while many of its competitors fear its technological capacities, the University of Phoenix's advantage may come more from its skill at targeting people that traditional schools have kept at a distance.

A DISTANT PROSPECT

Excitement about the reach of technology and the potential of a worldwide market make it tempting to pay attention to geographical distance almost exclusively. Curiously, such attention fails to see how the success of much new technology on campus has little to do with geographical distance at all. A good deal is used so people can interact across time rather than space.[30] Escaping the temporal confines of the classroom, class Web sites provide students and teachers access to documents separately and in their own time.[31] They also help class documents to grow incrementally over time, making changes (by both teachers and students) available for all in the class to see and annotate. In this way, these sites are powerful resources for a community of interpretation. But they are usually an extension of, not a replacement for, face-to-face meetings of such a community. Their usefulness is not primarily a matter of geographical distance.

These technologies may also help address the effects of certain types of social distance. In particular, teachers report that on-line and asynchronous interaction allows students who are reluctant to speak in face-to-face classes to have their say. This can benefit nonnative speakers, the disabled, minorities, and women. (Men are notorious for dominating classroom discussions.)

Despite these successes, however, the technological reach that conquers distance doesn't necessarily provide the reciprocity that allows people to form, join, or participate in worthwhile learning communities. Yet it can seem to. Certainly, the word *community* crops up all over the Web sites of distance courses. But often it refers to groups that are communities in little more than the sense that eBay is a community. More generally, the 'Net can give the appearance of membership or access that it does not provide in any meaningful way. (The ability to send a message to <president@whitehouse.gov>, for example, can give the illusion of much more access, participation, and social proximity than is actually available.)

So, despite the buzz about on-line learning and communities, it can be difficult to form suitably dense communities to support learning in cyberspace. Dan Huttenlocher, professor of computer science at Cornell, argues that digital technologies are adept at maintaining communities already formed. They are less good at making them. Hence, paradoxically, technologies may do a better job on the conventional campus than on the virtual one.[32]

Thus while plans to give every student a laptop may be a good start, they are only a start. There is, in every sense, a long way to go from there. If society ignores the need to address both geographical and social distance (or assumes that Moore's Law will fix the problem), new technologies may only polarize further an already divided educational system. The more expensive, conventional campus, with its rich and respected resources, is unlikely to disappear. It provides a highly effective setting for students to access multiple communities, directly and indirectly, purposefully and serendipitously. On the conventional campus, on-line activities complement the off-line. They do not replace them. Consequently on-line degrees that only provide half of this mixture are unlikely to be regarded as fully equivalent to those that provide the whole. And, as we have indicated, the marketplace can discriminate quite finely between better and worse degrees.

In consequence, despite the concern about "have nots" lacking access to technology, there is a danger that technology will become the *only* access they have to experiences whose full value actually develops through complementary on- and off-line practices. People able to afford conventional campuses, which will continue to get comparatively more expensive, are likely to have the best of both worlds.[33] Meanwhile, the people who now commute on the old highways to commuter colleges may be pushed onto the digital highway but remain the same distance from the benefits of the conventional campus as before.

To avoid this sort of polarization, distance and delivery should be set aside as primary technological goals. Instead the aim should be access. Like the home workers that we discussed in chapter 3, the more isolated learners are, whether physically or socially, the more they need access to peers, communities of practice, and other social resources.

A SENSE OF PLACE

The geographical reach of technology presents learners with another problem, too. As we said in chapter 1, certain kinds of disintermediation concentrate control in fewer hands and shift decision making from the periphery of institutions to the center. There are signs of this centralizing tendency in higher education. For-profit schools often centralize course design. Neither learners nor teachers have much local input into what is taught.

The new technologies with their power of ubiquitous delivery only tempt people to concentrate further. A Coopers and Lybrand report argues that twenty-five packaged courses can take care of half of community college and one third of four-year college enrollments. The race is clearly on among several of the 4,008 accredited colleges to provide some or all of these twenty-five.[34]

Inevitably, this sort of centralization overlooks the significance of place and the location of knowledge. If we consider the bulk of what we learn, it is remarkably local. Not only do U.S. students learn U.S. history and literature, but Midwestern students tend to learn more about prairies than oceans, West Coast students more about plate tectonics than the Gulf Stream. Texans learn more Spanish than Minnesotans, and art students in Washington State learn more about Oriental art and less about European art than art students in Washington, D.C.[35]

It would be unfortunate to return to the days when, as the art critic Robert Hughes remembers, young Australians were taught a curriculum created at the center of the empire in Britain. "They were made," Hughes writes, "to read the novels of Walter Scott and the deeds of Sir Francis Drake, to recite like parrots the names of English kings, the dates of unexplained events like the Rump Parliament and the Gunpowder Plot, the lengths of European rivers they would never see."[36]

Questions about the locality of knowledge are far from trivial. As we argued in chapter 6, universities play a vital role in knowledge ecologies. These ecologies have a distinct regional character. Submitting students to the curriculum of the global village may neglect the needs of the ecology.[37] There are good reasons why the University of California at Davis has a strong enology department (it's close to the Napa Valley), UC Berkeley has a strong computer science department (it's close to Silicon Valley), and UC Los Angeles has a strong film department (it's close to Hollywood). A policy of regional devolution is important if regions are to develop their own strengths supported by universities. Centralization pulls in the opposite direction.

RECOMPUTING DISTANCE

Hughes's remark about learning at the far end of an empire indicates that distance education is not new. In the nineteenth century, students from Scotland to Singapore and Aberdeen to Adelaide took courses and external degrees from the University of London, most without ever leaving home.

The university presided over a comparatively devolved system that balanced centralization and decentralization. The external degree allowed students and teachers to form or join relatively autonomous local groups of like-minded participants thousands of miles from the degree-granting university. High schools and libraries around the world opened their facilities to nearby students so that local scholars could provide university-level courses in places without a university.[38]

This devolved system of higher education involved both local and remote scholars and communities. Consequently, students were neither dislocated from local networks, nor trapped by the limitations of local resources. Local communities gave students opportunities for authentic access and membership, while, from a distance, the university provided oversight, materials, standards, and credentials. Consequently, students could draw on strengths of both the metropolis and the periphery.

This arrangement, furthermore, addressed both types of distance. Clearly it dealt with geographical distance. But it also provided educational opportunities for women in Britain, the poor, and Third World residents all of whom lacked access to universities as much on account of who they were as how far they were from a university. The London external degree provided people from these neglected groups with recognized and respected credentials.

REORGANIZING

As we emphasized at the opening of this chapter, the whole system of higher education is under tremendous pressure to change. Moreover, despite appearances to the contrary in some ivied exteriors, colleges and universities are changing significantly. Changing the directions of organizational vessels as large as universities, however, produces a fair amount of thrashing and churning. Consequently, it remains hard to see the ultimate directions that educational organizations might take.

Those directions may be of interest to more than people directly connected to the system—those taking or thinking of taking courses and degrees, those working in the system, and those who would work with or employ the system's graduates. The reorganization of colleges and universities for the twenty-first century may provide a useful means to think about change occurring elsewhere in society. So, with these interests in mind, we attempt here to see through some of the churning.

Universities are concerned with the communication of knowledge. So radical innovation in communications technologies inevitably suggests radical change in universities. And equally inevitably, technological change gives rise to the sort of 6-D thinking embedded in the IBM ad and other discussions of virtual and distance education. But as we have tried to show in the course of this chapter, other significant, social pressures are also at work.

These less visible pressures make it a mistake to think of institutional change as a linear descent from complex institutions and organization to individuals put into "direct" touch with information by information technologies. New, interactive technologies are undoubtedly starting to pick away at some previously invisible seams that run through institutions like the university. But other forces prevent the whole from simply disintegrating into a pile of loose threads. So we prefer to think of change as loosening, but not severing, the bonds that have held the components of conventional universities together for some time.

These bonds have not always held the university together in its recent form. So while most eyes are on the technology and the future, we suspect that attempts to rethink the university in the context of distance technology could learn a little from older configurations like that of the University of London. That example suggests what a worthwhile reconfiguration of the modern university might require. It needs, in particular, to overcome the limits of the parochial. Yet in so doing, it also needs to steer a path between the academy's (and technology's) centralizing tendencies, on the one hand, and the optimistic faith that technology will overcome distance (in all its forms) and create a devolved system, on the other.

UNPICKING THE THREADS

A few years ago, allergic though we may seem to futurology, we explored this idea of the devolved university.[39] At the time, it met with strong resistance. In Europe, it was portrayed as the "view from California," as if that was a synonym for outlandishness. In the States, people who read drafts suggested that we keep everything but the discussion of devolution, which clearly had lost touch with reality.

In presenting a similar account again now, we face a different challenge. Higher education has changed so far and so fast that what seemed ridiculous in 1996 seems commonplace today. We present it nonetheless. On the one hand, it may offer a simple measure of how far the apparently unchanging system has changed. And on the other, its failings as much as its strengths may help point through the churning to underlying directions.

Our discussion so far suggests that learners need three things from an institution of higher education: access to authentic communities of learning, interpretation, exploration, and knowledge creation; resources to help them work with both distal and local communities; and widely accepted representations for learning and work. Change in the system still needs to honor those constraints.

The conventional university has achieved this by arranging five distinct constituencies and components of the university: students, faculty, research, facilities, and an institution able to provide formal, accepted representation of work done. The conventional system sewed these together into one predominant type. New technologies are helping to pull those seams apart. As the seams come apart, we believe, these constituencies and components will probably remain interconnected, but in a looser configuration.

Several of the new forms of higher education that are springing up almost daily often appear to disregard one or more of these components. Some seem to suggest that, with a powerful Web site and some packaged "content," they can do away with everything but students, who they address individually, and fees, which lie at the core of their business models. As we noted with the unplug-and-pay models, however, such radical revisions often rely heavily on the continued existence of the conventional institutions. The Web site teaching Accounting 101 at a cut-rate price still relies on the old full-service colleges to recognize the ensuing course credits. As such, these radical revisions are perhaps not so radical after all.

By contrast, many of the conventional schools that are turning their eyes to alternatives, seek to keep all but the students tightly bound together. Far-flung students, it's assumed, can be reached with the help of distance education technology. From their old to their new guise, the conventional schools continue to regard learning as a matter of delivery. As we have argued, it is not. The old system, however, with its campuses and classrooms, nonetheless provided plenty of opportunities for students to "steal" knowledge from teachers and construct knowledge with peers, even though that was not necessarily the intention of the design. The new system, however, designs these opportunities out. The secure, narrow channels of digital technology make theft and collective construction much harder. Putting the pedagogy of the conventional classroom on line, that is, cuts out the hidden resourcefulness of the conventional classroom.

The history of the external degree, with its central credentialing but distal teaching, suggests that other configurations, focusing less on individuals and information and relying less on delivery models of teaching, are possible. With that in mind, we suggest that the university's constituencies and components may reconfigure along the following lines.

Students

The students, as we have said, are changing their demands on the university in response to changing demands on them. They need universities that can address their short-term, long-term, and lifelong needs and that can support them not only as they change careers but also as they change locations. They need opportunities both for ever-more-extensive association and ever-more-intensive application. And, in particular, they need universities that will provide them with robust credentials. For work without credentials is often little better than credentials without work.

Degree-Granting Bodies

To provide adequate credentials through adequate learning (with adequate amounts of misrepresentation) is the responsibility of the degree-granting function of universities. This function may develop in an increasingly independent direction with a variety of degree-granting bodies (DGBs) emerging to assume a degree-granting role. These would need, on the one hand, to attract students, and, on the other, to retain public trust.

A DGB could take on as many or as few students and faculty as they thought wise, becoming smaller than a liberal arts college or larger than an entire state system. They could set degree and core course requirements as they saw fit. And they would continue to play a critical part in ensuring access for students. Nonetheless, a DGB would be essentially an administrative body, with little need to own much beyond its administrative competency, public trust, and a building to house its (administrative) staff. Its loyalties might be to a locale or a region or to a field or a profession. It might then be principally local, regional, national, or international.

Subject to accreditation, private institutions could set up their own DGBs; states could set up their own. Some DGBs might try to be exclusive, others inclusive. Each would over time develop its particular reputation, attracting faculty and students through the exchange value of their degrees. Groups concerned about education in their field might try to establish themselves as DGBs—for example, the AMA, MLA, or Computer Scientists for Social Responsibility. Each would become aware that, as we suggested earlier, degrees reflecting too much concentration, representing too accurately the work involved, might well fall in value compared to those misrepresenting greater diversity.

Faculty

While DGBs oversee access, it is their faculty who provide it. Faculty would then need to find a DGB to sanction their teaching. (They might find more than one to do this.) DGB sanction would allow students who study with a particular scholar to gain credit for work done toward a degree from the DGB. Scholars might contract individually or in teams. But, as distinct from the current system, they wouldn't be tied to one campus. There is no reason for all the faculty of a DGB, nor even all the members of a team, to be in the same place. Some could be on the East Coast, some on the West Coast, and some overseas. They might teach students on-line or in person, through tutorials, lectures, or seminars, or any combination of these. The number and range of faculty a DGB might warrant this way would no doubt reflect the degree of extensivity (contact with multiple fields) or intensivity (depth within particular fields) they offered to students.

Research

Research would remain integral to the mission of several universities for a number of reasons.[40] First, for students it is important to have access to practitioners as they go about their work. Second, it is also important to have people active in their fields teaching. And third, a good deal of research depends on student labor.

Corporate or independent research labs offer many of these capabilities. University research, however, is at its most effective when it conducts research that the private sector is unable or unwilling to pursue.[41] (Much early Internet research falls into this category.) Conversely, it is at its weakest when it merely duplicates research going on elsewhere. Competition from the for-profit sector is likely to push university research into this complementary role to the benefit of innovative ecologies as a whole.[42] Both students and faculty would then stand to gain from new research ventures that would couple corporate and academic research in innovative, complementary ways.

Facilities

For both teaching and research, faculty could find their own facilities. Some faculty would require extensive facilities, with labs, equipment, and libraries. Others might only need a class-room. People running small, local tutorial groups or on-line classes might need few facilities beyond an Internet access or a seminar room. The latter, rather like branch libraries, might be dispersed across towns and cities, positioned for the convenience of faculty and students. The campus centers of the University of Phoenix are spread around in this way.

Despite the loss of a tied academic administration and faculty, physical facilities, under such an arrangement, would no doubt look very much like the campus of today. A campus would have to compete for faculty and students in the region, using the quality of its facilities to attract them. Both faculty and students using a particular facility might come from several DGBs. The facility itself might thus become a regional magnet for staff, students, and DGBs. If this were the case, it would be in a city's or a region's interest to maintain a high standard of facilities such as libraries, laboratories, and technologically dense learning environments.

Neither faculty nor students would necessarily want to travel to their DGB. Superior facilities might entice them to travel, however. On the other hand, neither faculty nor students would be locked into one set of facilities. In well-endowed areas, some faculty and many students might use more than one facility. DGBs, faculty, and students might not use campus facilities at all. We would imagine, however, that given the needs for socialization, most DGBs and many faculty might insist that candidates, as part of their degree, spend a set amount of time on campus in groups rather than on-line individually. DGBs that didn't might find their degrees rapidly falling in value and competitive worth.

Looking Beyond the Campus

Student choices would expand significantly in any reconfiguration of this sort. More choices, of course, are likely to mean more complex decisions. The central choice would involve finding a suitable DGB. Perhaps a student would choose one that insists on conventional campus life—and one that had faculty on a campus. Perhaps one that made no campus demands. Perhaps one that included certain faculty. Perhaps one that had faculty in the various regions the student expected to work in over the next few years: northern Scotland, Singapore, or San Francisco. A student might choose a DGB whose degree in an area of interest is known to have a high exchange value or one that was prepared to validate certain kinds of in-work experience. But a student wouldn't be committed to working with the faculty of a single campus or a single region; he or she would have the opportunity to work with local communities of excellence whose credentials under present arrangements are not accepted by universities.

In this way, a distributed system might allow much greater flexibility for local sites of professional excellence—research labs, hospitals, architects' offices, law firms, engineering offices, and the like—to contribute to and benefit from the educational component of a regional matrix. They could offer mentoring programs that give students practical experience and course credits simultaneously. Regions that lacked conventional academic facilities might then start to attract students through the quality of mentors in their conventional workforce. Students in forestry, viticulture, mining, conservation, or ocean science would, for instance, be able to get credit for working with experts in their field, however far this might be from conventional academic centers.

Tying these sites of learning more closely to the university has additional benefits, for it opens up a two-way street. On the one hand, it allows students more extensive and intensive access to working communities. On the other, it can give people in those communities access back to the university and its resources. It is through these links that the university's role in "lifelong learning," much talked about though less explored, might be expanded.

Reaching people beyond the campus, schools can, for example, provide alumni and other professional communities with which they work access to their inherent knowledge base. This might include not only formal classes, but ideas generated in the daily round of seminars, colloquiums, lectures, and so forth. New means for capture—such as live-boards (classroom blackboards that retain a digital copy of what's written on them) and multimedia recordings—and for dissemination across the 'Net could provide a dynamic, responsive archive out of what have formerly been transient or broadcast practices.

As we note in the Afterword, these resources will require more than unedited dumps of classroom exchanges.[43] To be useful, different types of indexing and annotation, new and versatile search tools, and moderated channels for response may be needed. In this area, schools might further develop links between students on campus (with time rather than money on their hands) and students off campus (with money rather than time). Students attending classes on campus could help index recordings in real time (these might be thought of as the multimedia equivalent of those exemplary class notes that classmates find so valuable today) and respond to the issues raised by off-campus students through the interactive links.

Essentially, a student's university career in such a system would no longer be through a particular place, time, or preselected body of academics, but through a network principally of their own making, yet shaped by a DGB and its faculty. A student could stay home or travel, mix on-line and off-line education, work in classes or with mentors, and continue their learning long after taking a degree.

Direct funding through fees wouldn't change much. DGBs would take tuition fees, while arrangements for faculty and facility per capita payments could be negotiated in a variety of ways. Fees would be likely to vary depending on the type of teaching offered—lecture, tutorial, research seminar, lab, or in-work training for graduate, undergraduate, or extension students. DGBs might pay a per capita fee to reward a teacher's ability to attract high-quality students to the DGB. Or, like eighteenth-century academics, scholars might collect a fee from the students they attract. Or again, a DGB might pay for matriculating students while auditors could pay teachers directly. (An option like this might help ensure that the structure and content of a course were not shaped by degree and exam requirements alone.)

More indirect funding sources raise different issues. Conventional universities, as we have noted, maintain their edge over more unconventional rivals in part through the deep pockets of their endowments. Alumni play a significant part in keeping these pockets filled. And alumni also tend to be a significant force against changes in their alma mater. But as alumni themselves come increasingly to need the sort of after-graduation lifelong learning that new configurations may better provide, alumni, too, may join the forces for change.

DEVOLVING IMPLICATIONS

This sketch is not a road map for the future. We intend it more as a catalyst for further conversation. It seeks to make clear that the radical changes occurring in a university's environment, from the reconstitution of its student body to the reengineering of its technological infrastructure, will require different institutional arrangements than those found today. Despite predictions about the end of the campus as we know it, we suspect that the university of the digital age may not *look* very different. It will still require classrooms, labs, libraries and other facilities. Nonetheless, we are sure that organizationally it will be very different.

In looking at university change for its own sake or as an indicator of institutional change more generally, no one should underestimate the remarkable staying power of these institutions.

They have been around, as we noted at the outset, for more than 1,000 years. In that time, they have survived many revolutions and may survive more yet, including the digital one.

Beyond Information

WE SAID AT THE OUTSET that we wanted to avoid rushing to solutions. And some 240 book pages later, we still have few to offer. We write this afterword in the spirit of the great lexicographer Samuel Johnson, who called the final chapter of his novel *Rasselas,* "The conclusion, in which nothing is concluded."[1] We do, however, want to draw together some of the threads that run through several of these chapters but are not necessarily emphasized in any one.

RESOURCES AND CONSTRAINTS

First we want to emphasize the complex character of resources and constraints. These, like good and bad people, don't always fall into two mutually exclusive groups. Sometimes there is some confusing overlap. Many of our criticisms here have been directed at cases in which this overlap has been overlooked. In such cases, new techniques and technologies often aim to remove a surface constraint (objects, organizations, practices, institutions) without appreciating their submerged resourceful-ness. When this happens, the old resourcefulness often wins, to the frustration of technologists and futurologists. Cases of stub-born resistance, then, while of interest in themselves, may also reflect a more general problem with technological design.

In particular, a tunnel-like focus on information, self-evident and free of context, remains too loyal to the digital presumption of a binary world. So it takes, for example, the useful clues involved in restraining information as merely clutter—the husk to be discarded rather than deployed. Remember, for example, the vinegar-scented letters we mentioned in chapter 7. The scent of vinegar undermined not only Paul's interpretation of the letters, but also his easy assumptions about where informa-tion begins and carrier ends, about dividing text from context.

Like separating context from text, separating constraints from resources can be specially difficult with familiar objects because people come to rely on recurring technological constraints to pro-vide social and institutional resources. So while paper may seem a constraint on the circulation of information, readers and writers have made it a powerful resource for making, shaping, warranting, interpreting, and even protecting information. The example of paper suggests to us that, for design more generally, before an apparent constraint is dismissed, it's important to consider the social resource that people may have developed around it.

Conversely, designers might look at ways to turn constraints into resources. To offer a small but concrete example, consider a project called the Madcap at Xerox PARC. The work is based on the simple observation that at PARC, as in so many places, we record many of the talks people come to give. These tapes are available—hours and hours, miles and miles of them—yet rarely used. It's curiously harder to listen or watch a whole talk on a tape than to attend the talk itself, and it's nearly impossible to skim it the way you might skim a document. On the other hand, conventional transcribing or annotating is an intensive and demanding process. So people rarely bother to use them at all.

So the Madcap project attempts to annotate these tapes dynamically. For instance, it attaches notes that people in the audience were taking, using time stamps to cross-reference the two. You can look at a note and cut straight to the point on the tape where the note was written.

Madcap also uses background noise—which might otherwise have been regarded as a constraint, something to be kept off or cleaned off the tape—as a resource. It capitalizes on audience noise, laughter, clapping, and the like—collective social responses to the event—using them to make an index of significant moments in the talk, moments to which someone reviewing the tape might want to skip.

Constraints that are also resources, as we have been trying to show throughout this book, are not necessarily physical materials, like paper or noise on a tape. They may also include such things as social groups, organizations, and institutions. There are good reasons to change all these, and new technologies now give us the means to do so. But if their resourcefulness is overlooked, the constraint may stick around, sometimes in its most obtuse form. On the other hand, once understood, such constraints may not block the way ahead, but rather point it out. For example, we have argued in chapter 8 that overlooking the resources provided by the face-to-face classroom—opportunities for "stealing" knowledge and collectively constructing understanding—may undermine distance learning technologies. Conversely, understanding those resources may make for much more powerful, socially useful learning technologies.

Ignoring these kinds of resources, we have also tried to argue, can lead to technologies that emphasize reach at the expense of reciprocity, spontaneity at the expense of structure. Reciprocity and structure may undoubtedly involve constraints, but these may also be resourceful constraints.

THE EVOLUTION OF INSTITUTIONS

In an age that emphasizes individual freedoms, institutions are often portrayed merely as constraints on this freedom. In particular, they are portrayed as monolithic, static, even stagnant constraints. Yet, because they are human creations, they rarely are just that. They change as people change. And they adapt to serve social needs. Overlooking their usefulness and their adaptability makes it very hard to understand social change in general. Yet, paradoxically, those who denounce institutions most loudly are often those who proclaim an interest in the future and the changes it will bring.

The social critic Raymond Williams draws attention to the evolutionary character of institutions when he suggests that society is always grappling with the mixed influence of dominant, residual, and emergent institutions.[2] The dominant institutions of the day tend to be the most obvious, affecting society most directly. The institutions of the free market, popular democracy, and intellectual property, for example, are all around us and the subject of debate.

They have not always been there. They emerged to replace older institutional forms. Mercantilism and monarchism, for example, preceded the free market and popular democracy in many places. Intellectual property institutions developed as an extension of other property rights. As new forms develop, older, residual institutions don't immediately disappear. The older often continue to make themselves felt residually. Mercantilism, for example, lives on in the opposition to free trade, vestiges of monarchism in class distinctions. But because such residual institutions are assumed to have faded out of existence, their effects can be hard to see or understand. We hope that greater awareness of institutional evolution rather than simple extinction might help bring if not the end of endism, then a little less of it.

While these ideas about institutions might seem abstract and vague (they are certainly hard to write about), the institutions themselves, in all their passing phases, nonetheless shape human actions and technologies in significant ways. Consequently, it is important to understand them. When people are championing the decline of old institutions and the rise of new ones, for example, it's always worthwhile to look around to see if there are any old ones that sweeping visions take for granted.

For instance, while many people talk about the new landscape of business and finance, it's worth noting that the "bottom line" is a 600-year-old relic from double-entry bookkeeping. The institutions of profit-and-loss accounting still exert remarkable influence over our thinking. Reengineers may have told us all to "forget all we know," but few of those caught up in reengineering were allowed to forget the bottom line.

Or, again, while people rightly talk so enthusiastically about the new economics of e-business, the power of the Web, and the emerging markets, it's worth noticing how much is predicated on the continuation of advertising. Many Web business plans assume the continuing existence of large companies shelling out very large sums to advertise on the Web. Yet those same business plans also champion the end of those same large companies and the availability of "perfect" information. Like some of the unplug-and-pay course providers, they want both to destroy and to preserve the same institutions. To extend Geoffrey Nunberg's metaphor, they hope to blow out the dam and sail on the lake at the same time.

It's equally easy for people to dismiss as residual institutions that have a good deal of dominating life in them. Some lawyers, for example, have promoted the idea of a "law of cyberspace." But there's little reason to believe that the old-fashioned law of material people and places has exhausted its writ yet. E-commerce relies on quite conventional laws to do with warranties, checks, misrepresentation, contracts, and the like.

Code of Code

Many people have claimed that the law of copyright barely merits even the term *residual*. Copyright developed as principally a document-based phenomenon. Society took the constraint of paper and built a resourceful institution around it. The law relied on the difficulty of copying texts to do much of its enforcement work for it. It was undoubtedly impractical to think of tracking down individuals who hand copied a few lines of a document. Given the demands of printing and distribution, however, anyone who wanted to copy on a large scale presented a large enough target for the law to pursue.

Digital technology has undermined these implicit assumptions. Where we might need a sizable operation to make a thousand copies of the Microsoft Word manual, we could send out thousands of copies of the software from our PCs with little more than a flick of the wrist. Still, it's too early to proclaim that copyright is dead. It still makes Bill Gates a very rich man. It will probably continue to do so. For while copying and distributing are easily achieved on the 'Net, so are bots to track down sources of large-scale digital distribution. What the material resources of paper once constrained is now constrained by the software code inherent in digital objects.[3]

This deployment of the constraints of software has led Larry Lessig of Harvard Law School to talk of "the code of code."[4] The legal code, instead of emerging from the resourcefulness of physical objects, now reflects software code. Looking from this perspective suggests that copyright and its institutions are not disappearing. Rather, they are mutating. As a result, the digital codification of copyright is likely to shift the institutional equilibrium that paper once helped achieve.

Until now, copyright has been a paradoxical and changing compromise between public and private good. In the name of the public's right to knowledge, copyright law curiously gave producers the right to withhold their knowledge from the public as they chose. And in defense of an individual's intellectual property, copyright insisted on the public's right to that property after a certain number of years. Society and copyright owners offered each other a quid pro quo.[5]

Software code respects the quid (protection of property) without yielding the quo (the public interest). Code now makes it possible to decide in fine degrees of detail not only who can or cannot use a certain digital text, but also how it can be used. It can prevent you from listening to a piece of music for a second time, pasting a text into another document, or sending an image to a friend. But it can also prevent the public from getting ultimate access to a copyrighted object forever. The "public domain" and all the public goods connected to it have no part in the new encoded balance.

Who these changes will favor remains unclear. Some critics

suggest that, though they are being done in the name of the individual creator, they are more likely to favor large organizations that can control the necessary software and hardware to manage the code and its enforcement. If this is the case, then again society seems to be going forward to the past. It took more than a century and a half to wrest control over intellectual property from the hands of publishers in the Stationer's Register and place it in the hands of individual authors. Now, despite the talk of the 'Net's disintermediation, it may be swinging back toward publishers and corporate ownership.

For us this debate, unresolved and ever-changing as it is, principally serves to highlight the way in which the language of information and technology can blind people to social and institutional issues. Here, that language can suggest that information is indifferent to institutions, organizations, and material constraints, while the constraints of software are actually enabling shifts in institutional power and control over such things as intellectual property. As Peter Lyman, the former university librarian at Berkeley, has argued, attending to the informational side of intellectual property and not the social and institutional side will not make the latter go away. It will merely produce bad policy, bad law, and weak public institutions.[6]

Beyond the Ecology

Dismissing institutions inevitably blinds people to the need to try to change and reform them. The regional knowledge ecologies that we discussed in chapter 6 help show the sort of issues that may arise from this blindness.

Two types of endism make the relevant institutions hard to see here. The first is the end of institutions: If institutions are going to die, there is no need to worry about them. If, however, we simply assume they will die, but they do not, they are likely to bite back unseen. The second endism concerns the end or death of distance. This claim makes nonsense out of regional advantage. But regional advantage is not nonsense. It is a significant economic factor, one moreover that both reflects and is reflected in regional institutions.

For those who do acknowledge the importance of regions and their institutions, it becomes important to ask what happens when people or organizations have to operate between regions, in particular between regions with distinct institutions. Institutions that might be a resource for organizations within the region can become a constraint when dealing with people outside.

On a very large scale, the clash between Europe and the United States over personal information suggests the sort of clash we might expect. Europeans are pursuing a code of tight and highly restricted privacy, preventing organizations from divulging information about their customers. North Americans, by contrast, are less concerned about the commercial use of personal information, though much more concerned about government use. The contrasting approaches reflect different cultures and histories. Europeans in general are more suspicious of business than of government. North Americans in general are more suspicious of government than business.

Anyone trading between the two has increasingly to deal with such differences, which can put deep ridges in the supposedly smooth surface of the global economy. Historically, trading across different regions and different institutional "regimes" has called for institutional and organizational creativity that goes well beyond formal, governmental regulation—and moves much more swiftly.[7] It has called for interesting articulations of firms and formal institutions. We suspect it will again. Those who insist that neither regions nor institutions are significant, that distance and organizations are dead, will have trouble coping with this sort of innovation. To play with boundaries—of firms, networks, communities, regions, and institutions—as innovation increasingly seems to demand, requires first acknowledging them.

These issues about resources and constraints, structure and spontaneity, reach and reciprocity, and about dominant, residual, and emergent institutions are ones that affect design—from the design of digital appliances to the design of transnational organizations and institutions. In the conditions in which we live, we are all, as we suggested at the beginning, both producers and consumers of designed objects. So such questions and their implications affect us all, presenting themselves to us with greater speed and greater urgency than ever before. As we said at the outset, we do not have solutions to offer. We only know that solutions will be much harder to find if we drive at the problems with tunnel vision—if, to repeat our long list, peripheries and margins, practices and communities, organizations and institutions are left out or swept out of consideration.

Notes

A Note on URLs

As much of this book concerns the popular portrayal and popular perception of information technology, we have deliberately drawn on popular, rather than scholarly sources wherever possible. We have used newspapers, magazines, radio broadcasts, and, most important, the World Wide Web. Moreover, wherever we could, we have also provided URLs (Uniform Resource Locators) for print material that appears on the Web as well.

In directing readers to these Internet sources, we face the problems that every seasoned Internet user will recognize. Publishing is a slow, deliberative process. The 'Net, by contrast, is lightning fast, its content often shifting or disappearing. (We discuss this contrast in chapter 7.) Trying to pin down references in these conditions is remarkably difficult.

Nonetheless, where we have used the Web as a source we have provided URLs indicating that source. Before sending our manuscript to the press in July 1999, we attempted to revisit each of these URLs. Where we were successful, we have given the date (1999, July 21). Often, inevitably, we were not successful. Several pages we cite or quote have since been taken down, moved, changed. In such cases, we give the date when we last successfully visited that site.

Still, some URLs with the July date will not necessarily lead to the page cited for a variety of reasons. Frames technology, for instance, does not identify different pages separately. Some sites will maintain a URL but change the page's content. And several sites (Wired.com and CNET.com among them) will not let you go directly to individual pages. On these sites, you must go to their "front door" and, generally, use their search engine.

Acknowledgments

1. See Brown and Duguid, 1996a, 1996b.

Introduction: Tunneling Ahead

1. Terkle, 1995.
2. Cutting off such resources can make a significant difference. Consider, for example, the historic Nixon–Kennedy debates of 1960. The majority of those who listened to the radio, who heard only the voices, apparently inclined to judge Nixon the winner. Those who watched television, who saw Kennedy's ease and Nixon's unease, leaned the other way.
3. Tenner, 1997.
4. Duguid, 1996b.
5. The term "infomated" comes from Zuboff, 1988.
6. Nor does widening the "bandwidth"—a standard strategy of adding more information when things go wrong—offer the solution. (See our notion of "Moore's Law" solutions in chapter 1).

Chapter 1: Limits to Information

1. Gates, 1995, p. 21; Gordon Bell and James N. Gray, quoted in Nardi and O'Day, 1999; Phillips, quoted in Napoli, 1999.
2. SETI stands for Search for Extra Terrestrial Intelligence. For more information, see http://seti.ssl.berkeley.edu [1999, July 21].
3. The notion of the "third wave" comes from the futurist Alvin Toffler's (1980) book of the same name.

4. Indeed, the degree to which we complain about such technologies when they do go wrong indicates the extent to which we have all become dependent on them to go right. The apprehension about the Y2K bug, which some predict may allow tiny embedded chips to bring huge social institutions to a halt, is itself a sign of how deeply enmeshed these things are in our lives.

5. Sometime around 2012, it has been predicted, Moore's Law will come up against the physical limitations of current microchip components, though by then solid-state components may well have been replaced.

6. Kelly, 1997.

7. Negroponte, 1995. John Tukey coined the term *bit*. It stands for "binary digit."

8. It's worth remembering that formal information theory, while it holds the bit as a central concern, is indifferent to meaning. Claude Shannon, who with Warren Weaver laid the foundations of modern information theory, is quite clear about this: "the semantic aspects of communication are irrelevant to the engineering aspects" (Shannon and Weaver, 1964, p. 8).

9. The pervasive image of the new open frontier only works if we forget the presence on the old frontier of the U.S. Army, the Church of Latter-Day Saints, and myriad other organizations and institutions large and small (let alone its native inhabitants) that shaped the frontier.

10. For "electronic frontier," see Rheingold, 1993; for "global village," see McLuhan, 1962; and for "electronic cottages," see Toffler, 1980, and chapter 3.

11. The phrase "information wants to be free" is usually attributed to the author Bruce Sterling.

12. Castells, 1996.

13. The SETI project (see note 2), after all, acknowledges that the universe has long been capable of producing raw information. Finding intelligence in its midst is a different matter.

14. *Business Week*, 30 June 1975, p. 48.; Toffler, 1980, p. 205.

15. Negroponte, 1995, p. 187.
16. For the dismissal of the pencil, see Petrosky, 1990, p. 331.
17. See the IBM advertisement in the *New York Times*, 30 June 1999, sec. C, pp. 13–20.
18. Gates, 1995, p. 5.
19. The idea is certainly a tempting one to the weary business traveler and is echoed in the curious enigma of the laptop. Ads for these suggest that laptops can be so "loaded" with communications software that you can travel anywhere and remain a virtual presence in your own office. Yet in suggesting this possibility, they make you wonder why you need to travel at all.
20. Reagle, 1996.
21. Readers of Toffler's (1980) *Third Wave* will recognize the first three terms here, particularly the first, *demassification*, to which Toffler adds three subtypes: demassification of media, production, and society. Notions of *disintermediation* and *decentralization* are features, for example, in the work of George Gilder or Kevin Kelly's (1997) writing on the "new economy." There are more "Ds" that could be added, such as Kevin Kelly's *displacement* and *devolution*.
22. Downes and Mui, 1998.
23. Coase, 1937. Coase's theory should be seen not so much as an attack on neoclassical individualism as an attempt to save it from itself. We return to transaction cost theory briefly in our discussion of the future of the firm in chapter 6. There we take a "knowledge based," rather than transaction cost, view of the firm.
24. Among the targets of early, landmark trust cases were Northern Securities (1911), Standard Oil (1911), and American Tobacco (1911). In November 1998, Philip Morris acquired several brands from the Ligget corporation.
25. *The Economist*, 13 December 1997.
26. Daniel, 1996, table 3.2. We take up this topic again in chapter 8.
27. The concentration of media ownership was the subject of a

special edition of *The Nation* (March 13, 1997). The picture drawn there recalled Frank Norris's famous image of the railroads as an "octopus," but, as with any list we might produce, the *Nation*'s octopus is already well out of date.

28. Paul Krugman, quoted in Kelly, 1998.

29. The appearance of the fax provides a conventional example of network effects at work. At first, for most people, it was hardly worth owning a fax machine because so few others did. But with each new buyer, owning a fax became more useful and so more valuable. Each addition to the network meant that everyone had more people to fax to and receive faxes from. By the late 1980s, the network had grown to such a size that owning one became almost a necessity.

The fax spread on the back of nonproprietary standards that allowed many different firms to compete in the fax market, as they still do. But if someone had owned those standards, the results would have been quite different. Here the obvious example is not the fax, but the video recorder and the battle between VHS and Betamax. This battle was in effect a race between the two to establish network effects. In such races, a small lead can produce a "tipping" effect, where whoever gets ahead can quickly end up taking it all. In such conditions, firms will grow, not shrink.

30. Raik-Allen, 1998.

31. Sassen, 1996, p. 38.

32. With the rise of the Internet, many people argue that information can travel straight from its producer to its consumer, without need for any intermediaries. Kelly (1997), for example, envisages music going from musicians to listeners and then leaps to gourmet coffee from producers to drinkers. Undoubtedly disintermediation along these lines is happening; however, there's a good deal of wishful endism here, too. Specific examples always seem to include unpopular professions that people want to see ended, with banking and real estate falling in behind travel agents and car salespeople. One curious example

of a job relentlessly pushed off the stage yet refusing to sing its own swan song is that of the humble meter reader. Most recently, Jeremy Rifkin (1995) sang a requiem for this job in 1995. Curiously, so did articles on the effects of computers in 1970 in *National Geographic*, and as far back as 1952 in *Fortune*.

33. Fukuyama and Shulsky, 1997, p. 63

34. Attewell, 1994, p. 36.

35. Fukyama and Shulsky, 1997, p. 11.

36. Innis, 1991. For a case study of previously decentralized business organizations that were later centralized, see Duguid and Silva Lopes, 1999.

37. Fidler, 1997.

38. The same long arm of technology has led to the direct intervention of politics into battlefield planning; for example, though President Bush said he would leave decisions in the Gulf War to local commanders, the White House began to exercise veto power and control over the conduct of the war, after a smart bomb went astray and drew bad press.

39. Shoshona Zuboff, quoted in Lohr, 1996.

40. Meanwhile, Royal Dutch/Shell, one of the most well known and widely applauded decentralizers of the past decade, has announced that it will recentralize its "treasury." Decentralization had been too costly and inefficient. More generally, the *Economist* magazine's "Intelligence Unit" has noted a trend toward "shared services" in large corporations—and what they describe reads very much like recentralization.

41. Negroponte (1995) suggests that "a few strokes of the keyboard" will close the generation gap (p. 203).

42. Nunberg, 1996. Coffman and Odlyzko (1998) show how many projections about the current and future growth of the 'Net extrapolate from a particularly rapid point in its development, failing to note that both before and after this point, the growth curve, though impressive, was far less steep.

43. Hobsbawm, 1977, pp. 61–62. The spread of the telephone was more dramatic, growing from 14 miles in 1845 in the United

States to 670,000 in 1886, but the infrastructure of the telephone was far easier to build than railway lines. The spread of the radio was more impressive yet.

44. See Campbell-Kelly and Aspray, 1996.
45. Wellman (1988) provides one of the few worthwhile studies of the effects of information technologies on social communities and networks.

Chapter 2: Agents and Angels

1. Distinguishing a computer from a human is the essence of the famous Turing test, developed by mathematician Alan Turing (1963). He argued that if you couldn't tell the difference then you could say the machine was intelligent. Shallow Red is not quite there yet. Indeed, the continuation of the exchange suggests that Shallow Red is still rather shallow (though pleasantly honest):

   What are VSRs?
   The botmaster has not provided me with a definition of "VSRs." Thank you for asking. The botmaster shall provide me with an appropriate definition.

   Shallow Red could be found at http://www.neurostudio.com [1998, October 21]. It has since been upgraded to Red, though it is not yet quite as deep as that promotion might suggest.
2. The lists you get if you shop for other people or buy gifts online make it clear that tastes and tracks are different things.
3. The study, done at Yale, was reported on National Public Radio's *All Things Considered*, 18 November 1998.
4. Leonard, 1997, p. 186.
5. Hoggdon, 1997, p. 15.
6. Though less so, perhaps, than with the telegraph, which the president of the Magnetic Telegraph Co., W. M. Swain, suggested might be the fulfillment of scriptural prophecy.

7. These quotations come from IBM's research into intelligent agents, reported on the 'Net at: http://www.networking.ibm. com/iag/iagwp1.html [1998, November 16]. IBM has since abandoned this work and taken down the site. (See http:// www.networking.ibm.com/iag/iaghome.html [1999, July 21].)

8. Gates, 1995, p. 83.

9. See Franklin, [1995]; for a taxonomy of agents, see Franklin and Graessner, 1996.

10. People familiar with the old programs of artificial intelligence (AI) will recognize some of these redefinitions. For classic AI, it eventually became apparent that such activities could not be reduced to notions of mental representation and thus made computationally tractable. The real strength of AI came from recognizing that computers were not like people.

11. Pretext Forum, 1997.

12. Maes, Guttman, and Moukas, 1999. See also Jonkheer, 1999.

13. It has been suggested, for example, that if bots can match learners' needs with teachers' capabilities, then the distance university will be no more than a software program with an income stream (Chellappa, Barua, and Whinston, 1997). See chapter 7 for a further discussion of this point.

14. For more on this see chapter 8.

15. None, unfortunately, took us to the alternative and more usual spelling, *knowbot*.

16. In all, visions of automated brokering often trivialize the complexities of a broker's work.

17. The Polish economic historian, Witold Kula (1986) tells the fascinating story of the standardization of measurements and how important that was to international trade. Another historian, Theodore Porter (1994), has shown how standardized grades enabled the Chicago Corn Exchange to broker deals between farmers in the old West and merchants around the world.

18. De Long and Froomkin, 1999.

19. Maynard, 1998; Markus, 1997.

20. These quotations come from the IBM intelligent agent research (see note 7).
21. Of course, this sort of breakdown is not always accidental. The opening of *Romeo and Juliet* reminds us that rivals can deliberately refuse this sort of implicit negotiation.
22. Indeed, part of the process of negotiation involves negotiating what sort of behavior, formal or informal, is appropriate. People have to understand what rules apply, for identical behavior can have different consequences depending on the situation. A wave across a room might welcome a friend or make you highest bidder at an auction. Recently, a young boy was discovered to be highest bidder in an eBay on-line auction. He bid $900,000, believing, apparently, that he was taking part in an on-line game. ("13-Year-Old Makes $3 million in Bids on eBay," *USA Today Online* [Online], 29 April 1999. Available: http://www.usatoday.com/life/cyber/tech/ctf027.htm [1999, July 21].)
23. Lave, 1988.
24. "No tolerance" policing refuses to turn such a blind eye. Its critics have argued that while such policing may meet short-term goals, it can be profoundly damaging to the social fabric, destroying for example, police relations with minority communities.
25. Jeffrey Kephart quoted in Schwartz, 1998, p. 72. See also Ward, 1998. Work of the HEDG group at MIT (http://www.lucifer.com/~sasha/HEDG/HEDG.html [1999, July 21]) suggests that cooperation among bots may help offset these wild swings, but there is significant debate among scientists about what cooperation entails.
26. De Long and Froomkin, 1999.
27. These quotations also come from the IBM intelligent agent research (see note 7).
28. In Oakeshott's (1967) words:

> By "judgement" I mean the tacit or implicit component of knowledge, the ingredient which is not merely unspecified in propositions, but which is unspecifiable in propositions. It is

> *the component of knowledge which does not appear in the form of rules and which, therefore, cannot be resolved into information or itemized in the manner characteristic of information. (p. 167)*

29. Humphrys, 1997.
30. Jennings et al., 1996.
31. This may turn out to be the biggest challenge in adjusting Y2K problems.
32. These quotations also come from the IBM intelligent agent research (see note 7).
33. Quoted in Quittner, 1995.
34. Those who are unhappy, by contrast, can express their rage by posting messages to the microsoft.crash.crash.crash or microsoft.sucks newsgroups.
35. The car, by the way, found a buyer within a week.
36. Lyman, 1997.
37. Quittner, 1995.
38. Leonard, 1997, p. 192.
39. "Collaborative tracking" of this sort can easily fall prey to Goodhart's law, which states that statistical regularities break down when used for control. Because the digital footprints people leave across the Web can provide guidance, people have an interest in creating fake footprints.
40. Markoff, 1999.
41. See chapter 1 for our discussion of Moore's Law solutions.
42. Geer, 1998.
43. To illustrate his point by analogy, Geer (1998) reveals that, while conventional handwritten signatures are a relatively reliable means of verification, "actually verifying handwritten signatures" is so costly that banks generally bother only for checks over $20,000. Below that they are willing to incur the risk of insecurity rather than the cost of security. With digital signatures, too, banks must balance their risk against the costs of the full organizational and institutional infrastructure of verification. The encryption may be more or less the same for

both high- and low-risk transactions, but the important procedural formalities (the weak links in the chain) will be quite
different.

44. Giddens, 1990, p. 170.
45. The SETI project, which we mentioned in chapter 1 (see
chapter 1, note 2), is an interesting case in point. Thousands of
people are downloading data over the Internet and letting it
run on their machines in the belief that they are processing
data from outer space. It is the reassuring presence of the University of California in the arrangement that keeps at bay the
idea that our machines might be processing data for the
National Security Agency (NSA) or even providing data for a
major marketing venture.

Chapter 3: Home Alone

1. http://www.microsoft.com/QUESTIONS/who_motivates_
us/Lusk_text.htm [1999, July 21].
2. Toffler, 1980, p. 221. For *gemeinschaft*, see Tonnies, 1963. Some
of the predictions of the new pastoral life recall the enthusiasm for "garden cities" at the turn of the century, and some
the gap between promise and reality that Dickens's (1968)
Martin Chuzzlewit found on the new frontier.
3. See Barlow, n.d.
4. See http://www.uli.org/pubs/LUD/landus27.htm [1999, May
17], reporting a survey of office vacancy by CB Commer-
cial/Torto Wheaton Research.
5. Lyon, 1988.
6. Forester, 1988, p. 229.
7. Edwards and Field-Hendry, 1996.
8. The often-repeated 41 million figure appears to come from a
Pacific Bell survey. Telecommunications companies inevitably
have a strong interest in promoting telecommuting.
9. See Varma et al., 1998.
10. Dix, 1994.

11. Berger, 1999.

12. Council on Environmental Quality, 1993, ch. 7.

13. See our discussion of this in chapter 1.

14. Toffler, 1980, pp. 212–13.

15. In fairness to Toffler, we should note that he claims that "social forces" are behind moves toward the electronic cottage. Yet, what he offers as examples of social forces are employees who "hate" their office, accumulate "frustration," and are "willing" to work at home. These forces are undoubtedly important, but they are individual and psychological rather than social.

16. On the release of Macintosh's system 8.5 software, newspapers quoted an Apple employee saying triumphantly, "And my machine hasn't even crashed yet." The exclamation nonetheless suggests how fragile the technology still is. (We wish, by the way, that we could say the same.)

17. In this case, an effortless installation required two computers, two ISPs, two phone lines, a fax, and significant Internet experience to get the job done. Both that technology and experience are often beyond someone trying to set up a small business. Six months later the diarist decided to change to another ISP with worldwide access numbers. While the ISP's own software was again buggy, attempts to override it were met with the response from the ISP that "if you don't use our software, we will not provide technical support for your problems."

18. Dix, 1994.

19. Berger, 1999.

20. Anderton, 1998.

21. Despina Katsikakis, quoted in Anderton, 1998.

22. Brand, 1994.

23. At the time it was introduced, some feared that the installation of Windows 95 might contribute to a slowdown in national productivity in the United States (Fried, 1995).

24. Strassmann, 1997, p. 77.

25. Toffler, 1980, p. 215.

26. Mundie, quoted in *Wired* 6.12 (December) 1998.

27. The family is often one of the missing "distractions" in young people's lives. Talk about the home office often overlooks how hard it can be to work at home with young people in the house.

28. Odlyzko, 1998. The word *migration* is often used to describe the process whereby content moves from outdated software to a current version. It may thus conjure up the image of people with neatly packed trunks waiting on the wharf for an ocean liner to take them to a promised land. The reality of technological migration, however, often appears more like the flight of refugees grabbing what little they can while escaping marauding invaders.

29. Berger, 1999.

30. *Wall Street Journal*, 30 April 1998.

31. Jaroff and Ratan, 1995.

32. Harris, 1994, p. 2.

33. David, 1990.

34. Louis Uchitelle, "Productivity Set Fast Pace in Late 1998," *New York Times*, 10 February 1999, sec. C, p. 1. Strassmann (1999) argues that the recent boom in productivity can be attributed almost entirely to interest rates.

35. Wells, 1902. The comments about Niagara Falls appear in Wells, 1986.

36. Engelbart, interviewed on National Public Radio's *Morning Edition*, 11 December 1998.

37. Downes and Mui, 1998, p. 29.

38. This argument offers another case of separating a logic of information from the logic of humanity (see chapter 1). It's hard to know who measures the "exponential" progress of technology if not humanity—unless technology is allowed to set its own standards.

39. Carey, 1989.

40. Mokyr, 1990.

41. These developments of electricity and computers show on a

large scale something of the perennially difficult process from invention to innovation, during which technologies are socialized, grand ideas trimmed, and practical uses developed. The Internet has taken more than twenty years to socialize, and it too has a way to go. We take up the topic of innovation in chapter 6. These problems don't bedevil "high" technologies only. According to *Prospect*, a British magazine, a study by the British Department of Trade and Industry found that the time from invention to application of the ballpoint pen was fifty-eight years, the zipper thirty-two (*Prospect*, 5 January 1999, p. 5).

42. Occasionally the lack of social resources in the home may be recognized but not well understood. As we note in chapter 4, British Telecom tried to overcome the isolation of its home-working operators by piping the sound of background chatter into their home offices (Walsh and Bayma, 1995).

43. In his experiments that produced the telephone, Bell had actually been trying to advance the cause of the telegraph. It was almost by chance that he discovered an alternative use.

44. Pool et al., 1977; Kraut, 1994.

Chapter 4: Practice Makes Process

1. Hammer, 1996, p. 17.

2. The economist Stephen Roach estimated that despite huge investment, information technology was only contributing about 0.16 percent to productivity growth in the early 1990s, which was less than its contribution in the previous decade. See Lester, 1998, p. 40.

3. In his book *The Rise of the Network Society*, Castells (1996) describes the ideal feedback loop as follows:

    A networked, deeply interdependent economy emerges that becomes increasingly able to apply its progress in technology, knowledge, and management to technology, knowledge, and management themselves. Such a virtuous circle should lead to greater productivity and efficiency, given the right conditions of equally dramatic organizational and institutional changes. (p. 67)

4. Hammer and Champy, 1993. The phrase "the crisis that will not go away" is theirs (p. 7).

5. Shao, 1995.

6. See Blair, Taylor, and Randle, 1998.

7. GM, for example, effectively reengineered production in creating the Saturn line. But it was prepared to wipe billions off the books in doing so. Strassmann (1997) points to the low correlation between IT investment and results.

8. Nynex, for example, shed 25 percent of its workforce during reengineering. "Re-engineering Europe," 1994.

9. De Cock and Hipkin, 1997.

10. Sabel, quoted in Lester, 1998, p. 62.

11. March, 1991, p. 111.

12. Wenger, 1998.

13. See, for example, Wenger's explanation of the "C, F, & J thing" (1998, pp. 35–38), where processors are told to manipulate some figures according to a company algorithm without any further explanation.

14. See Davenport, 1993, p. 12: "Because large firms' structures do not reflect their cross-functional processes, only those in positions overlooking multiple functions may be able to see opportunities for innovation."

15. Hammer, 1996, p. 117.

16. This process-without-people viewpoint may indeed account for what some critics regard as business process reengineering's callous disregard for human rather than economic capital. The maxim "Forget all you know" doesn't show much interest in accrued human capital.

17. Walsh and Bayma, 1995.

18. Orr, 1996.

19. As the workplace sociologist Stephen Barley (1996) of Stanford

University argues, these reps are in many ways models of the new knowledge worker. They work alone, with sophisticated technology, supported by extensive information resources.

20. Hammer also briefly discusses tech reps, but he gives little sense of how they develop understanding or deal with the unexpected. He primarily affirms that reengineering helps them. Hammer, 1996, pp. 26–28.

21. At the time, that documentation was mostly kept on paper. It was ripe, however, for digitization.

22. Orr, 1996, p. 1.

23. As noted in chapter 1, many prognostications about the way people should work in the information age tend to assume that people are unpredictable but machines are not.

24. Our own favorites come from the popular e-mail software, Eudora, which occasionally produces messages that include "No one is listening, so you might as well stop typing" or, following an unintelligible error report, "And a fat lot of good that does you."

25. Reps also had to make sense of the machines to explain problems to customers. Without a coherent explanation, it is hard to keep the customer's confidence in the rep, the machine, or the corporation. "It's not in the documentation" is unacceptable on all fronts. Orr argues that reps also have to work on the social system of which the machine is but a part. This is common practice for most people in jobs like this. You can see it in the word computer technicians use for problem, *bug*, which is interestingly ambiguous. It can refer to a problem in the software. But computer support personnel also use it to refer to the complaint about a problem. To fix a bug then, may require working on the software, or it may require working with the user to sort out their difficulties, which most technicians realize is the important matter to clear up. (The observation about *bug* comes from Bret Pettichord via *Red Rock Eater News Service* [Online], 24 November 1998. Available: http://www.egroups.com/list/rre [1999, July 21]).

26. For a criticism of the notion of knowledge as tool, see Lave, 1988.

27. Their linear structure also distinguishes stories from collections of information, providing, for example, different properties from hypertext though the "information" both contain might be the same.

28. This division between discovery and retelling inevitably oversimplifies the subtleties of storytelling. For example, in telling a story to pass along an insight, it's quite common to discover something you didn't understand before.

29. As the historian Brian Stock (1983) points out, the orthodox and the dissenters often share the same stories; it's interpretation that separates them. See also our discussion of Stock in chapter 7 and Stanley Fish in chapter 8.

30. Toulmin, 1972, p. 35.

31. Orr, 1996, p. 161.

32. See Bowker and Star's (1999) important study. Etienne Wenger's (1998) study of the insurance claims processors shows the challenge of this form filling, routine though it may seem. What Wenger reveals is less routine than routinization as the processors' struggle to produce order and consistency out of the highly disordered and inconsistent flows of information coming into the company. They have constantly to decide what, on the one hand, anomalous as it may seem, is actually routine at base, and what, on the other, straightforward though it might appear, should be marked for special attention. By transforming the individual demands of clients, with all the peculiarities and idiosyncrasies the situation and the health of each brings, into the general categories that the organization is geared to deal with, processors negotiate the distance between the environment and company while striving to keep both customers and supervisors happy.

33. It's similar to the need to punch key 5½—i.e., not quite 5 or 6—on a telephone menu.

34. Suchman, 1996, p. 415.

35. Evolutionary economics looks closely at routine, as does Stinchcombe (1990) on whose ideas we lean here.

36. From the perspective of process, however, it may appear that members of an organization divide between the two categories. Most are expected to follow routine. Some—those in R&D, corporate strategy, and the like—are expected to improvise. But again, in practice, things don't break down so easily. People in the labs, for example, have to learn to tie their improvisations to company routine, otherwise their work detaches itself from the company and its goals. (We'll discuss this tension within innovation in chapter 6.)

37. This sort of processing is evident in the shoppers Lave (1988) studied. See chapter 3.

38. Hammer and Champy, 1993.

39. *FAQ* stands for "frequently asked questions."

40. Andrea Hornett, in preparation. See our discussion of Networks of Practice in chapter 6.

41. Granovetter, 1985, p. 502.

42. Ellen O'Connor, 1999.

Chapter 5: Learning—in Theory and in Practice

1. http://www.microsoft.com/exchange/community/lotus_km.asp [1998, December 20]; http://www.microsoft.com/mcsp/coreso.htm [1998, December 20].

2. Donkin, 1998.

3. On its Microsoft Exchange Web site, Microsoft formerly accused its competitor Lotus of merely rebranding old-fashioned groupware to claim relevance in the escalating knowledge wars (http://www.microsoft.com/exchange/community/lotus_km.asp [1998, December 20]). In response, Lotus admitted that it has relabeled its groupware, but argued that this merely showed that Lotus had always been concerned with knowledge: "But knowledge management is nothing new. It's a different label applied to something that Lotus has been

working on for years" (http://www.lotus.com/news/topstories. nsf/a1d792857da52f638525630f004e7ab8/ee02468b55e0824b8 5256598004a827d?OpenDocument [1999, July 21]).

4. See chapter 7 for a further discussion of related "conduit" metaphors. As Reddy (1979) notes, these metaphors make it easy to overlook questions of meaning in discussions of information.

5. Shannon and Weaver, 1964.

6. Davenport and Prusak (1998) use the Ford example to talk about "corporate amnesia" (p. x).

7. Professor Amin Rajan, quoted in "Managing Knowledge Is Latest Business Buzz," 1998.

8. Stewart, 1997, p. 88.

9. Leonard-Barton, 1995, p. 7.

10. Cole, 1999, see chapter 8, "Adoption, Adaptation, and Reaction at Hewlett Packard."

11. This is how the story is commonly told. O'Dell and Grayson (1998) trace the remark to Junkins, CEO of Texas Instruments, who said, "If TI only knew what TI knows." It was then echoed by Pratt, chairman of HP, who said, "I wish we knew what we know at HP."

12. "Managing Knowledge Is Latest Business Buzz," 1998.

13. Lotus made the same shift to information but, adding in expertise to the equation, is a little more cautious about making technology the central issue: "Knowledge Management [is] the systematic leveraging of information and expertise to improve organizational innovation, responsiveness, productivity and competency" (http://www.lotus.com/home.nsf/welcome/ km [1998, December 20]).

14. Lave and Wenger, 1993.

15. See, for example, Karin Knorr Cetina's (1999) study, *Epistemic Cultures.*

16. Heart interviewed in Gates, 1998.

17. Ryle, 1949.

18. The last example helps overcome conventional divisions between theory and practice. A management theorist is a

practitioner. But his or her practice is the practice of theorizing, whereas a manager's is the practice of managing. Consequently, each has different "know how."

19. Miller and Gildea, 1987.

20. Whalen and Vinkhuyzen, forthcoming.

21. Jack Whalen, interview with authors, 16 June 1998.

22. Polanyi, 1966.

23. Dickens, 1969, p. 1. Part of the enjoyment of the passage is that Mr. Gradgrind's lecture, while trying to form the mind of a reasoning animal, contains not one fact, only opinion and imperatives.

24. Bandyopadhyay, 1989.

25. Quoted in Bandyopadhyay, 1989, p. 45.

26. Too often the technology people work with, while designed for learning, produces this sort of damaging isolation, allowing people little insight into where their work goes, what it means, or why it matters. A couple of years ago a young architect wrote an article in *Architecture* complaining that spending her day in front of a CAD (computer aided design) machine prevented her from gaining any understanding of the practice of architecture and the path that leads from clients to buildings. All she executed were tasks, and in isolation they gave no real insight into how they had arisen or what role they played. *Architecture* 185 (1): 30.

27. Orr understands the Xerox reps, for example, in terms of their collective development of the identity of a rep. The company, however, often addresses them as though the identity they are developing is that of a Xerox employee. The two may be quite distinct.

28. Dretske, 1981.

29. Bateson, 1972.

30. Hayek, 1988, pp. 114–16. Hayek's claim primarily reflects the idea that everything is social, so adding the word *social* serves no real purpose. A recent book on Hannah Arendt, arguing that she used the word so capriciously that it could mean

almost anything, was called *The Attack of the Blob: Hannah Arendt's Concept of the Social* (Pitkin, 1998). The word *blob* in the title stands for Arendt's use of *social*.

31. The first thing to remember, of course, is that Crusoe is a fictional character.

32. Marx, 1947, p. 48.

33. Sartre, 1957, quoted in Warnock, 1960, pp. 127–28.

34. See Feenburg (1995) for an insightful discussion of the social character of illness.

35. These examples are from Dorothy Leonard-Barton and Silvia Sensiper (1998) and Kenneth Arrow (1984), respectively.

36. See van Maanen and Barley (1984) for "occupational communities"; Strauss (1978) and the following chapter for "social world."

37. Listservs are e-mail lists that forward messages sent to a single address to everyone who subscribes to that list. Members of large lists rarely know who the other members are. Some lists are edited so that only messages approved by the editor are forwarded.

38. This demand for explicit communication puts a strain on that communication. Creating the insights from which tips are written is part of the practice of Xerox reps. Turning these insights into written tips for the reps' database, however, is another practice that reps don't necessarily find easy.

39. Weick, 1976.

40. Here we are using *negotiation* in the *implicit* sense that we outlined in chapter 2.

41. Hammer and Champy, 1993.

42. Sitkin and Stickel, 1996.

Chapter 6: Innovating Organization, Husbanding Knowledge

1. Professor Arturo Pérez Reyes interviewed on National Public Radio's *Morning Edition*, 3 June 1999.

2. The $436 million figure comes from the Internet Index 14

(July) 1996 [Online]. Available: http://www.openmarket.com/
intindex/96-07.htm [1999, July 21]. Commerce department
figures from http://www.ecommerce.gov/pressrelease.html
[1999, July 21].

3. Gurley, 1998.
4. Many of the papers from this meeting appeared in a special
issue of *California Management Review*, Spring 1998.
5. See Smith and Alexander, 1988.
6. O'Connor, 1999.
7. Wilson, 1955; J.Whyte, 1956.
8. If homogenization were more successful in practice, there
would perhaps be less need for all the exhortations for members to join or form a community.
9. The organization, in this regard, resembles an "imagined community" (Anderson, 1991; see chapter 7 for a discussion of this
notion). People are aware of and identify with their common
membership and organizational identity, but that does not
override their local loyalties or restrict the firm's diversity.
10. Smith's (1937) *Wealth of Nations* opens with the famous example of the pin maker. Working alone, Smith estimated, a
laborer could make perhaps 20 pins a day. With the labor
divided among different specialties, the output per laborer was
4,800.
11. Becker and Murphy (1993) suggest that the coordination
problems involved here impose limits on the extent of the
division of labor.
12. Bennis and Biederman, 1997, p. 78.
13. Jacobson and Hillkirk, 1986, pp. 69–72.
14. Von Burg and Kenney, in preparation, p. 16.
15. Quoted in Lester, 1998, p. 120.
16. Descriptions of the group at PARC are very much those of a
community of practice. Alan Kay, one of the central
researchers, talks of the dynamics of the group as, "like those
on a good basketball team. Everybody has to be able to play
the whole game. Each person should have certain things

they're better at than the others, but everyone should be pretty good at anything" (Hiltzik, 1999, p. 16). And Michael Hiltzik compares them to "orchestra members composing and rehearsing a symphony at the same time" (ibid., p. 225). Hiltzik's description gets at the near simultaneous production and deployment of knowledge within such a group.

17. Quoted in S. Levy, 1994.

18. Carlton, 1997.

19. One of the most critical organizational, systemic decisions— to integrate hardware and software—remains highly contentious twenty years later, though it is again a central part of Apple's strategy. Some people claim it is the source of Apple's success, others of its failure, and yet others of both. Among other things, Apple's decision to work in the world of software and hardware puts one foot in the world of increasing returns and one in the world of diminishing returns.

20. Brown, 1991.

21. Porter (1996) describes organizations in complementary terms.

22. Rosenberg, 1994, p. 143.

23. Chandler; 1977; see also North, 1981.

24. Campbell-Kelly and Aspray, 1996 (information systems), and Yates, 1989 (documentation).

25. We develop our idea of the matrix from Dan Alpert's (1985) model of the university.

26. Marshall, 1916, p. 269.

27. See, for example, Porter, 1998; Saxenian, 1996.

28. Marshall, 1916, p. 271.

29. Saxenian, 1996.

30. Von Burg and Kenney, in preparation, p. 12.

31. Marshall, p. 272; Saxenian, 1996.

32. Mounier-Kuhn's (1994) analysis of the French computer industry reached similar conclusions.

33. Kenney and von Burg, 1999.

34. Conventional wisdom sees the large as sclerotic and the small

as agile. The small may be agile because they are more tightly coupled. If so, they and their members will bear all the burdens that come with tight coupling, in particular, lack of autonomy. The sociologist Anthony Giddens (1990) argues that "Rather than tending inevitably towards rigidity, [formal] organizations produce areas of autonomy and spontaneity—which are actually often less easy to achieve in small groups" (p. 138).

35. Kogut, Walker, and Kim, 1995.

36. Kenney and von Burg, 1999.

37. The phrase *knowable community*, comes from William (1973), though he does not use it quite this way.

38. Marshall, 1916, p. 273.

39. The grandfather of all these discussions is by the Dutch physician-turned-philosopher Bernard de Mandeville (1714). In the eighteenth century, he wrote a wonderful book called *The Fable of the Bees, or, Private Vices, Publick Benefits*. Mandeville used the example of the beehive to suggest that the best society emerges from each individual bee pursuing its own needs rather than consulting the needs of others. (People who follow in Mandeville's footsteps perhaps forget that neither Mandeville's ideal society nor the hive lacked hierarchy. Mandeville's England was, like the hive, a highly structured society ruled by a queen.)

40. Fukuyama and Shulsky (1997) point out that ideological enthusiasm often hides behind the appeal to "nature." While work on complex adaptive systems, they argue,

> *Is highly suggestive, it is a body of theories that can easily be abused, . . . turning from a descriptive scientific hypothesis into a prescriptive social doctrine. . . . Whether many real-world organizations can in fact be run in a completely non-hierarchical fashion seems dubious. (p. 8)*

41. Shapiro and Varian, 1999.

42. This battle between geometric growth and arithmetic growth is an interesting echo of the discussions of the growth of technology and human society that we discussed in chapter 3.

43. The sociologist Anthony Giddens has long emphasized the importance of reflection to human society. Emphasis on human reflexivity doesn't lurk in the "softer" social sciences alone. It appears in the work of the financier George Soros and in such obscure economic issues as "moral hazard." It is certainly hazardous to exclude it from accounts of human society.

44. Spender and Grant, 1996, p. 9.

Chapter 7: Reading the Background

1. Bits may be environmentally friendly, but computers, of course, are not. The European Community has issued a directive (Directive on Waste from Electrical and Electronic Equipment) demanding that manufacturers take responsibility for postconsumer recycling in order to limit the problem of computer trash (Vernon, 1999).

2. Paper figures from the American Forest and Paper Association, *Statistical Roundup* (Washington, D.C.: National Forest Products Association).

3. The literary critic I. A. Richards (1960), grandfather of "New Criticism," long ago called the book a "machine to think with."

4. Baker, 1994.

5. Hiltzik, 1999, p. 192.

6. For the language of replacement, see Duguid, 1996b.

7. See Noll, 1996. Softpress's "Softbook" allows readers to download the *New York Times* onto their electronic book every day.

8. For the *Chronicle*, see http://sfgate.com [1999, July 21]. The *Guardian* Web site (http://www.newsunlimited.co.uk [1999, July 21]) looks both naïve and ambitious, a common Web trait and often a winning one. We get back to the question of immediacy and archiving at the end of this chapter.

9. Bush, 1945. Intriguingly, Bush hoped that Memex would control the "growing mountain" of information, whereas the Web seems to have accelerated that growth.

10. See Project Gutenberg's on-line history, http://www.guten berg.net/history.html [1999, July 21]. Undoubtedly, Project Gutenberg is not a very sophisticated project. But that might be to its advantage. More sophisticated attempts to turn print into digital form have recognized more sophisticated problems. Project Gutenberg reproduces books as linear text— more or less turning books back into scrolls. Researchers looking for a better digital representation are made increasingly aware of the integrity behind the book's division into pages, chapters, and other recognizable chunks. There is still much debate about how best to address these.

11. See Robert Wilensky in Pretext Forum, 1997.

12. One of the most talked about contributions to the public library of recent years has been the admirable gift of computers and software to libraries by the Gates Foundation. As Geoffrey Nunberg (1998) points out, however, no one quite knows how libraries will afford to maintain such equipment. The unforeseen hunger of library technology often leads to bites out of the book budget, thus setting potentially complementary systems against one another.

13. One of paper's most intriguing complementary properties is endurance. Digital documents do not last very long. See Binding Issues, later in this chapter.

14. The promotional literature for Everybook makes this distinction (see http://www.everybk.com [1999, July 21]). Most electronic books also plunge into the book's abandoned past by offering leather bindings.

15. The German philosopher Hegel says somewhere that history's Owl of Minerva takes flight at dusk. As the light has dimmed around the library, people have begun to notice (in many instances, been forced to notice) its subtlety and versatility. And today, the library continues to change shape. It has not sat still to present an easy technological target. Similarly, as dusk threatened each, the book, the newspaper, "print culture," and the like have become the focus of historical investigations that

provide a rich understanding of the uses of documents and the usefulness of paper.

16. Quoted in Nunberg, 1996, p. 103.

17. McLuhan, 1962.

18. Now there is another measure of importance. Some stories appear only on a paper's Web site. Those thought more important or more reliable appear both there and in the conventional paper.

19. Such claims resemble the problem faced by Epimendes in the famous "Cretan Paradox." Epimendes announced "I am a Cretan, and all Cretans are liars." (This turned out, the mathematical philosopher Bertrand Russell showed, to be a key insight into the problems of mathematical set theory.) People cannot declare themselves to be lying because, as the poet John Donne wrote long ago, "if he say true, he lies."

20. Because these are important indicators, sumptuary laws once regulated economic life. People were not allowed to display more wealth than they could actually maintain because this could convey a false image of their creditworthiness. The businessman and, ultimately, bankrupt César Birotteau in Balzac's (1989) novel *The Rise and Fall of César Birotteau* about nineteenth-century business lives in fear that his wife's proud extravagance will lead him to be prosecuted under such laws.

21. In the eighteenth century when cheap and pirated editions flooded the book market in England, several established publishers sought to distinguish themselves by putting out increasingly expensive works, favoring dictionaries, encyclopedias, and annotated and complete editions that helped elevate their authority over that of their cheaper rivals. See Innis, 1991.

22. O'Brien, 1977, p. 22.

23. Rhiengold, 1993.

24. An O'Brien-like Web-handling service would, we suppose, insert impressive sites into an Internet browser's list of favorite sites and create an elaborate Web history, while removing the traces of ESPN.com and Playboy.com.

25. Libraries face the interesting question, for example, of what to do with marginalia. In general, they strongly discourage handwriting in books and seek "clean" copies. When the annotator is famous, however, they collect it. Cambridge University's library, for example, has a special collection of *adversaria*—annotated books. See Sherman, 1995.
26. Fidler, 1997; Rheingold, 1993; Dibbell, 1999.
27. Strauss, 1978.
28. Rudolf II, emperor of the Holy Roman Empire, might plausibly be thought of as the first great scientific patron for his role in developing Europe's first reliable postal service. See Kronick (1976) for this point and others developed in this section.
29. Price, 1961.
30. Kronick, 1976.
31. The quantum physicist John Ziman (1967), like sociologists of science after him, has argued that scientific communication is not a secondary occupation, conducted after the science is over, but a central part of what scientists do.
32. Scientific research has to a significant degree been built upon a gift economy. It may change dramatically if technology pushes it toward a genuine marketplace of ideas.
33. The French *Journal des Sçavans* appeared in the same year (Kronick, 1976).
34. According to Kronick (1976), early issues contained an extraordinary miscellany, ranging from Hooke's "spot on one of the belts of Jupiter," an account of a "Very Odd and Monstrous Calf" forwarded by Boyle, some inquiries from "An Inquisitive Physician," and notes on "New American Whale-fishing about the Bermudas." As Geoffrey Nunberg (1995) points out, this range is not very different from that found on some apparently scientific Internet lists.
35. Stock, 1983.
36. Anderson, 1991.
37. The population of the colonies and new nation was highly literate for the time, but widespread literacy wasn't necessary for

communities to form around documents. When Cubans struggled against the Spanish empire *lectores* read nationalist newspapers, letters, and pamphlets in cigar factories and similar places. These readings, again, gave a sense of a revolutionary movement as much as information about the movement.

38. In 1832, Frances Trollope (1984) wrote of the "universal reading of newspapers" (p. 76). In 1839, Frederick Marryat (1962) noted in amazement that "[t]he number of papers published and circulated in Great Britain, among a population of twenty-six millions, is calculated at about three hundred and seventy. The number published in the United States, among thirteen millions, are supposed to vary between *nine and ten thousand* [emphasis in original]. . . . Every man in America reads his newspaper" (pp. 406–40). Charles Dickens, who felt himself roughly handled by the American press when he visited in 1842, made the numerous, raucous New York newsboys the centerpiece of his first impression of the States in the novel *Martin Chuzzlewit*: "'Here's this morning's New York Sewer!' cried one [newsboy]. 'Here's this morning's New York Stabber! Here's the New York Family Spy! Here's the New York Private Listener! Here's the New York Peeper! Here's the New York Plunderer! Here's the New York Keyhole Reporter! Here's the New York Rowdy Journal! Here's all the New York papers!'" (Dickens, 1968, p. 318).

39. Quoted in Henkin, 1998, p. 151.

40. Longfellow, 1966–1982, vol. 2, pp. 481–82.

41. Innis, 1991, p. 157.

42. Innis, 1991, p. 84.

43. Tocqueville, 1945, vol. II, p. 119.

44. Huizinga, 1972, p. 243.

45. We borrow these terms from our colleague David Levy (1994).

46. Latour, 1986.

47. They remain open, of course, to changing interpretation. Playing on the French phrase "plus ça change, plus c'est la même chose" [the more it changes, the more it stays the same],

the French theorists Pierre Bourdieu and Roger Chartier (1985) suggest that with documents, the more it stays the same the more it changes.

48. See our note on URLs at the beginning of the Notes section.

49. Barlow, 1994.

50. MP3, the technology that allows high-quality sound reproduction across the Web also challenges the fixity on which music copyright relies.

51. Davenport and Prusak, 1998, p. 106.

52. Dynamic preference matching raises some interesting questions about fixed or fluid in this regard. You can send someone to Amazon.com, but you can't send them to your list of preferences there—valuable though that may be. You can't send anyone to a digital store that provides a personalized "store window" and expect them to see the "same" store window or even the same goods on offer at the same prices.

53. See Hesse, 1997, for the importance of "deferral" in human communication and deliberation.

54. Innis, 1991.

55. In addition to monitoring footsteps across the Web, the Alexa project attempts to take periodic snapshots of the Web for posterity. It recently delivered a 2-terabyte record to the Library of Congress. See http://www.Alexa.com [1999, July 21].

Chapter 8: Re-education

1. See "A farmer's supposed to dig in his home sod—not burrow through libraries half way around the world." http://www.ibm.com/sfasp/locations/italy/index.html [1999, July 21].

2. "Higher education," the National Commission on Costs of Higher Education (NCCHE, 1998) announced bluntly, "is a product, a service and a life-long investment bought and paid for, like others."

3. Palattella, 1998.

4. While initially disdainful of for-profit competitors, many major universities have now formed for-profit subsidiaries.
5. Winston, 1999.
6. For the importance of regional complementarity, see Clustered Ecologies in chapter 6.
7. Education is one of what the economist William Baumol (1993) calls the "stagnant services." These are service industries (they include law, medicine, postal services, and police) that are labor intensive, where increases in productivity are hard to come by. A doctor can see only so many patients an hour. A teacher can get only so many students in a classroom. Consequently, as productivity improves elsewhere, prices in the stagnant sectors rise disproportionately. Hence their clients suffer "sticker shock"—which talk of "stagnant services" doesn't readily calm down. So the idea of making future, large gains in productivity is seductive. Meanwhile, in the period of transition, the old excuse that fees were high because of lack of technology can be eased aside by the more attractive excuse that fees are high because of the cost of technology. "It was nice to go for 100 years at a stretch without having to change the infrastructure," said the president of New York University, offering by implication an irresistible excuse for why college tuition was outpacing inflation (quoted in Bronner, 1998).
8. Rossman, 1992.
9. Chellappa, Barua, and Whinston, 1997, p. 56.
10. Arenson, 1998.
11. See Etienne Wenger's (1987) impressive survey for a summary of these systems and their underlying assumptions.
12. See Feenberg, 1999.
13. See http://www.california.edu/about.html [1999, July 21].
14. California now also boasts a digital library. The core of this, too, however, is a catalogue. This useful resource points to some 9,874,027 titles in the University of California libraries and the California State Library and to 878,074 periodical

titles (see telnet:melvyl.ucop.edu [1999, July 21]). A trip to the library is still required to read most of these.

15. http://www.psu.edu/dept/cac/news/nlsp98/worldcampus. html [1999, July 21].

16. We shouldn't underestimate simple conservatism. Faculty, as we have seen, may respond to change with claims of tradition. They are not alone. Alumni and parents often resist strongly, too. People who have paid a lot for a chunk of tradition will usually resist attempts to dismember it. (In a whirl of medieval costumes and dead languages, commencement invests both parents and alumni with the value of tradition.) See Arenson, 1995. Nor does business, if we take example from the campuses of Motorola and McDonald's universities, suggest a future very different from the past. Moreover, students, often a vanguard for change, have recently taken to fighting the commercialization of campus education. See Noble, 1998.

17. NCCHE, 1998.

18. For college essays, see http://www.ivyessays.com [1999, July 21]. Anyone with an e-mail account will have received the following sort of spam:

From: 73477.2104@compuserve.com
To: run78@aol.com
Subject: per request
X-UIDL: dd1408876ad530fc4e589ee64dc0b2cc
UNIVERSITY DEGREE PROGRAMS

Increase your personal prestige and money earning power through an advanced university degree. Eminent, non-accredited universities will award you a degree for only $200.

Degree granted based on your present knowledge and experience. No further effort necessary on your part.

Just a short phone call is all that is required for a BA, MA, MBA, or PhD diploma in the field of your choice.

---

19. For this argument, see Arrow, 1984.
20. Trow, 1996. The balance point for these issues of institutional trust and misrepresentation shifts as supply shifts to the for-profit sector. There, where responsibility is not to society but to shareholders, some of the slack in the system disappears. Undoubtedly there may be slack worth losing. But too great a loss can lead to a certain narrowness of vision. What narrowness in this regard might entail is perhaps best summed up by both what was said and left unsaid on the early versions of the Web site for the Western Governors' Initiative, outlining plans for a virtual university supported by the western states: "We sometimes view distance education too narrowly, as merely a way to save money. We should expand our vision . . ." the proclamation began. It seems an admirable sentiment, and certainly one we would applaud. The last sentence, however, is incomplete. In full, it read, "We should expand our vision and look for opportunities to make money." Whether that is the best way to maintain public trust remains to be seen. (http://www.westgov.org/smart/vu/faq.htm#1 [1997, March 7].)
21. See Lessig, unpublished ms., for an example of this.
22. Jaspers, 1959.
23. See Lave and Wenger, 1993, for "communities of practice"; Toulmin, 1972, for communities of concepts.
24. Gibbons, Pannoni, and Orlin, 1996.
25. Fish, 1980.
26. Gibbons, Pannoni, and Orlin, 1996.
27. Cameron and Heckman, 1993.
28. Cameron and Heckman, 1993; Duke and Marriott, 1973. Much of the difference here can be traced to the socialization that colleges provide. See also Peter Cappelli, 1995.
29. Fish, 1980.
30. In Innis's (1991) terms, they are "time binding" rather than "space binding." See chapter 7.
31. Hesse's (1997) notion of "deferral" and delay rather than

immediacy, which we noted in the chapter 7, are parts of education.

32. See Brown and Duguid, 1996b.

33. For the comparative expense of education, see note 7 above.

34. See Feenberg, 1999.

35. Local constraints are more evident in the professional curriculums. Many countries that the distance teachers of the economically advanced nations hope to reach have only a limited need for the medicine of heart disease or liposuction, the law of tax avoidance, or the architecture of luxury housing. Equally, providers may know too little about medicine with limited resources, the economics of community lending, or small-holding agronomy.

36. Hughes, 1986, p. 599.

37. We should acknowledge that the famous essay, "The Idea of a University" by John Henry Cardinal Newman (1987), talks about universal knowledge. Newman, however, defined such knowledge as, in practical terms, useless.

38. Bell and Tight, 1993.

39. We first presented this model in 1996 (Brown and Duguid, 1996b). It then drew some very sharp reactions primarily because we described the changes under way in universities by analogy with HMOs just at the time when HMOs' unpopularity was soaring. Since then, the term educational maintenance organization (EMO) has come into being. We present our earlier model here again, with a few modifications, and no references to the bedeviled HMOs.

40. The Open University, though a distance university, has developed a strong graduate research component.

41. Jaspers (1959) argues that universities deserve funding principally because they do what others don't or won't do.

42. See chapter 6 for more on complementarity.

43. See the discussion of the Madcap Project in the Afterword.

Afterword: Beyond Information

1. Johnson, 1976.
2. Williams, 1983.
3. Rose, 1995.
4. Lessig, unpublished ms.
5. Jaszi, 1991.
6. Lyman, 1998.
7. Duguid and Silva Lopes, 1999.

Bibliography

See "A Note on URLs" at the beginning of the Notes section.

Alpert, Dan. 1985. "Performance and Paralysis: The Organizational Context of the American Research University." *Journal of Higher Education* 56 (3): 242–81.

Anderson, Benedict. 1991. *Imagined Communities: Reflections on the Origins and Spread of Nationalism.* Rev. ed. London: Verso.

Anderton, Frances. 1998. "Virtual Officing Comes in from the Cold." *New York Times,* 17 December, sec. F, p. 1.

Arenson, Karen W. 1995. "Alumni Generosity Has a Catch." *New York Times,* 15 March, sec. E, p. 5.

———. 1998. "More Colleges Plunging into Uncharted Waters of Online Courses." *New York Times,* 2 November, sec. A, p. 16.

Arrow, Kenneth J. 1984. "Information and Economic Behavior." In *Collected Papers,* edited by Kenneth J. Arrow, 136–52. Cambridge: Harvard University Press.

Attewell, Paul. 1994. "Information Technology and the Productivity Paradox." In *Organizational Linkages: Understanding the Productivity Paradox,* edited by D. Harris, 13–53. Washington, DC: National Academy Press.

Baker, Nicholson. 1994. "Discards." *The New Yorker,* 4 April, 65–86.

Balzac, Honoré de. 1989. *The Rise and Fall of César Birotteau.* Translated by Ellen Marriage. New York: Caroll & Graf.

Bandyopadhyay, P. 1989. *Rabrindrath Tagore.* Calcutta, India: Anglia.

Barley, Stephen R. 1996. "Technicians in the Workplace: Ethnographic Evidence for Bringing Work into Organization Studies." *Administrative Science Quarterly* 41 (3): 401–44.

Barlow, John Perry. 1994. "The Economy of Ideas." *Wired* [Online] 2.03 (March). Available: http://www.wired.com/wired/archive/2.03/economy.ideas.html [1999, July 21].

———. N.d. "Declaration of the Independence of Cyberspace." [Online]. Available: http://www.eff.org/~barlow/Declaration-Final.html [1999, July 21].

Bateson, Gregory. 1972. *Steps to an Ecology of Mind*. New York: Ballantine Books.

Baumol, William. 1993. "Do Health Care Costs Matter: Anatomy of an Illusion." *New Republic* 209 (November): 16–19.

Becker, Gary S., and Kevin M. Murphy. 1993. "The Division of Labor, Coordination Costs, and Knowledge." In *Human Capital: A Theoretical and Empirical Analysis, with Special Reference to Education*, edited by Gary S. Becker, 229–322. 3d ed. Chicago: University of Chicago Press.

Bell, Robert, and Malcolm Tight. 1993. *Open Universities: A British Tradition?* Bristol, U.K.: Society for Research into Higher Education and Open University Press.

Bennis, Warren, and Patricia Ward Biederman. 1997. *Organizing Genius: The Secrets of Creative Collaboration*. Reading, MA: Addison-Wesley.

Berger, Warren. 1999. "Lost in Space." *Wired* [Online] 7.02 (February). Available: http://www.wired.com/wired/archive/7.02/chiat.html [1999, July 21].

Blair, Helen, Susan Grey Taylor, and Keith Randle. 1998. "A Pernicious Panacea: A Critical Evaluation of Business Reengineering." *New Technology, Work, and Employment* 13 (2): 116–28.

Bourdieu, Pierre, and Roger Chartier. 1985. "La Lecture: Une Pratique Culturelle." In *Pratiques de La Lecture*, edited by Roger Chartier, 218–39. Marseille, France: Rivages.

Bowker, Geoffrey C., and Susan Leigh Star. 1999. *Sorting Things Out: Classification and Its Consequences*. Cambridge: MIT Press. Forthcoming.

Brand, Stewart. 1994. *How Buildings Learn: What Happens after They're Built*. New York: Viking.

Bronner, Ethan. 1998. "College Tuition Rises 4% Outpacing Inflation." *New York Times*, 8 October, sec. A, p. 18.

Brown, John Seely. 1991. "Research that Reinvents the Corporation."

Harvard Business Review, January–February, 102–11.

Brown, John Seely, and Paul Duguid. 1993. "Stolen Knowledge." *Educational Technology* 33 (3): 10–15. Available: http://www.parc.xerox.com /ops/members/brown/papers/stolenknow.html [1999, July 21].

———. 1996a. "The Social Life of Documents. *Release 1.0,* October (special issue): 1–19. Available: http://www.parc.xerox.com/ops/ members/brown/papers/sociallife.html [1999, July 21].

———. 1996b. "The University in the Digital Age." *Times Higher Education Supplement,* 10 May (multimedia supplement): iv–vi. Available: http://www.parc.xerox.com/ops/members/brown/papers/university. html [1999, July 21].

Bush, Vannevar. 1945. "As We May Think." *Atlantic Unbound* [Online]. Available: http://www.theatlantic.com/unbound/flashbks/compute/ bush.htm [1999, July 21].

Cameron, Stephen, and James Heckman. 1993. "The Nonequivalence of High School Equivalents." *Journal of Labor Economics* 11 (1): 1–47.

Campbell-Kelly, Martin, and William Aspray. 1996. *Computer: A History of the Information Machine.* New York: Basic Books.

Cappelli, Peter. 1995. "Is the Skills Gap Really about Attitudes?" *California Management Review* 37 (4): 108–24.

———. 1996. "The British Experience with Youth Apprenticeship." *Phi Delta Kappan* 77 (10): 679–82.

Carey, James W. 1989. *Communication as Culture: Essays on Media and Society.* Boston: Unwin Hyman.

Carlton, Jim. 1997. *Apple: The Inside Story of Intrigue, Egomania, and Business Blunders.* New York: Times Business Books.

Castells, Manuel. 1996. *The Rise of the Network Society.* Vol. 1 of *The Information Age: Economy, Society, Culture.* Oxford, U.K.: Blackwell.

Cetina, Karin Knorr. 1999. *Epistemic Cultures: How the Sciences Make Knowledge.* Cambridge: Harvard University Press.

Chandler, Alfred D. 1977. *The Visible Hand: The Managerial Revolution in American Business.* Cambridge: Harvard University Press.

Chellappa, Ramanath, Anitesh Barua, and Andrew B. Whinston. 1997. "E3: An Electronic Infrastructure for a Virtual University." *Communications of the ACM* 40 (9): 56–58.

Coase, Ronald H. 1937. "The Nature of the Firm." *Economica* NS 4 (16): 386–405.

Coffman, K.G., and Andrew M. Odlyzko. 1998. "The Size and Growth Rate of the Internet." *FirstMonday* [Online] 3 (10). Available: http://www.firstmonday.dk/issues/issue3_10/coffman/ [1999, July 21].

Cole, Robert. 1999. *Managing Quality Fads.* New York: Oxford University Press.

Council on Environmental Quality. 1993. *Environmental Quality: The Twenty-fourth Annual Report of the Council on Environmental Quality.* Washington, DC: Department of the Environment.

Daniel, John S. 1996. *Mega-Universities.* London: Kogan Page.

Davenport, Thomas H. 1993. *Process Innovation.* Boston: Harvard Business School Press.

Davenport, Thomas H., and Laurence Prusak. 1998. *Working Knowledge: How Organizations Manage What They Know.* Boston: Harvard Business School Press.

David, Paul. 1990. "The Dynamo and the Computer: An Historical Perspective on the Modern Productivity Paradox." *American Economic Review* 80 (2): 355–61.

De Cock, Christian, and Ian Hipkin. 1997. "TQM and BPR: Beyond the Beyond Myth." *Journal of Management Studies* 34 (5): 659–76.

De Long, J. Bradford, and A. Michael Froomkin. 1999. "The Next Economy?" In *Internet Publishing and Beyond: The Economics of Digital Information and Intellectual Property*, edited by Deborah Hurley, Brian Kahin, and Hal Varian. Cambridge: MIT Press. Forthcoming. Available: http://www.law. miami.edu/~froomkin/articles/newecon.htm. [1999, July 21].

Dibbell, Julian. 1999. *My Tiny Life: Crime and Passion in a Virtual World.* New York: Owl Books.

Dickens, Charles. 1968. *The Life and Adventures of Martin Chuzzlewit.* Harmondsworth, Middlesex: Penguin Books.

———. 1969. *Hard Times.* Harmondsworth, Middlesex: Penguin Books.

Dix, David. 1994. "Virtual Chiat." *Wired* [Online] 2.07 (July). Available: http://www.wired.com/wired/archive/2.07/chiat.html [1999, July 21].

Donkin, Richard. 1998. "Disciplines Compete for a Newcomer." *Financial Times*, 28 October, p. 14.

Downes, Larry, and Chunka Mui. 1998. *Unleashing the Killer App: Digital Strategies for Market Dominance*. Boston: Harvard Business School Press.

Dretske, Fred. 1981. *Knowledge and the Flow of Information*. Cambridge: MIT Press.

Duguid, Paul. 1996a. "Lavradores, Exportadores, Comissários, e Capitalistas: Os Componentes da Região do Vinho do Porto." *O Douro* 1 (2): 201–24.

————. 1996b. "Material Matters: The Past and the Futurology of the Book." In *The Future of the Book*, edited by Geoffrey Nunberg, 63–102. Berkeley, CA: University of California Press. Available: http://www.parc.xerox.com/ops/members/brown/papers/mm. html [1999, July 21].

Duguid, Paul, and Teresa Silva Lopes. 1999. "Ambiguous Company: Institutions and Organizations in the Port Wine Trade, 1814–1834." *Scandinavian Journal of Economic History* 47 (1): 84–102.

Duke, Christopher, and Stuart Marriott. 1973. *Paper Awards in Liberal Adult Education: A Study of Institutional Adaptation and Its Costs*. London: Michael Joseph.

Edwards, Linda N., and Elizabeth Field-Hendry. 1996. "Home-Based Workers: Data from the 1990 Census of Population." *Monthly Labor Review* [Online] 119 (November). Available: http://stats.bls.gov/ opub/mlr/1996/11/art3full.pdf [1999, July 21].

Feenberg, Andrew. 1995. *Alternative Modernity: The Technical Turn in Philosophy and Social Theory*. Berkeley, CA: University of California Press.

————. 1999. "Distance Learning: Promise or Threat?" [Online]. Available: http://www-rohan.sdsu.edu/faculty/feenberg/TELE3.HTM [1999, July 21].

Fidler, Roger. 1997. *Mediamorphosis: Understanding New Media*. Thousand Oaks, CA: Pine Forge Press.

Fish, Stanley. 1980. *Is There a Text in This Class? The Authority of Interpretive Communities*. Cambridge: Harvard University Press.

Forester, Tom. 1988. "The Myth of the Electronic Cottage." *Futures* 20 (3): 227–41.

Franklin, Stan. [1995] "Autonomous Agents, Mechanisms of Mind." [Online]. Available: http://www.msci.memphis.edu/~franklin/aagents.html [1999, July 21].

Franklin, Stan, and Art Graessner. 1996. "Is It an Agent, or Just a Program? A Taxonomy for Autonomous Agents." *Intelligent Agents 3: Agent Theories, Architectures, and Languages.* Proceedings of the ICAI '96 Workshop, Budapest, Hungary, August 12–13, 1996. New York: Springer-Verlag. Available: http://www.msci.memphis.edu/~franklin/AgentProg.html [1999, July 21].

Fried, John. 1995. "The Techno-Productivity Slump." *Journal of Commerce,* 17 February, sec. A, p. 1.

Fukuyama, Francis, and Abram Shulsky. 1997. *The "Virtual Corporation" and Army Organization.* Santa Monica, CA: Rand.

Gates, Bill. 1995. *The Road Ahead.* New York: Viking.

Gates, Dominic. 1998. The Pretext Interview: Frank Heart Talks to Dominic Gates. *Pretext* [Online]. Available: http://www.pretext.com /mar98/columns/intview.htm [1999, July 21].

Geer, Dan. 1998. "Risk Management Is Where the Money Is." *The Risks Digest* [Online] 20 (6). Available: http://catless.ncl.ac.uk/Risks/20.06.html [1999, July 21].

Gibbons, Jim, Rob Pannoni, and Jay Orlin. 1996. "Tutored Video Instruction: A Distance Education Methodology that Improves Training Results." Paper presented at the American Society of Training and Development International Conference and Exposition, Orlando, FL, June 3, 1996. Available: http://www.cs.cmu.edu /afs/cs/user/jhm/15–601/tvi.html [1999, July 21].

Giddens, Anthony. 1990. *The Consequences of Modernity: The Raymond Fred West Memorial Lectures.* Stanford, CA: Stanford University Press.

Granovetter, Mark. 1973. "The Strength of Weak Ties." *American Journal of Sociology* 78 (6): 1360–80.

———. 1985. "Economic Action and Social Structure: The Problem of Embeddedness." *American Journal of Sociology* 91 (3): 481–510.

Gurley, J. William. 1998. "How Low Can You Go?" *Above the Crowd Dispatch*

[Online] 21 December. Available: http://www.news.com/Perspectives/Column/0,176,282.00.html. [1999, July 21].

Hammer, Michael. 1996. *Beyond Reengineering: How the Process-Centered Organization Is Changing Our Work and Lives.* New York: Harper-Business.

Hammer, Michael, and James Champy. 1993. *Reengineering the Corporation: A Manifesto for Business Revolution.* New York: HarperBusiness.

Harris, Douglas H. ed. 1994. *Organizational Linkages: Understanding the Productivity Paradox.* Washington, DC: National Academy Press.

Hayek, Friedrich A. 1988. *The Fatal Conceit: The Errors of Socialism.* Vol. 1 of *The Collected Works of F. A. Hayek,* edited by W. W. Bartley. Chicago: University of Chicago Press.

Henkin, David M. 1998. *City Reading: Written Words and Public Spaces in Antebellum New York.* New York: Columbia University Press.

Hesse, Carla. 1997. "Humanities and the Library in the Digital Age." In *What's Happened to the Humanities?,* edited by Alvin Kernan, 107–21. Princeton, NJ: Princeton University Press.

Hiltzik, Michael A. 1999. *Dealers of Lightning: Xerox PARC and the Dawn of the Computer Age.* New York: HarperBusiness.

Hobsbawm, Eric J. 1977. *The Age of Revolution, 1789–1848.* London: Abacus.

Hoggdon, Paul N. 1997. "The Role of Intelligent Agent Software in the Future of Direct Response Marketing." *Direct Marketing* 59 (9): 10–18.

Hornett, Andrea. In preparation. "Cyber Wars: Organizational Conflicts of a Virtual Team." Department of Business, Pennsylvania State University, draft June 1999.

Hughes, Robert. 1986. *The Fatal Shore: The Epic of Australia's Founding.* New York: Knopf.

Huizinga, Johan. 1972. *America: A Dutch Historian's Vision, from Afar and Near.* New York: Harper.

Humphrys, Mark. 1997. "AI Is Possible . . . but AI Won't Happen: The Future of Artificial Intelligence." Paper presented at the symposium "Science and the Human Dimension," Jesus College, Cambridge, August 29.

Innis, Harold. 1991. *The Bias of Communication.* Toronto: University of Toronto Press.

Jacobson, Gary, and John Hillkirk. 1986. *Xerox: American Samuri*. New York: Macmillan.

Jaroff, Leon, and Saneel Ratan. 1995. "Age of the Road Warrior: In the Virtual Office Paper Has Disappeared—And So Have the Employees." *Time* (special issue: "Welcome to Cyberspace") 145 (12): 38.

Jaspers, Karl. 1959. *The Idea of the University*. Translated by H. Reiche and T. Vanderschmidt. Boston: Beacon Press.

Jaszi, Peter. 1991. "Toward a Theory of Copyright: The Metamorphoses of 'Authorship.'" *Duke Law Journal* 2: 455–502.

Jennings, N. R., P. Faratin, M. J. Johnson, T. J. Norman, P. O'Brien, and M. E. Wiegand. 1996. "Agent Based Business Process Management." [Online]. Available: http://gryphon.elec.qmw.ac.uk/dai/projects/adept/jcis96/introduction.html#top [1998, December 16].

Johnson, Samuel. 1976. *The History of Rasselas, Prince of Abissynia*. Harmondsworth, Middlesex: Penguin Books.

Jonkheer, Kees. 1999. "Intelligent Agents, Markets, and Competition: Consumers' Interests and Functionality of Destination Sites." *First-Monday* [Online] 4 (6). Available: http://firstmonday.org/issues/issue4_6/jonkheer/index.html [1999, July 21].

Kelly, Kevin. 1997. "New Rules for the New Economy." *Wired* [Online] 5.09 (September). Available: http://www.wired.com/wired/archive/5.09/newrules.html [1999, July 21].

———. 1998. "New Economy? What New Economy?" *Wired* [Online] 6.05 (May). Available: http://www.wired.com/wired/archive/6.05/Krugman.html [1999, July 21].

Kenney, Martin, and Urs von Burg. 1999. "Technology and Path Dependence: The Divergence between Silicon Valley and Route 128." *Industrial and Corporate Change* 8 (1): 67–103.

Kogut, Bruce, Gordon Walker, and Dong-Jae Kim. 1995. "Cooperation and Entry Induction as an Extension of Technology Rivalry." *Research Policy* 24: 77–95.

Kraut, Robert R. 1994. "Demassification and Community: Lessons from the Telephone." *Human–Computer Interaction* 9 (1): 91–93.

Kronick, David. 1976. *A History of Scientific and Technical Periodicals: The Origins and Development of the Scientific and Technical Press, 1665–1790*.

2d edition. Metuche, NJ: Scarecrow Press.

Kula, Witold. 1986. *Measures and Man.* Translated by R. Szerter. Princeton, NJ: Princeton University Press.

Latour, Bruno. 1986. "Visualization and Cognition: Thinking with Eyes and Hands." *Knowledge and Society* 6 (1): 1–40.

Lave, Jean. 1988. *Cognition in Practice: Mind, Mathematics, and Culture in Everyday Life.* New York: Cambridge University Press.

Lave, Jean, and Etienne Wenger. 1993. *Situated Learning: Legitimate Peripheral Participation.* New York: Cambridge University Press.

Leonard, Andrew. 1997. *Bots: The Origin of New Species.* New York: Penguin Books.

Leonard, Dorothy, and Silvia Sensiper. 1998. "The Role of Tacit Knowledge in Group Innovation." *California Management Review* 40 (3): 112–32.

Leonard-Barton, Dorothy. 1995. *Wellsprings of Knowledge: Building and Sustaining the Sources of Innovation.* Boston: Harvard Business School Press.

Lessig, Lawrence. Unpublished ms. "The Law of the Horse: What Cyberlaw Might Teach." Available: http://cyber.law.harvard.edu/works/lessig/LNC_Q_D2.PDF [1999, July 21].

Lester, Richard. 1998. *The Productive Edge: How U.S. Industries Are Pointing the Way to a New Era of Economic Growth.* New York: W. W. Norton.

Levy, David. 1994. "Fixed or Fluid?: Document Stability and New Media." In *ECHT '94: European Conference on Hypertext Technology '94,* 24–31. Edinburgh, Scotland: ACM.

Levy, Steven. 1994. *Insanely Great: The Life and Time of Macintosh, the Computer That Changed Everything.* New York: Viking.

Lohr, Steve. 1996. "The Network Computer as the PC's Evil Twin." *New York Times,* 4 November, sec. D, p. 1.

Longfellow, Henry W. 1966-1982. *The Letters of Henry Wadsworth Longfellow.* 4 vols. Edited by Andrew Hillen. Cambridge: Harvard University Press.

Lyman, Peter. 1997. "Documents and the Future of the Academic Community." Paper presented at conference on Scholarly Communication and Technology, Emory University, April 24–25. Available: http://www.dlib.org/dlib/july98/07lyman.html [1999, July 21].

————. 1998. "The UCC2-B Debate and the Sociology of the Information Age." *Berkeley Technology Law Journal* 13 (3): 1063–86. Available: http://www.sims.berkeley.edu/~plyman/articles/BJLTfinal.pdf [1999, July 21].

Lyon, David. 1988. *The Information Society: Issues and Illusions.* Oxford, U.K.: Polity Press.

Maes, Pattie, Robert H. Guttman, and Alexandros G. Moukas. 1999. "Agents That Buy and Sell." *Communications of the ACM* 42 (3): 81–91.

"Managing Knowledge Is Latest Business Buzz." 1998. *Newsday,* 19 October, sec. C, p. 17.

Mandeville, Bernard de. 1714. *The Fable of the Bees, or, Private Vices, Publick Benefits.* London: Printed for J. Roberts.

March, James G. 1991. "How Decisions Happen in Organizations." *Human–Computer Interaction* 6 (1): 95–117.

Markoff, John. 1999. "Intel Goes to Battle as Its Embedded Serial Number Is Unmasked." *New York Times,* 28 April, sec. C, p. 1.

Markus, Edward. 1997. "Low Bid Alternatives Earning Respect." *American City and County* 112 (9): 22–25.

Marryat, Frederick. 1962. *A Diary in America.* Westport, CT: Greenwood Press.

Marshall, Alfred. 1916. *Principles of Economics.* 7th ed. 2 vols. London: Macmillan.

Marx, Karl. 1947. *Capital: A Critical Analysis of Capitalist Production.* 3 vols. Edited by Friedrich Engels. Translated by Samuel Moore and Eduard Aveling. New York: International Publishers.

Maynard, Michael. 1998. "Architects Oppose California Initiative." *Architecture* 87 (4): 26.

McLuhan, Marshall. 1962. *The Gutenberg Galaxy: The Making of Typographic Man.* Toronto: University of Toronto Press.

"Mentors." 1997. *Architectural Record* 01 (January): 30.

Miller, George, and Patricia Gildea. 1987. "How Children Learn Words." *Scientific American* 257 (3): 94–99.

Mokyr, Joel. 1990. *The Lever of Riches: Technological Creativity and Economic Progress.* New York: Oxford University Press.

Mounier-Kuhn, Pierre E. 1994. "Product Policies in Two French Computer

Firms: SEA and Bull (1948–64)." In *Information Acumen: The Understanding and Use of Knowledge in Modern Business*, edited by Lisa Bud-Frierman, 113–35. London: Routledge.

Napoli, Lisa. 1999. "Turning 'Sticky Traffic' into Advertising Dollars." *New York Times*, 10 May, sec. C, p. 4.

Nardi, Bonny A., and Vicki L. O'Day. 1999. *Information Ecologies: Using Technology with Heart*. Cambridge: MIT Press.

National Commission on Costs of Higher Education (NCCHE). 1998. *Straight Talk about College Costs and Prices*. [Online]. Available: http://www.eriche.org/Library/ncche.html [1999, July 21].

Negroponte, Nicholas. 1995. *Being Digital*. New York: Basic Books.

———. 1998. Foreword to *Unleashing the Killer App: Digital Strategies for Market Dominance*, by Larry Downes and Chunka Mui. Boston: Harvard Business School Press.

Newman, John Henry. 1987. *The Idea of a University*. Chicago: Loyola University Press.

Noble, David F. 1998. "Digital Diploma Mills: The Automation of Higher Education." *FirstMonday* [Online] 3 (1). Available: http://www.firstmonday.org/issues/issue3_1/noble/index.html [1999, July 21].

Noll, A. Michael. 1996. "When Electronic Newspapers Fail, It's Not News." *The Sunday Star-Ledger*, 23 June, sec. 10, p. 5.

North, Douglass C. 1981. *Structure and Change in Economic History*. New York: W. W. Norton.

Nunberg, Geoffrey, 1995. "Gimcrack Nation." *Natural Language and Linguistic Theory* 12 (4): 767–75. Available: http://www.parc.xerox.com/istl/members/nunberg/gimcrack.html [1999, July 21].

———. 1996. "Farewell to the Information Age." In *The Future of the Book*, edited by Geoffrey Nunberg, 103–38. Berkeley, CA: University of California Press. Available: http://www.parc.xerox.com/istl/members/nunberg/Farewell.html [1999, July 21].

———. 1998. "Will Libraries Survive?" *American Prospect* 41, November-December, 16–23. Available: http://epn.org/prospect/41/41nunb.html [1999, July 21].

Oakeshott, Michael. 1967. "Learning and Teaching." In *The Concept of Education*, edited by R. S. Peters, 156–77. London: Routledge and Kegan Paul.

O'Brien, Flann [Myles na Gopaleen]. 1977. *The Best of Myles*. London: Picador.

O'Connor, Ellen. 1999. "The Politics of Management Thought: A Case Study of the Harvard Business School and the Human Relations School." *Academy of Management Review* 24 (1): 117–31.

O'Dell, Carla, and C. Jackson Grayson. 1998. "If Only We Knew What We Know: Identification and Transfer of Internal Best Practice." *California Management Review* 40 (3): 154–74.

Odlyzko, Andrew. 1998. "Smart and Stupid Networks: Why the Internet Is Like Microsoft." *ACM netWorker*, December, 38–46. Available: http://www.research.att.com/~amo/doc/stupid.networks.pdf [1999, July 21].

Orr, Julian. 1996. *Talking about Machines: An Ethnography of a Modern Job*. Ithaca, NY: IRL Press.

Palattella, John. 1998. "The British Are Coming, The British Are Coming." *University Business* [Online] July/August. Available: http://www.universitybusiness.com/9807/british.html [1999, July 21].

Petrosky, Henry. 1990. *The Pencil: A History of Design and Circumstance*. New York: Alfred A. Knopf, 1990.

Pitkin, Hanna F. 1998. *The Attack of the Blob: Hannah Arendt's Concept of the Social*. Chicago: University of Chicago Press.

Polanyi, Michael. 1996. *The Tacit Dimension*. Garden City, NY: Doubleday.

Pool, Ithiel de Sola, Craig Decker, Stephen Dizard, Kay Israel, Pamela Rubin, and Barry Weinstein. 1977. "Foresight and Hindsight: The Case of the Telephone." In *The Social Impact of the Telephone*, edited by Ithiel de Sola Pool, 127–57. Cambridge: MIT Press.

Porter, Michael. 1996. "What Is Strategy?" *Harvard Business Review*, November–December, 61–78.

———. 1998. "Clusters and the New Economics of Order." *Harvard Business Review*, November–December, 77–90.

Porter, Theodore M. 1994. "Information, Power, and the View From Nowhere." In *Information Acumen: The Understanding and Use of Knowledge in Modern Business*, edited by Lisa Bud-Frierman, 217–31. London: Routledge.

Pretext Forum. 1997. "A Panel of Thinkers and Technologists Debate the Future of Libraries." *Pretext* [Online] October. Available: http://www.pretext.com/oct97/columns/forum.htm [1999, July 21].

Price, Derek John de Solla. 1961. *Science Since Babylon.* New Haven, CT: Yale University Press.

Quittner, Joshua. 1995. "Automata Non Grata." *Wired* [Online] 3.04 (April). Available: http://www.wired.com/wired/archive/3.04/irc.html [1999, July 21].

Raik-Allen, Georgie. 1998. "Garage Door Slams Shut." *Red Herring Online* [Online] November 3. Available: http://www.redherring.com/insider/1998/1103/garagedoor.html [1999, July 21].

Reagle, Joseph M., Jr. 1996. "Trust in Electronic Markets: The Convergence of Cryptopgraphers and Economists." *FirstMonday* [Online] 1 (2). Available: http://www.firstmonday.dk/issues/issue2/markets [1999, July 21].

Reddy, Michael. 1979. "The Conduit Metaphor." In *Metaphor and Thought*, edited by Andrew Ortney, 284–324. New York: Cambridge University Press.

"Re-engineering Europe." 1994. *The Economist* 330 (February): 63–65.

Rheingold, Howard. 1993. *The Virtual Community: Homesteading on the Electronic Frontier.* Reading, MA: Addison-Wesley.

Richards, Ivan A. 1960. *Principles of Literary Criticism.* London: Routledge and Kegan Paul.

Rifkin, Jeremy. 1995. *The End of Work: The Decline of the Global Labor Force and the Dawn of the Post-Market Era.* New York: Putnam.

Rose, Lance. 1995. "The Emperor's Clothes Still Fit Just Fine." *Wired* [Online] 3.02 (February). Available: http://www.wired.com/wired/archive/3.02/rose.if.html [1999, July 21].

Rosenberg, Nathan. 1994. *Exploring the Black Box: Technology, Economics, and History.* New York: Cambridge University Press.

Rossman, Parker. 1992. *The Emerging Worldwide Electronic University: Information Age Global Higher Education.* Westport, CT: Greenwood Press.

Ryle, Gilbert. 1949. *The Concept of Mind.* London: Hutchinson.

Sartre, Jean-Paul. 1957. *Being and Nothingness: An Essay on Phenomenological Ontology.* Translated by Hazel E. Barnes. London: Methuen.

Sassen, Saskia. 1996. *Losing Control: Sovereignty in an Age of Globalization.* New York: Columbia University Press.

Saxenian, AnnaLee. 1996. *Regional Advantage: Culture and Competition in Silicon Valley and Route 128.* Cambridge: Harvard University Press.

Schwartz, Evan I. 1998. "Shopbot Pandemonium." *Wired* [Online] 6.12 (December). Available: http://www.wired.com/wired/archive/6.12/mustread.html [1999, July 21].

Shannon, Claude E., and Warren Weaver. 1964. *The Mathematical Theory of Communication.* Urbana, IL: University of Illinois Press.

Shao, Maria. 1995. "Beyond Reengineering." *Boston Globe,* 12 November, sec. A, p. 21.

Shapiro, Carl, and Hal R.Varian. 1999. *Information Rules:A Strategic Guide to the Network Economy.* Boston: Harvard Business School Press.

Sherman, William H. 1995. *John Dee:The Politics of Reading and Writing in the English Renaissance.* Amherst, MA: University of Massachusetts.

Sitkin, Sim B., and Darryl Stickel. 1996. "The Road to Hell: The Dynamics of Distrust in an Era of Quality." In *Trust in Organizations: Frontiers of Theory and Research,* edited by Roderick M. Kramer and Tom R. Tyler, 196–215. Thousand Oaks, CA: Sage.

Smith, Adam. 1937. *An Inquiry into the Nature and Causes of the Wealth of Nations.* New York: Modern Library.

Smith, Douglas K., and Robert C. Alexander. 1988. *Fumbling the Future: How Xerox Invented,Then Ignored, the First Personal Computer.* New York: Morrow.

Spender, J-C., and R. M. Grant. 1996. "Knowledge and the Firm: Overview." *Strategic Management Journal* 17 (1): 5–9.

Stewart, Thomas A. 1997. *Intellectual Capital:The New Wealth of Organizations.* New York: Doubleday.

Stinchcombe, Arthur L. 1990. *Information and Organizations.* Berkeley, CA: University of California Press.

Stock, Brian. 1983. *The Implications of Literacy:Written Language and Models of Interpretation in the Eleventh and Twelfth Centuries.* Princeton, NJ: Princeton University Press.

Strassmann, Paul A. 1997. *The Squandered Computer: Evaluating the Business Alignment of Information Technologies.* New Canaan, CT: Information Economics Press.

————. 1999. "Is There a Computer Paradox?" Private Briefing to the Board of Governors of the Federal Reserve System, Washington, DC, April 15. Available: http://www.strassmann.com/pubs/frb-041599.pdf [1999, July 21].

Strauss, Anselm. 1978. "A Social World Perspective." *Studies in Symbolic Interaction* 1 (1): 119–128.

Suchman, Lucy. 1996. "Supporting Articulation Work." In *Computerization and Controversy: Value Conflicts and Social Choices*, edited by Rob Kling, 407–23. 2d ed. San Diego, CA: Academic Press.

Tenner, Edward. 1997. *Why Things Bite Back: Technology and the Revenge of Unintended Consequences*. New York: Vintage Books.

Terkle, Sherry. 1995. *Life on the Screen: Identity in the Age of the Internet*. New York: Simon and Schuster.

Tocqueville, Alexis de. 1945. *Democracy in America*. 2 vols. Translated by Henry Reeve. New York: Vintage Books.

Toffler, Alvin. 1980. *The Third Wave*. New York: William Morrow.

Tonnies, Ferdinand. 1963. *Community and Society*. Translated by C. Loomis. East Lansing, MI: Michigan University Press.

Toulmin, Stephen. 1972. *Human Understanding: The Collective Use and Evolution of Concepts*. Princeton, NJ: Princeton University Press.

Trollope, Frances. 1984. *Domestic Manners of the Americans*. Oxford: Oxford University Press, 1984.

Trow, Martin. 1996. "Trust, Markets, and Accountability in Higher Education: A Comparative Perspective." *Higher Education Policy* 9 (4): 309–324.

Turing, Alan. 1963. "Computing Machinery and Intelligence." In *Computers and Thought*, edited by Edward A. Feigenbaum and Julian Feldman, 11–35. New York: McGraw-Hill.

Van Maanen, John, and Stephen R. Barley. 1984. "Occupational Communities: Culture and Control in Organizations." In vol. 6 of *Research in Organizational Behavior*, edited by Barry M. Staw and Larry L. Cummings, 287–365. Greenwich, CT: JAI Press.

Varma, Krishna, Chan I. Ho, David M. Stanek, and Patricia L. Mokhtarian. 1998. "Duration and Frequency of Telecenter Use: Once a Telecommuter, Always a Telecommuter." *Transportation Research* 6 (1): 47–68.

Vernon, Mark. 1999. "No Longer a Side Issue." *Financial Times*, 3 February, 13.

Von Burg, Urs, and Martin Kenney. In preparation. "There at the Beginning: Venture Capital and the Creation of the Local Area Networking Industry." Department of Applied Behavioral Sciences, University of California, Davis, draft, October 1998.

Walsh, John P., and Todd Bayma. 1995. "The Virtual College: Computer-Mediated Communication and Scientific Work." *The Information Society* 12: 343–63.

Ward, Mark. 1998. "Wired for Mayhem." *New Scientist* [Online] 159 (July). Available: http://www.newscientist.com/ns/980704/nwired.html.

Warnock, Mary. 1960. *Ethics since 1900*. London: Methuen Books.

Weick, Karl E. 1976. "Educational Organizations as Loosely Coupled Systems." *Administrative Science Quarterly* 21: 1–19.

Wellman, Barry. 1988. "The Community Question Reevaluated." In *Power, Community, and the City*, edited by Michael Peter Smith, 81–107. New Brunswick, NJ: Transaction Books.

Wells, H. G. 1902. *Anticipations of the Reaction of Mechanical and Scientific Progress upon Human Life and Thought*. New York: Harper and Brothers.

———. 1986. *The Future in America*. London: Granville Publishing.

Wenger, Etienne. 1987. *Artificial Intelligence and Tutoring Systems: Computational and Cognitive Approaches to the Communication of Knowledge*. Los Altos, CA: Morgan Kauffman.

———. 1998. *Communities of Practice*. New York: Cambridge University Press.

Whalen, Jack, and Erik Vinkhuyzen. Forthcoming. "Expert Systems in (Inter)Action: Diagnosing Document Machine Problems over the Telephone." To appear in *Workplace Studies: Recovering Work Practice and Informing Systems Design*, edited by Christian Heath, Jon Hindmarsh, and Paul Luff. New York: Cambridge University Press.

Whyte, William H. 1956. *The Organization Man*. New York: Simon and Schuster.

Williams, Raymond. 1973. *The Country and the City*. New York: Oxford University Press.

Index

A.B. Dick, 159
Aetna, 175
Age of the Smart Machine, 30
Alexa.com, 188
Amazon.com, 148
    acquisitions activities of, 25
    bot use on, 37, 44, 45, 47–48
American Airlines, 45
American Notes, 195
Anderson, Benedict, 194, 197
AOL, acquisitions activities of,
    25, 26
Apple Computer, 70, 87
    innovativeness of, 159–160
    relations with PARC, 151,
        157, 163, 166
    structure of, 154
AT&T, 178
    downsizing by, 122
    reengineering of, 92
    relations with Microsoft, 25, 28
Attewell, Paul, 29
Autonomous agents, 36–37
    and delegation, 53–54
    negotiation and, 48–52

and representation, 54–56
strengths and limitations of,
    41–56
unethical use of, 56–59
See also Bots

Babbage, Charles, 86
Barlow, John Perry, 66, 198
Barnard, Chester, 114
Barnes & Noble, 148
Bateson, Gregory, 138
Being Digital, 15
Bell, Alexander Graham, 87–88
Bell, Gordon, 11
Berkeley, University of California
    at, 228
Bots (autonomous agents), 36–37
    and delegation, 53–54
    future of, 39–41, 61–62
    negotiation and, 48–52
    as representative, 54–56
    strengths and limitations of,
        41–56
    unethical use of, 56–59

About the Authors

JOHN SEELY BROWN is the Chief Scientist of Xerox Corporation and the Director of its famous Palo Alto Research Center (PARC). Over the years, his research has focused on human learning and the management of radical innovation. His additional research interests include digital culture, ubiquitous computing, user-centering design, and organizational learning.

Brown is a cofounder of the Institute for Research on Learning, a member of the National Academy of Education, and a Fellow of the American Association for Artificial Intelligence. He also serves on numerous advisory boards and boards of directors. His many awards include the 1998 Industrial Research Institute Medal for outstanding accomplishments in technological innovation, the 1999 Holland Award in recognition of the best paper published in *Research Technology Management,* and a bronze medal at the Charleston International Film Festival for the film *Art • Lunch • Internet • Dinner,* of which he was an executive producer. His publications include the book *Seeing Differently: Insights on Innovation* and nearly one hundred papers in a range of scientific journals.

PAUL DUGUID is a historian and social theorist affiliated with the University of California, Berkeley, and the Xerox Palo Alto

Research Center. He was formally a member of the Institute for Research on Learning in Palo Alto. His interest in multidisciplinary, collaborative research has led him to work with social scientists, computer scientists, economists, linguists, management theorists, and social psychologists.

His writing has appeared in a broad array of scholarly fields and journals including anthropology, business and business history, cognitive science, computer science, design, education, economic history, human-computer interaction, management, organization theory, and wine history. Duguid has also written essays and reviews for a variety of less specialized publications, including the *Times Literary Supplement,* the *Nation,* and the *Threepenny Review.* While continuing to address the issues reflected in this book, he is currently also investigating the historical development of the institutions that shaped international trade in the eighteenth century.